ONENESS PERCEIVED

OMEGA BOOKS

The OMEGA BOOKS series from Paragon House is dedicated to classic and contemporary works about human development and the nature of ultimate reality, encompassing the fields of mysticism and spirituality, psychic research and paranormal phenomena, the evolution of consciousness, and the human potential for self-directed growth in body, mind and spirit.

John White, M.A.T., Series Editor of OMEGA BOOKS, is an internationally known author, editor, and educator in the fields of consciousness research and higher human development.

MORE TITLES IN OMEGA BOOKS

BEYOND THE HUMAN SPECIES: The Life and Work of Sri Aurobindo and
the Mother, *Georges van Vrekhem*

KUNDALINI: EMPOWERING HUMAN EVOLUTION
Selected Writings of Gopi Krishna, *edited by Gene Kieffer*

KUNDALINI EVOLUTION AND ENLIGHTENMENT
Edited by John White

LIFECYCLES: Reincarnation and the Web of Life
Christopher M. Bache

THE MEETING OF SCIENCE AND SPIRIT
Guidelines for a New Age, *John White*

THE RADIANCE OF BEING: Understanding the Grand Integral Vision; Living
the Integral Life
Allan Combs, Foreword by Ken Wilber

THE SACRED MIRROR: Nondual Wisdom and Psychotherapy
Edited by John Prendergast, Ph.D., Peter Fenner, Ph.D., and Sheila Krystal, Ph.D.

ONENESS PERCEIVED

A WINDOW INTO ENLIGHTENMENT

JEFFREY S. EISEN, PH.D.

Published in the United States by

Paragon House
2285 University Avenue West
St. Paul, Minnesota 55114

Copyright © 2003 by Paragon House

The Omega Books series from Paragon House is dedicated to classic and contemporary works about human development and the nature of ultimate reality.

Library of Congress Catalog-in-Publication Data

Eisen, Jeffrey S., 1940-
  Oneness perceived : a window into enlightenment / Jeffrey S. Eisen.--
1st American pbk. ed.
    p. cm.
  ISBN 1-55778-826-X (pbk. : alk. paper)
  1. Consciousness. 2. Experience. I. Title.
  BF311 .E39 2003
  150.19'8--dc21
                          2003005334

10 9 8 7 6 5 4 3 2 1
For current information about all releases from Paragon House,
visit the web site at www.paragonhouse.com

DEDICATIONS

To Dr. Jean Derousseau Eisen, the person I talk with most. Without your critiquing and editing this book would have been far less coherent. Without our fifteen year dialogue on enlightenment, evolution, living systems, consciousness and reality this book might never have been written. Without your presence, I would not have become the person I am today. Thank you for being in my life.

To John White M.AT., author, editor and enlightened spirit, whose right work in this world is championing the highest truth, whoever speaks it...thank you for seeing me.

CONTENTS

SECTION FOUR: SELF / PSYCHE

SECTION FIVE: CONSCIOUSNESS

SECTION SIX. THE INTELLIGENCE OF THE UNIVERSE

AFTERWORD: Towards Original Perception

APPENDIX

FOREWORD

TOWARD A NEW PARADIGM OF ENLIGHTENED THOUGHT

THOSE OF US CONCERNED WITH SPIRITUAL GROWTH AND societal transformation sometimes base our ideas for personal and planetary change on the assumption of enlightenment, as if the workshops we have all taken and books we have read have fully enlightened us. There is no doubt that there has been a great enlightenment in social attitudes since the psychedelic sixties. We have revised the ways we work, love, eat, raise our kids, and recycle our waste. However, this does not mean that we have become enlightened in the strict sense of the word.

Enlightenment is a specific state of being, difficult to define and arduous to attain. Many traditional esoteric writings on this subject are obscure, even misleading. In light of this, it is understandable if most of us are content with enlightened attitudes. While from the point of view of social good, this is usually an advance, it is by no means the real article. This becomes all too clear when newly enlightened attitudes come up against old residues of self-interest, creating conflict and even hypocrisy.

People have been attracted to enlightenment for thousands of years but few people agree on what it is. From Jesus to Buddha, enlightenment has always suggested paranormal faculties, if not godlike powers. The possibility of acquiring these powers is one of the attractions of the spiritual quest. Among the more useful of the powers attained by some enlightened beings are healing and extrasensory perception. However, most spiritual teachers have minimized the importance of these psychic powers saying that they are not the point. Powers may sometimes emerge on the road to enlightenment, but they are a side effect, not to be confused with enlightenment itself. What's more, the teachers warn, if powers are sought, the spiritual journey becomes sidetracked. But if enlightenment is not about developing psychic powers, what is it about?

Another common idea is that enlightenment is a state of transcendent unflappability. If anything can upset us, we must not be fully enlightened. But this too seems off the mark. Being unemotional can be the result of many things: drugs, depression, a schizoid personality, or plain not giving a damn. On the other hand, we have stories of enlightened beings from all traditions who cared ferociously and dedicated their lives to a noble cause. They also could laugh, play, overeat, and when appropriate, get righteously angry.

Another common idea is that enlightened beings are benign, and enlightenment is a matter of politically correct behaviors and attitudes: altruism, harmlessness, moderation, nondiscrimination, even vegetarianism. However, in the early years the Buddha wouldn't let women join his order, nor were women among Jesus's disciples. So Buddha and perhaps Jesus could be called sexist by contemporary standards. What's more, Bodhidharma, the first Zen patriarch, held that the enlightened man can be a butcher or snatch the food out of the mouth of a starving man, but as long as he knows his real nature no harm or bad karma will come out of it. So if Bodhidharma's hyperbole is to be given credence, admirable behavior, however desirable, is not essential to enlightenment. In fact, it may have nothing whatsoever to do with it. Perversely, outwardly despicable behavior may prove to be enlightened once we understand its purpose. In fact, there is a tradition of teachers acting as harsh and irascible taskmasters. Bodhidharma, on the other hand, gives us a real clue to what enlightenment is when he says "as long as a man knows his real nature." Enlightenment has something to do with knowing your real nature.

What is this real nature, and how does one go about discovering it? One time-honored means of pursuing it, advocated by the Advaita sage Ramana Maharishi, is to repeatedly inquire "Who am I?" But when most people ask themselves this question, the only answer they get is a set of identities, nested like Chinese boxes: man, Jew, husband, father, teacher, therapist, wit, etc. Surely, the secret to enlightenment is not to be found in those identities. Of course, Maharishi had something else in mind, probably very similar to what Bodhidharma had in mind when he said that the key to enlightenment is in discovering one's real identity. Obviously we need to go further.

To really understand enlightenment it will be useful to go to Buddha, who said that the real problem with life is *dukkha*. *Dukkha* is commonly translated as suffering, but its literal meaning isn't that at all. *Dukkha* simply means twoness. Life is twoness, and from that essential twoness all the problematic aspects of life somehow emerge, of which suffering certainly is one. But to say that suffering is the basic problem of life is a half-truth. It is like saying the world is made up of fire, water, air, and earth. It does not address the problem on a sufficiently fundamental level. Sadly, however, much of popular Buddhism and much of our misunderstanding of the nature of enlightenment is based on that mistranslation.

Going back to a reading of *dukkha* as twoness is one starting point for the understanding of our real nature and subsequent enlightenment. What Buddha referred to as *dukkha*, twoness, is what is known in Western philosophy as duality. The Vendanta tradition of India also has at least two major branches that specifically identify dualism as the heart of the problem: Advaita, which is literally the philosophy of dualism, and Kashmir Shaivism, a philosophy that originated in Kashmir.

What is duality, where does it come from, what is its relationship to reality, how does it give rise to the problematic aspects of our life, how can it help us discover our real nature, and what is its relationship to enlightenment? Only after answering these questions can we know what enlightenment is and how it can live up to its promise of making us somehow godlike. These questions are the essence of the perennial investigation into the nature of Self and existence, that perennial investigation that is at the heart of Vedanta, Kashmir Shaivism, Advaita, Taoism, and Buddhism as well as the esoteric branches of most other wisdom traditions and religions. They also are at the heart of the book you are about to read, *Oneness Perceived*. Let us answer these questions one by one.

What is duality?

Duality refers to the way all known things, whether they be sensory qualities or cognitive concepts, come in the form of polar opposites. Hot and cold, near and far, in and out, health and sickness, rich and poor, beautiful and ugly, etc., are all polar opposites, negative and positive. They are polarized around a point of perception, a projection of the corresponding quality in the perceiver. Thus, things are hotter or cooler than, nearer or farther than, and richer or poorer than the perceiver.

Where does duality come from?

Duality comes from perception—and perception only. Whenever perception takes place, duality is created. Duality, twoness, occurs whenever a person or any sentient being, by the act of perceiving, splits Oneness, the unknowable unity of existence, into poles relative to itself. This is the way that Oneness is transmuted into experiencable form. This also is the entry point of the book you are about to read.

What is the relationship of duality to reality?

Duality is illusory. It is the appearance that emerges subsequent to perception. Hot and cold do not exist independently; they exist only in perception relative to the perceiver. This does not deny reality to existence. Existence exists. But it does say that all sensory and cognitive experience is only appearance, what it seems to the perceiver. It is illusory as to the existence underlying it. The very thingness of things is illusion, an artifact of perception. All experience is illusory! All experienced reality is virtual reality.

How does duality give rise to the problematic quality of our lives?

If all the qualities of ourselves, all the things of the world, and all the dimensions and laws of reality that we experience are illusory, what does that mean? It means that all the hard realities that make life problematic and create suffering are illusory as well. They are not real! They have no existence independent of us as perceivers.

Pleasure and pain, sick and well, rich and poor, gain and loss—none have meaning or reality except to us as perceivers. Space and time, location, even causality only have meaning relative to ourselves as perceivers. Yet what are we? Our very selves, not as they exist in Oneness but as we ordinarily know them, are illusory. They also are perceptions, self-perceptions, things that also exist in duality, the duality of self and other. Even life and death, some of the enlightened masters tell us, are illusory. They also are a duality, perceptual poles that exist outside of that real space—that Self—which we come to inhabit when we realize our real nature.

So it is being mesmerized by this illusory world of duality, this illusory world only meaningful to our illusory selves, which is creating the problematic quality of our lives and which in turn is creating our suffering. Correspondingly, it is getting out of this self-created loop of creating illusion from our illusory selves that will end our suffering. So it becomes clear that suffering is not the base of the problem, but the result. Twoness, duality, is the base of the problem.

How can understanding duality help us discover our real nature?

The understanding of duality and illusion can help us discover our real nature by warning us where not to look and how not to look. If we understand that our individual selves, like all perceptions, are illusions, that will save us lifetimes of looking into the illusion of ourselves for our real nature. This real nature, the answer to the question "who am I?" cannot be found in the roles we play or the ideas we have of who we are!

Furthermore, if we understand that all the products of our mind and our senses—in fact, anything we perceive or conceive—is illusion, that will save us lifetimes of examining external illusions to find our real nature. Therefore, even science, at least in the way it is commonly conceived, cannot provide the answer. Science is involved with explaining the illusory appearance of things as if they are real, and using the illusory laws of nature to do it.

What is the right place and the right way to look? The only way that is left. After we give up looking in the wrong place and the wrong way, like a bull left staring bewilderedly into the emptiness that remains after the matador has swept the muleta from his line of sight, there is our real nature.

Finding our real nature requires an examination of aperceptual reality. But how do you examine a reality that you cannot, see, hear, even conceptualize. Actually, there are a few routes left to us, but they are subtle—subtle and difficult. They are inquiry, surrender, and spontaneous revelation. This book explores one of these paths, inquiry, and lays the groundwork for surrender. Spontaneous revelation cannot be transmitted in words, only courted by meditation.

Inquiry

The path of inquiry is a deep contemplation of the principle of perceptual duality and its implications for the nature of reality. It repeatedly asks the question, "What is reality?" Going deeper and deeper, it turns the high beam of integrative intellect on every discipline of human thought with this question in mind. This is the direction this book takes.

Surrender or letting go

Surrender is one of the most misunderstood principles of spirituality. It is commonly thought of as letting go of your will to the will of God, as if God is an external entity that has a will of his own to which you are supposed to sacrifice your will. However, what if, in aperceptual reality, we are all God? Then who should we surrender our will to—ourselves?

Seems ridiculous, but properly understood, in the paradox of the

ridiculous lies the sublime. If all that lies between us and enlightenment are the illusions of the dual mind, then these selfsame illusions
are all that separates our personal will from God's will.

In turn, letting go of these illusions reveals the reality of our
Self, of our real nature, of our identity. It reconciles our dual mind
with One mind, our personal will with God's will. It accomplishes that
because we realize our identity with the One mind and the One will. I
am going to explore this subject extensively in subsequent books.

What is the relationship between duality and enlightenment?

The first task of the path of inquiry is to attain a deep understanding
of *dukkha*, twoness, duality, illusion. Whatever way that understanding is deepened—through study, thought, meditation, koan practice,
any way at all—enlightenment will deepen with it. Enlightenment
progresses as more and more fundamental dualities, all the illusions
of our life, become transparent to the underlying unity, the underlying truth. Enlightenment is a process that starts someplace and
progresses somehow, gradually consuming all of the illusions we
hold dear in the flame of reality. First, it works on our ideas of what
is. Gradually it shifts to our ideas of who we are, then imperceptibly
shifts to transform what we are…from the illusion of our perceptions to the reality that we were all the time. So enlightenment can
start with the process of understanding duality and ripen into being
transformed by that understanding, thus coming into one's real nature. This is a rigorous process, one that requires not only inspiration
and meditation, but in the words of Ramana Maharishi, "an intellect
capable of discerning truth from illusion."

What is our true nature? What is left after withdrawing attention and importance from the senses and the mind? Only awareness
of Self. In that awareness there is nothing, no colors, no forms, no
smells, no images, no time, no space, no thoughts, not even desires,
no things at all. Buddhists call this awareness the void, mystic
Christians call it the godhead, cabalists call it *ein soph*. Every mystic tradition recognizes and names it. In this awareness there is no
one, no person, no you, just consciousness with thoughts arising and

subsiding within it. However, go there anyway, for that no thing at all is a window into reality and a window into the unknowable. Go there and stay. When you catch yourself wandering into the world of thoughts and things, return. As you rest in the reality of your Self, enlightenment will gradually dawn.

One question remains; why we should bother. One answer, certainly one of the best, is for freedom. Enlightenment brings us freedom from...from ignorance, fear, folly, and delusion, freedom from the bondage of ideas, maybe even a measure of freedom from suffering. Enlightenment also brings us freedom to...to be spontaneous, to see the humor in all things (most of all ourselves), to explore the oldest questions for the first time, to trade attachment for perspective, to be happy, serene, unfettered, balanced, even carefree among the cares of life.

There is another reason to seek enlightenment, for comprehension, for a new paradigm of enlightened thought. All branches of human activity and human inquiry, from the exploitation of the earth to the pursuit of objectivistic science, are reaching their limits, reaching the end of the illusion.

What illusion is this? First it is the illusion of separateness, of self and other. As science reports that the PCBs we released into the atmosphere have come back to us in the milk of nursing mothers, the realization is thrust upon us that there truly is no other. There is only Self, and we are all it, together with the cosmos we inhabit. To paraphrase Arthur Koestler, "every boundary is a connection." We are all swimming in the infinite hierarchy of the All.

Second, it is the illusion that reality is the way we perceive it, a world of tangible things imbued with sensory qualities, separate things revolving around the separate self we perceive ourselves to be, instead of the infinite, interconnected skein of unknowable existence it is. (Unknowable because it has no perceptual qualities by which it can be known.)

Ultimately we need to understand that all "things" are illusions created by the very act of perception that knows them, and that all things, upon examination, resolve into the unknowable One, the One that is not a thing. We as perceivers, both individually and collectively, are centers that create our subjective worlds. We project the reality of the selfsame illusion that we embody. Man's world is made not in God's image, but in his own. In order to remake the world in God's image, we first have to realize the God in ourselves.

But what is this God in ourselves? It is nothing but the reality behind the illusion, if only we will see it. From our point of view we are the center of the universe; from any other point of view we are just "out there," a thing along with every other thing. But in Oneness there can be no point of view. That is the ultimate key to understanding the mystery. From no point of view there are no separate things and no places where these things arise; there is just here, everywhere. There is just Oneness itSelf. You and I, the animals and the plants, the earth and the stars, are equally and inexplicably that Self. And that One Self, in all its mysterious workings, in all its glory, is God, should you choose to call it that.

That is the ultimate paradigm of enlightened thought, enlightenment to reality, enlightenment to our true nature, enlightenment to God. It is all one and the same. All is One Self and we, no more and no less than anything else, are also Self. The only possible difference, for what it's worth, is a level of awareness. Our advantage as humans is that we can be aware that we are the One Self, but our handicap is that it is far easier to be aware of the illusion. In the final analysis, it is which awareness we choose to act on that separates the men from the Gods.

—Santa Barbara, California
May 20, 2001

PREFACE

THIS BOOK COMES OUT OF MY ATTEMPTS TO UNDERSTAND what reality is. The realms of science, philosophy, and religion are, of course, filled with such volumes. They used to be made up of them, one man's speculations, one man's attempt to put it all together. Since the advent of specialization, as academics and granted research have made thinking a profession, these volumes have become rarer. The men that have inspired me are men like Lao-tzu, Chung-tzu, Gautama Buddha, Darwin, Einstein, and Jean Piaget. These men have sat down with a problem and gotten up with a new worldview. They have other things in common, too. They were all of a contemplative or meditative disposition and were all concerned with one or another of the two great themes concerning the nature and origin of reality.

These themes first came down to us through Buddha and Lao-tzu. One is the illusoriness of perceived reality, and how we create the world by our perception. The other is the evolutionary dialectic, or universal process, which was set forth in its most pure form as Tao, the way. It is notable that these two great themes, more appropriate to science and philosophy than they are to religion, came down to us from two of the greatest contemplative metaphysicians of all time, presumably accessed through meditation rather than rational thought (although, of course, we really don't know this), and are part of the "religion" of the East.

Tao's statement of the alternation of yin and yang as the evolutionary dialectic preceded Western science by thousands of years. The evolutionary dialectic first came to the attention of Western science through the work of Darwin. It was extended into psychology by Jean Piaget, who started as a teenage molluscologist and whose work on the evolutionary development of cognitive stages paralleled the Hegelian theory on the evolution of the idea.

The other great theme, the illusoriness of all perceived phenomena, has not yet penetrated Western science to the same extent, maybe because it threatens the entire foundation of Western science, based as it is on the study of phenomena as real. In philosophy, Kant stated it in his distinction between phenomena and noumena, although he did not comment on the dynamics of perceptual dualization. In science, Einstein came closest to it in his discoveries of the relationships and equivalances between such apparently separate phenomena as space, time, mass, energy, light, gravity, and acceleration. Being a physicist, not a metaphysicist, he did not see that these were all dualisms, illusory appearances of Oneness, part of the thousand and one things. Instead, he reified them and tried to form a unified field theory at the level between perception and Oneness. However, discovering the equivalencies was a great advance toward reconciling physics and metaphysics. I don't know how science could be constructed on the base of all perceived qualities being illusory; maybe it cannot. I do know, however, that the failure to do this constitutes making a science out of illusions.

These men I have mentioned have one other thing in common. They have all pursued a crack in the universe. Sometimes two concepts in the accepted view of things just don't quite fit. There is a little incongruity, a little offset like you get in an old-fashioned, split-level range finder when the camera is out of focus. This little offset, where things don't quite meet, is a crack. It's really nothing much, and most practical minds don't bother with it, reasoning that either they don't understand fully or that the explanation will be forthcoming someday. But some people worry about these cracks, and sometimes they open up suddenly and there again appears the abyss, the vast unknown to be explained yet another time.

Relativity theory started with one of these cracks. Einstein asked himself, what is simultaneity? If two bolts of lightning strike exactly the same place at the same time, that is clearly simultaneity. But what if they strike two different places at the same time, is that simultaneity? Is the distance between them a factor? What about the time it takes for light to travel from them to an observer? If the observer is equidistant between them, seeing both at the same time, that seems to be simultaneity, but what if the observer is a foot from one and ten thousand miles from the other, thus seeing the strike at two different times? Is that still simultaneity? You can't answer these questions without getting into the relationships between space, time, and the speed of light. Darwin started with another of these cracks, namely the absence of a mechanism to account for the assumed transmission of acquired characteristics.

A crack in my understanding led to the question that grew into this book. My wife and I were talking about Oneness and duality, and I realized that I didn't have a real understanding of how they were related to one another or to reality. So I began holding the question. In time the insight came to me that duality is the perception of Oneness, Oneness perceived. The relationship, once seen, was self-evident; however, it seemed somehow portentous as well. After additional weeks of mulling it over and discussing it with Jeanie, it began coming clear that if the relationship between Oneness and duality was perception, perception was the unifying factor in what I came to call the biofield or perceptual field. It was in some way the key to a unified field theory, not of physics but of consciousness. The unclear relationship between Oneness and duality was my crack in the universe. Questioning it and holding the question until the ground gave way opened the abyss that is explored in this book.

A word or two about my background and the way this book was written. I am a psychologist and psychotherapist by training, in addition to which I have always had an interest in Eastern meditative philosophies and martial arts. I am not a physical or biological scientist, nor do I have a formal background in philosophy. These limitations not withstanding, the speculations contained here plunge into those areas as well as explore psychology and Eastern thought.

Doubtless I have both made mistakes and rediscovered the wheel a few times. I ask the reader to forgive me, and instead of focusing on my errors and naïvetés, concentrate on the overall vision that is leading me. For although I am sometimes unsure of my facts and precedents, the overall correctness and importance of my message speaks for itself.

I'd like to say something about the writing as well. This book is a loose compilation of meditations on a theme (in the real sense of meditation). The style varies from poetic to academic to sutra-like. Basically I have written it as it came to me. Some passages were written laboriously, gropingly, then rewritten and rewritten until clarity came. Other passages were inspired. While not documented in the conventional sense, it is the synthesis of a lifetime of reading, discussing, and practicing different disciplines from meditation to the martial arts. I really don't know where some of the material came from. Everything I discovered seemed marvelous when I first thought of it, but obvious after I had gotten it down. All I really know is that it was and still is an exploration. It started with an answer to a question which led to another question and still another. It seems that if I held the questions long enough the answers came. Where they came from, I really don't know. I would like to take credit for them, but perhaps they were inspiration from a higher source. Mysteriously this book has taken me way beyond what I knew before writing it, yet it all came from me! Not a lot of research went into it. Also, it is in a very real sense of the word psychedelic, mind expanding. When I first wrote down the principles of *Oneness Perceived,* my mind was far ahead of my consciousness. I knew perception to be illusory, but my consciousness, my imagination, was still firmly rooted in the reality of appearances. Gradually, as I worked on the book, I developed an alternate way of seeing reality, one more like how I imagine Zen adepts see it. Now I shift back and forth from passionate to objective seeing more or less at will. But even now there are times when I am so caught up in the reality of appearances that I have difficulty grasping what I have written.

Every man has a path but few find it. In writing this book, embodying these insights, I have unexpectedly found my path. It started in front of my nose and all I had to do was take it where it led. I am on the path home, and it is the great adventure of my life. Join me.

A note on organization

I would like this book to be more organized. It just isn't! It was not written so much as it evolved over many years, and my depth of understanding evolved with it. Although some parts logically develop, others are paradoxical, poetic, or just plain quirky. In addition, the whole development is more like music than philosophy, with major and minor themes that emerge, develop, grow silent, and then are heard again in an expanded context.

I have attempted to reorganize it into tight chapters, but not only is it beyond my capacity, I don't even think it is a good idea. Every time I tried to do it, it deadened the writing and took the excitement of discovery out of it. Finally, I had the happy inspiration of abandoning all pretense of tightly organized chapters and instead reinstated their identity as short, standalone pieces, really meditations. Then I sorted these into sections and chapters as to their main ideas.

The same applies for consistency of tone. As I said, some parts are academic, others paradoxical, poetic, or quirky, occasionally even preachy. I have tried to even it out as much as possible, but the material and the way it was written just seems not to lend themselves to the effort. I don't want to labor to make it a worse book, so I just have to ask you to bear with me.

A note on state of mind

This is not an easy book to read, and it is an almost impossible one to speed-read. It requires patience, concentration, dedication to understanding, and above all meditative consciousness on the part of the reader. However, I believe that making the effort and getting into that place where the book makes sense will be a very powerful means of moving the reader toward enlightened understanding, as writing it did for me!

SECTION ONE

ONENESS AND PERCEPTION

1. ONENESS

All true spiritual traditions are closer to one another than to the religions derived from them, for they spring from one reality!

—Bob Russell

ONENESS

Oneness perceived presents a unified field theory of perception and reality. It is a theory of Oneness and duality, reality and illusion, as they affect, redefine, and unify such fundamental concepts as consciousness, knowing, evolution, time, space, and being.

It is a unified field theory, but because it deals with perception and aperceptual reality, it unites the biofield or perceptual field, the field of consciousness, and not the physical field. (Whether it will move us closer to a unified physical field theory as well is to be seen, but it will at least offer some clarification.) I call it aperceptual field theory.

3

Oneness Is Reality
Oneness Perceived Is Duality
Duality Is Illusion
Oneness Perceived Is Illusion*

THE GREAT INFERENTIAL

Oneness is the great inferential. In one sense we know it is there, it must be there, yet there is no way of getting primary information about it, no way of knowing it. Sometimes the idea that there is only Oneness and everything is connected seems improbable, a woolly-headed notion, a mystical construct. Other times it seems self-evident, a palpable reality, a truism so real that it shines out every-place one looks. What is this level on which all things are connected, on which all things are one? Call it the level of *being*. No matter how extensive the differences between things are, everything exists, everything is in a state of being. Existence…being…forms a continuum, inhabits a common dimension, saturates all possible separate dimensions, is all-inclusive, universal.

Oneness is reality. However, this too is an inference, a negative category. Oneness can be said to be reality only in the sense that it is not illusory, is not a perception, is not dualized, is not a relational quality. It is a reality that we cannot even prove exists. It must exist, otherwise we could not have anything to perceive, but we can no more prove it than know it. We think it's reality, the reality that underlies all appearances, but again this is just pure supposition, unacceptable in any scientific court of law. For now, let us just agree to discuss Oneness as if it exists and as if it is reality, aperceptual reality. For if it is not real and doesn't exist, then nothing is real and nothing exists.

Not that this is a compelling argument. One could take it the other way, reasoning that since there is no proof that Oneness is real or even exists and since we know perception is illusory, then perhaps

---

*By illusion I mean that the experienced quality of the perceived thing is not isomorphic to that underlying it, but rather is a projection of the perceiving organism. It does not mean there is nothing real, only that the experience does not correspond to the reality.

nothing is real and nothing exists. This opens up a difficult path. If nothing is real and nothing underlies perception, what does this say about the nature of existence...that nothing exists except illusion? As absurd and self-contradictory as this is on the face of it, it does dispassionately sum up the human predicament, or for that matter the condition of all sentient beings.

It also implies something else. It implies that the existence of Oneness and reality, to say nothing of the reality of Oneness, if believed in at all, have to be believed in as articles of faith, blind faith. We believe in them because we must, because without that belief the bottom would fall out of all higher human thought and endeavor. We would be trapped in a shifting maze of appearances with no direction even possible. However, this belief is more like religion than philosophy...to say nothing of science. To believe in Oneness the same way we believe in God, with no proof and no prospects of proof, just faith, is not a foundation for science but for superstition. The more we think about it, the more closely it resembles belief in God.

Can Oneness be considered the generic form of God?

Like God, Oneness is something that we suppose must be there, underlying all we can see, something we infer from all of the detailed and glorious illusions that make up our world and ourselves. Unlike God, however, Oneness is devoid of form and intention, and as such is devoid of the forms and intentions that almost all religions attribute to their gods.

If, however, despite the difficulties it makes for us, despite the abyss it throws us into, we choose to disbelieve, to be agnostic on Oneness, where does that leave us? Is it possible to construct a coherent worldview on the foundation that all there is is appearance, illusion, with no underlying reality? We would have to start with the premise that underlying perceptual illusion is just a more fundamental illusion. (Not the fundamental illusion, just a more fundamental illusion.) Now peculiarly enough, this is just what science finds. Beneath color perception we find the illusion (I say illusion because these are cognitive perceptions realized in the form of sensory analogs) of electromagnetic waves, behind that we find the illusion of packets of energy; behind that perhaps vibrating strings and behind that…nothing, at least nothing we have thought up yet. What is generating these levels of illusion if not Oneness, if not primal existence…nothing?

In a sense then, Oneness and nothingness can be held equivalent. Why is this and what does it mean? The solution to this apparent paradox resides in the realization that "thingness" is a perceptual category. Nothing, "no thing," doesn't mean absence of all existence, it simply means absence of perceptions, perceptual categories. I talk more about this in the chapter titled "Thingness and the Perceived Self." That nothing, "no thing," that no perceptual category seems ultimately to underlie the hierarchy of sensory and cognitive perceptions by which we account for things, could suggest an absence of fundamental existence, particularly if one does not recognize the difference between perceptual categories and underlying reality. However, it does not suggest that absence to me. Rather, it points to the existence of an aperceptual Oneness that is a perceptual void.

DUALITY AND ILLUSION

The relationship between Oneness and duality is wholly a matter of perception. Whenever there is perception, Oneness divides into a perceiver and a perceived, a subject and an object. In other words, Oneness becomes dual. Oneness and duality are the same thing from different points of view; as are reality and illusion.

More precisely, duality and illusion arise from any and all points of view, whereas Oneness and reality exist only from no point of view. A point of view is a necessary condition for perception. Perception without a point of view is as contradictory and meaningless as perception without a perceiver.

If reality exists only from no point of view, it is definitionally unknowable (that is, not perceivable). In that case, what can reality mean?

The dualism engendered by the sheer act of perception is an unbreachable wall, an irreducible fact, an impenetrable illusion that limits the human condition and, in fact, the condition of all bounded entities.

ILLUSION

All perception is illusory. Illusion is an inescapable consequence of the duality of perception, is the duality of perception. Illusion enters with the perceiver. The sheer existence of a point of consciousness in Oneness sensing another creates duality and illusion, which, of course, are merely the generic and specific forms of one another.

When one confronts himself with this premise, one confronts the ultimate dilemma of the human condition, the impossibility of knowing reality, perhaps even the problem of conceiving reality. This is because conception, at least meaningful conception, is closely tied to perception and equally built on sensory experiences. Throughout the history of mankind, contemplative people have tried to find a way out this limitation without fully appreciating why it is impossible. Alchemists and their successors, scientists, try to get around it by peering ever deeper into macrocosmic and microcosmic space, as if duality could be resolved just beyond the limits of resolution of our unaided senses. All sorts of experiential metaphysicians ranging from shamans to gurus to academic psychedelicians explore inner space through trance, meditation, or drugs. All attempts, however, are destined to fail because of the intrinsic limitations of perception.

Unfortunately, nonillusory perception is the perpetual motion machine of both physics and metaphysics. It seems intuitively possible, yet it can only run contrary to natural law, and that realm has yet to be discovered. The bright side of the matter, however, is that the pursuit of nonillusory perception has led not only to a great deal of nonsense, but to science and technology as well. However, as science progresses, the search for nonillusory perception is misleading us deeper into paradoxical wonderlands, quagmires of nonsense. It is time to accept the limits of perception, and consider what further limitations, in the pursuit of knowledge and the doing of science, these limits thrust upon us.

NONILLUSORY PERCEPTION

What could nonillusory perception be? Sometimes in altered states we think we experience it, but as soon as we try to hold on to it, to describe it, to claim it as ours, to know that we know it, it vanishes.

Is nonillusory perception possible?
The only way to have perception that is nonillusory is to have perception without a perceiver, without a point of perception, to have awareness without reference to an individual consciousness, without someone to be aware.
Is this a possibility?
Could a "you" experience it?
A person can be aware of the illusion of duality, but he cannot get free of it! A person can know about reality, but he cannot perceive it.

Can the observer be both subject and object?
Not and remain the observer, i.e., only at the sacrifice of separation.

Can you remember what you have never experienced, what you can never have experienced?

ISNESSING ISNESS

One sometimes has an experience that seems to have the portent of Oneness. Is it possible that this is real? Can one experience Oneness but not perceive it, or is this semantic nonsense?
Experiencing Oneness is imaginable by being in a state of pure awareness, not awareness of. How can this be accomplished, if indeed it ever is? Meditators suspend "perception of" by disidentifying, disassociating, or turning away from the presentations of the sensorium. The yogis withdraw from the senses entirely, whereas other meditative traditions teach techniques of disidentifying from them, or quieting the mind (stopping the cognitorium) by concen-

trating on a point, counting breaths, repeating a mantra, and so on.

What is left when we do this? Pure consciousness, experience without experiencing anything!

If anything is, this is the experience of Oneness. It is not Oneness out there, Oneness perceived. It is our inner, individual Oneness. Oneness known. But this is the turning of the circle…Oneness is Oneness…is all Oneness. By suspending perception and tapping into our inner Oneness, we experience universal Oneness…and that opens the gate.

There is a possible problem with this formulation of pure aperceptual consciousness as the experience of Oneness. Consider the possibility that consciousness does not exist in aperceptual reality, but it too is perceptual illusion, the reification of the experience of the sensorium or the cognitorium. If this is the case, can consciousness exist without anything to be conscious of? If consciousness is just one pole of the dualistic illusion, conscious/unconscious, then how can we attribute anything real to it? Even more to the point, how can we say that pure consciousness is the experience of Oneness, to say nothing of being Oneness itself.

One solution is to go beyond the intrinsically dual idea of consciousness as synonymous with awareness (consciousness / unconscious) to the definitionally nondual idea of Isness, that which just is, *resting in oneness*, neither known nor not known. But again can we experience Isness? If we can, is it not just another perception? Does any experience *of* it convert it into the illusion of consciousness? On the other hand, if we cannot experience Isness, how can it lead to the experience of Oneness? Obviously we are running up against the limitations of a dualistic language here.

Try this…what if we don't experience Isness? I don't mean being unconscious of it. That would just be the other pole of the duality, conscious/unconscious. What if we refuse to admit being either conscious or unconscious of it? What if we neither experience or not experience it? What if we isness it instead? What if we isness Isness? Is this possible or nonsense? Is it what the meditation masters do? I leave these as open questions as well.

Isness…As a new verb it is destined to remain forever incomprehensible!

What is the difference between being Isness, which we all, from the lowest to highest, can lay claim to, and isnessing Isness? What is the difference between a common man and a Buddha? Is it knowing or even remembering a state never perceived, in fact, unperceivable?

The fundamental question, the heart of the matter, is this. Do you, by suspending perception reside in your own fundamental self, the perceiver rather than the perception, thus touching your own unperceived reality, your own Oneness, which, of course, is also the Oneness of the universe; in this way coming to know unperceived reality? Or is this, too, this touching of your own self, your own Oneness, just a perception by a different eye, also an illusion, the innermost shell of a perceptual onion that has no core?

PERCEIVED REALITY

Is reality itself a perceptual illusion?
If we perceive it, it must be.
Everything else we perceive is.
But if that is the case
There must be infinite realities
just as there are infinite qualities
and infinite illusions.

Is there something real beneath that illusion we call reality?
How can we know it?
How can we call it?
The cosmic mystery!
The unperceived!

2.   THE IMPOSSIBILITY OF KNOWING

THE PROBLEM WITH THE DIRECT PERCEPTION OF REALITY

We humans are perceivers in quest of knowing. We extend the enve-
lopes of technology and consciousness in the search for reality, but
as close as we think we are coming, we ultimately always fail. The
problem with our quest to know reality is us. We want to know reality in the same sense that we know a perception; we want to know
what it looks, smells, tastes, sounds, and feels like, but it is not to be!
When science investigates reality, it always suffers from the same
problems. It asks things of things…things like what does it smell
like; what color is it; what is its size, shape, and mass; is it energy
or matter, wave or particle; how did it begin; what are its smallest
components and how can we measure them? It too "expects" the
answers to be qualitative, subjective, in terms of the qualities of sensory perception or their cognitive analogs. This is qualitative knowing, metaphorical knowing. However, a little thought will bring us
to the conclusion that real answers cannot be in illusory terms. The
only qualitative fact about reality that we can be reasonably certain
of is that it is not qualitative.

WHAT IS TANGIBLE IS ILLUSORY

When we know reality directly, what we are knowing is without content or form, without dimension, without qualities. We are really isnessing. Reality can never be known in perceptual, dualistic, linear, material, qualitative terms. Aperceptual reality, by definition, can never be known perceptually. It will never be tangible. It is what it is…aperceptual.

Perceiving Oneness makes it tangible but illusory. "Knowing reality" in the perceptual sense is an empty concept, a misconception, a misnomer, a fantasy, a doomed quest, a projection of the very quality of perception through which we create illusion in the first place. This particular kind of "knowing" to which we all aspire is an impossibility, a contradiction in terms, and an ego trip in the deepest sense. We can perceive. We can know about (in the sense of scientific models and concepts), but when we know reality directly, there is no thing there. There is a there, a presence, but there is no thing there. The essence of a thing cannot be abstracted from its being without losing its reality. Much less can the essence of everything be abstracted from every being, everywhere, throughout time. There is but one undistorted reality and that is Oneness, Isness itself. Any experience of, however extensive, is hopelessly fragmented and infinitely distorted by the occasion of its perceptual qualification.

Impossible as it may ultimately be, the quest to understand reality through perception has given rise to some of man's greatest accomplishments. However, we can make far better sense out of this universe that we are a part of by facing the limitations of perception, by balancing perception and knowing, than by remaining one-sided, blind, and willfully deluded. Acknowledgment of the limitations of perception and the need to balance it with knowing, is as old as Taoist philosophy. It has been expressed exquisitely and unequivocally by Lao-tzu in the first paradox of the Tao Te Jung.

> The Tao that can be told of
> Is not the absolute Tao;
> The names that can be given
> Are not the absolute names

The nameless is the origin of heaven and earth; *(Oneness)*
The named is the mother of all things. *(perception)*

Therefore:
Oftentimes, one strips oneself of passion *(meditates)*
In order to see the secret of life;
Oftentimes, one regards life with passion, *(ordinary
perception)*
In order to see its manifest forms.

These two (the secret and its manifestations) *(Oneness and
perception)*
Are (in their nature) the same;
They are given different names
When they become manifest.
They may both be called the Cosmic Mystery.

—The Wisdom of Laotse (Lao-tzu). Lin Yutang translator and editor.
Modern Library Edition, 1948
(Italics mine)

SELF AND OTHER

You cannot be self and know other. As self, you can only know self. On the other hand, if you cease to be self, there is no one to know other. To say there is knowing (other) without anyone to know makes nonsense out of the concept of knowing.

If there is anyone apart, that one is automatically isolated from knowing other and thus is dependent on perception.

Perceiving other is knowing the experiential quality of one's own senses; it is knowing the other as a projection of yourself. In this sense it is the ultimate anthropomorphism.

To know Oneness tangibly is the longing of the soul, the longing for that which is ever denied us, not because we are specifically human but just because we exist apart, because we are subjects, some-

ONES, because we are finite, individual, referent points in but apart from Oneness, because we are not everything everywhere. Knowing the One is denied us by our essential condition as separate perceivers.* The yearning for tangible knowledge of Oneness is the yearning for escape from that condition of separation, from the inherent limitations of our individual existence, of any individual existence.

This yearning, however, misdirects us. Real wisdom and understanding come not from trying to know Oneness qualitatively, as if it has qualities like "blue" and "warm," but from knowing from Oneness.

THE MIND OF GOD

God knows everything because he is everything…is everywhere… is all aspects of all things. He is not outside but inside, not separate but One. He knows through being, not through perceiving. He does not perceive but rather he is. Therefore he is not limited by subject-object duality. The limitation of God, on the other hand, is that he can't perceive. He can know but he cannot know that he knows. He knows but there is no "he" to know.

In this sense, all sentient creatures are the "he's" of God. All sentient creatures are the means by which God knows (in the perceptual sense). They are the eyes of God, also his ears, nose, tongue, and fingers. Mankind, however, is more, not only are we the eyes of God, we are also his mind!

We do not provide just another set of senses for him, but with our exquisitely developed powers of cognition and cognitive perception, we lend him with our capacity to question and understand, to reflect. For we, not God, for better or worse, are Homo sapiens sapiens, the creatures that do know that they know!

---

*I am talking about one level, the perceptual level. Of course there is another, simultaneous level on which we are "everything, everywhere."

3.   THE STRUCTURE OF ILLUSION

PRIMAL AND QUALITATIVE DUALISM

The very occasion of perception splits Oneness into perceiver and perceived. This is primal dualism. Any particular perception by a living being is through a sensorium which acts as a point of consciousness,* a zero point or a fulcrum, around which a duality is constructed by the perceiver. This is qualitative dualism.

Primal dualism divides the world into illusory opposites: subject and object, self and other, cause and effect, etc. Without a subject (perceiver), there can be no object (perception); with a subject, there must be an object. Without a self, there can be no other; with a self there must be an other. Without an effect, there can be no cause; with

*A word on point of consciousness. Any perceiver is a separate point in velocity-space-time. Just by virtue of coming from a physically separate point, perception creates numerous physical dualities, like self other, plus minus, before behind, slower faster, etc. This point can be thought of as the physical reference point of the perception. Other points that are projected are biological, sensory, and cognitive aspects of the perceiving organism. Points like sensed body temperature and learned responses are extensions of location in velocity-space-time. Because they sum in consciousness I refer to them as the points of consciousness of the perceiver. They are the points in consciousness from which the individual perceives and from which he creates the even more abstract dualities like hotter colder, and safer more dangerous, etc.

15

an effect, there must be a cause.

Qualitative dualism is a derivative or second level of primal dualism. Hot cold, near far, rough smooth, and all other perceptual qualities depend not only on the act of perception, but on the individual sensorium that is doing the sensing.

All perceivers create primal dualism equally just by being a viewpoint. Qualitative dualisms are specific to the individual qualities of the individual perceiver.

ORGANIC RELEVANCE

All life forms evolve categories of sensory perception on the basis of organic relevance. The perceiver's sensorium evolves to be selectively sensitive to those aspects of Oneness relevant to its survival and reproduction. Then, it encodes these organically relevant aspects into experiential categories: certain wavelengths of light into colors, certain chemical compounds into tastes and smells, certain intensities of molecular activity into a comfortable range of temperature. These experiential categories are qualities.

Thus, qualitative dualism is the subdividing of the perceptual field into synthetic, sensory qualities; qualities that are comprehensible, useful, and relevant to the perceiver, although completely illusory, qualities like heat, color, and smell. These qualities are strictly experiential and in their experience totally illusory (as far as Oneness is concerned), although they seem very real to the perceiver. Hence, the term "qualitative dualism."

THE CONTINUUM

The continuum of qualitative dualism is first determined by sensation. The organism (guided by organic relevance) selects certain modalities of Oneness to be sensitive to (stimulated by). Some of these are universal like temperature, some are almost universal like light, and some, like the presence of certain chemicals, are specific to only certain organisms.

What is sensed is always relative to the sensor organ and generally sensed along a continuum of intensity, i.e., cooler, louder, brighter. These are cognitive analogs to the sensory continuums, that are also interpreted as continuums, for example, distance.

THE REFERENCE POINT

Continuums of information, which is what sensory continuums are, neither inform the perceiver nor are useful to him without a point of reference...some marker around which it can be said the intensity of the quality in question is more or less. In perception, the referent point is the place or point of consciousness of the perceiver with regard to the quality under question.

In any sensed continuum, there is a place in which the sensing organism fits itself, according to the principle of organic relevance. For instance, in a temperature continuum there is the organism's ideal internal temperature; in a light continuum there is a level of illumination at which the eye switches from rods to cones.

This place where the organism fits (more or less) is the point of reference on the continuum of that sensed quality, and the modality in turn becomes dualized around the point of reference. Thus, temperature becomes hot and cold, light waves become light and dark, location becomes front and rear, near and far, all in relation to the perceiver.

The place where the perceiving organism is located (on the continuum) is called the point of consciousness of the perceiver.

NON-SELF-REFERENT THOUGHT IS DUALISTIC BY EXTENSION

Cognitions, thoughts, theories, etc. are not rooted in the sensation of the physical organism; therefore they are not directly self-referent. Instead, they are self-referent by extension. Cognition is an extension or metaphor of the perceptual field. However in cognition, as in perception, there is always an (implied) point of consciousness dualizing a continuum of information.

Such non-self-referential abstractions as zero in mathematics are metaphorical extensions of the point of consciousness. Zero, for instance, starts as a metaphor for the point of consciousness where we cannot perceive any of the quality in question. It then evolved to where it could be a point on a continuum separating a positive value from a negative one. Metaphorical extension also accounts for the cognition of nonperceptual qualities like X-rays. We conceptualize X-rays as being like light and the zero could be the point on the continuum of X-ray strength where human exposure is safe or where we can't measure any more X-rays.

Because of this metaphorical extension, we cognate as well as perceive dualistically. No matter how abstract, thinking about nonperceptual qualities is almost always a metaphor of perception. Even theoretical physicists, dealing with inferred phenomena, have to find arbitrary perceptual metaphors like wavicles, strings, flavors, spin, and field in order to ground their concepts.

LANGUAGE IS ALSO DUALISTIC BY EXTENSION

Language is a further extension of both perception and cognition. The structure of our language, like the structure of perception and cognition, is dualistic. As difficult as it is to conceive nondualistically, it is almost as difficult to conceive nonlinguistically. Our language is based on our perceptions and at the same time forms them. Subject and object, actor and act, cause and effect, past and future, and all other dualities are all intrinsic to the linguistic syntax by which we not only communicate but think!

THE WAY QUALITIES ORIGINATE

The location of one's point of consciousness or self, as the reference point on a sensed continuum, plus the dualization of that continuum around this reference point, is the completion of the perceived quality, the illusion, the experience.

It is the way qualities originate.

Conversely, the experience of a quality always implies an adjacent environmental event, sensed and perceptually interpreted, then viewed as a continuum with a reference point (although these implications are not always readily evident). Molecular activity is an adjacent environmental event, whereas the experience of heat, with its implications of hot and cold, hotter and cooler (perceived qualities around a reference point on the continuum of temperature) is a perceptual quality.

We must keep in mind that the event is not necessarily structured in the same way as the experience. A good example of this is color. Color perception in humans gives rise to a discontinuous spectrum, red, blue, etc., whereas light is a smooth continuum of frequency.

By the same reasoning, environmental events cannot be experienced in their reality, only inferred from the quality of sensory perception, i.e., we never experience molecular activity as such, but always process it into perceptions of heat or cold. Sensation is automatically converted into perception by the sensorium. The point of consciousness of the perceiver, as well as the perceiver's biological individuality, is automatically factored in. Perception is the ultimate in user friendly programming, the ergonomic triumph of that miraculous biocomputer, the brain.

Of course, we must keep in mind that there are no such things as adjacent environmental events. These are also perceptual illusions, limited aspects of the flux of Oneness, selected by the organism on the basis of self-relevance. But it is convenient to speak about them as events for the moment.

Therefore, when we refer to a quality, we have to bear in mind that the experience, the very qualitativeness of it, is a perceptual illusion, a complex selection of one aspect of Oneness by the sensorium, a transformation and structuring into appearance by the act of perception.

4. PERCEIVING THE MIND

Sensory perception is an illusory form of the real.
Cognitive perception is a real form of the illusory.

NOTE TO THE READER: This chapter has some difficult material in it that slows down the plot and which even my best friends have difficulty reading through. Prudence suggests I put this material in an appendix; however, logically it belongs right where it is. So I have compromised and put everything but the bare minimum for continuity in an alternate typeface *so that the impatient reader may know what he may skim without losing the continuity.*

SOME WORKING DEFINITIONS

These definitions are not meant to be scientific or universal but merely specify the way these terms will be used in this book.

Sensation is the physiological interface between organism and environment. It is the irritation of the skin boundary or stimulation of the senses by the environment. It is unconscious.

Sensory perception, on the other hand, is the interpretation or *experience* of sensation by the central nervous system.

Imagination and *cognition* are events in the central nervous system that are independent of external stimuli or sensation.

Cognitive perception is the experience of imagination and cognition combined with the experience of sensation. It can be thought of as the perception of perception.

Consciousness may be read as consciousness of, awareness or experience. These definitions pertain exclusively to chapters 4 and 5. Later in the book the definition of consciousness will be both expanded and refined.

Note that *sensory perception* and *cognitive perception* are similar in the location of the experience (CNN), but differ in the origin or location of the events experienced (the organism environment interface versus the CNN). Note, too, that whereas sensation has to be encoded into sensory-perceptual qualities by perception, the events of imagination and cognition already occur in illusory forms, i.e., as sensory-perceptual qualities. The experience (perception) of these qualities gives rise to a second level of awareness, or maybe just awareness where there was none before, and permits a second level of processing, i.e., thinking about your thoughts.

If cognitive perception is the perception of perception, and the further perception of that perception, what is cognition? The psychological literature uses cognition in the same way that I use cognitive perception, although loosely, without the structural specificity that I give to the process of cognitive perception. It also uses cognition to refer to all thinking and reasoning processes. This approximate usage frustrates my purposes so I am going to adapt a slightly different and more precise terminology. The "knowing or perceiving" usage of cognition I am going to keep referring to as cognitive perception. The "thinking or reasoning" usage, any activity that entails mental representation or manipulation of representation, I will term cognitive activity or just "cognition."

THE SENSORIUM AND THE COGNITORIUM

The sensorium creates perceptual experience. It is a specialization of that which started out, in cells and extremely simple organisms, as irritability of boundary membranes. I am using the term *sensorium* to refer to the totality of the sense organs and those areas of the brain that translate sensory neural inputs into qualities of experience (both relevant to and comprehensible by the organism), and then presents them to consciousness. The sensorium's function is to ascertain present conditions in the immediate sensory field.

Simpler forms of life, plants and animals with rudimentary nervous systems, work directly off of their sensoriums, and it is unknown what sort of intervening variables (in the form of consciousness or cognitive perception) come into play, if any. Therefore, the functioning of the sensorium itself, without the superimposition of consciousness, is sufficient to say that perception is taking place. This is a situation roughly analogous to somebody responding to a stimulus in their sleep. However, as animals evolved complex central nervous systems, first sensory perception, i.e., the experience or consciousness of the sensorium, and then cognitive perception, i.e., the experience of cognitive process and contents, emerged.

The cognitorium creates cognitive experience, the experience of all thought and imagination. It is an extension to the sensorium. It also is a means of perception, in that it too presents interpreted information or qualities to consciousness. Consciousness does not routinely differentiate between sensations, e.g., smells, and cognitions, e.g., thoughts, imaginings. (Sometimes, as in the case of hallucinations, it cannot.) They are all mental events in consciousness!

The cognitorium refers to the totality of cognitive processes, including those parts of the brain that perform them. As I have said, the sensorium perceives things in the present environment, and presents them to consciousness (and thus to the cognitorium) in the form of qualities. Similarly, the cognitorium perceives qualities from memories and the brain's activities, represents them, conserves them over time, and manipulates and processes them in various ways. It also synthesizes or imagines qualities, and processes these similarly.

Then it presents both the processes (in part) and their conclusions back to consciousness, where, in turn, they become available to the sensorium again.

What is important to remember (vis-à-vis discussions of illusion and reality) is that the sensorium gets its initial inputs from the environment and presents them to consciousness in the guise of qualities. The cognitorium on the other hand gets its initial inputs from memories and inner representations, where they are already in the form of qualities. So that the sensorium perceives (transforms) the environment into qualities, i.e., transforms Oneness into duality or illusion, whereas the cognitorium starts with these (illusory) qualities and conserves their intelligibility through a number of complex processes without transforming them further qualitatively. Thus, the sensorium perceives reality into illusion, whereas the cognitorium experiences illusion, transforms, conserves it, and reexperiences it. It takes the qualities of the sensorium, plucking them from the inner world, and returns them, processed and recombined but essentially unchanged qualitatively. Thus, it can be said that the sensorium transforms reality into illusion, but the cognitorium conserves this illusion unchanged through successive manipulations, therefore working with real illusion rather than illusory reality. The transformation and conservation of cognition corresponds to logic.

Consciousness as a Bidirectional Mediator

Consciousness, then, functions as a bidirectional mediator between the sensorium and the cognitorium, and a unifying stage for all perceptual phenomena.

(The path seems to be from the sensorium, to consciousness of the sensorium, to the cognitorium, to consciousness of the cognitorium.)

Sensorium > Consciousness > Cognitorium > Consciousness > Sensorium or Cognitorium.

COGNITIVE PERCEPTION AS AN EXTENSION OF SENSORY PERCEPTION

Cognitive perception, in addition to its other features, shares the structural features that characterize sensory perception, but with two differences. It doesn't necessarily start with the sensorium and it doesn't necessarily have organic relevance. Aside from that, it too has a point of perception or point of consciousness that acts like a reference point splitting a continuum, and, of course, it too is dual and illusory with reference to aperceptual reality.

Sensory perception takes information from the sensorium, from the perceiver's sensation of external events, and is rooted there. Cognitive perception, however, takes information from sensory perception and therefore is free to soar to the heights of abstraction, conjecture, concept formation, logic, imagination, and fantasy.

There are a number of reasons for this freedom. First, the reference point on the cognitive continuum is not tied to the perceiver's biocentric or physical point of consciousness. The point of consciousness can be projected into anything, the concept of zero, the speed of sound, Times Square. Second, the continuum need not be a continuum of sensation; it need only be known about, as is the case with ultraviolet light or pH. It can be observable by an instrument which functions in the place of the sensorium. Third, since the cognitive perception does not have to have organic relevance, the organism merely has to be involved in it conceptually.

We see then that cognitive perception can be greatly removed or abstracted from sensory perception.

COGNITIVE PERCEPTION AND DUALISM

Sensory perception is conscious experience of the isness of the sensorium. Cognitive perception is conscious experience of the isness of the cognitorium. The quality of consciousness is the same: the quality experienced is different.

These differences not-withstanding, the same perceptual dualism is at work in cognitive perception as in sensory perception, only the objective field consists of cognitive contents instead of sensory contents, while consciousness is the subjective field of both.

Sensory perception is primary illusion while cognitive perception is the awareness or perception of that illusion. To put it concisely... cognitive perception is the perception of perception. (It is also the perception of other cognitive events like thought and imagination.)

This perception of perception entails a folding over of perception onto itself, which takes place in a flash and repeats ad infinitum. This ability to fold onto itself again and again creates a potential increase in mental complexity limited only by the neural capacity of the brain, and rapidly proliferates thought forms. The rapidity and the unlimited potential of the process creates the demand that accounts for the evolutionary rapidity of cerebral cortex development, while the dynamic of the process itself suggests the morphology of the cerebral cortex as it physically folds over and over itself.

Furthermore, the fact that the cerebral cortex coevolved with cognition means that the cerebral cortex coevolved with and was based on illusion.

THE ROLE OF ILLUSION IN COGNITIVE PERCEPTION

The role of illusion in cognitive perception is different than its role in sensory perception. In sensory perception the sensorium creates the illusory quality (which is the way the perceiver "knows" Oneness) with real changes in the central nervous system. In cognitive perception the sensorium has already played its role. That which is cognitively perceived is no longer an aspect of Oneness, but composed of the very illusions of perception now coded in the central nervous system. These the cognitorium can experience directly without the need for further transformation.

This gives rise to the paradox that Oneness can only be known in illusion, but illusion can be known in reality. That is, cognitive perception experiences illusions as they are, as real illusions couched in the terms of sensory perception in the central nervous system (or their cognitive analogs). The events of imagination and cognition already occur in experienced or perceived forms, and the experience of them gives rise to a second level of awareness and processing, i.e., thinking about your thoughts.

THE COGNITIVE LOOP

Whenever someone manipulates a cognitive representation of any sort and then experiences the manipulation and/or its conclusion, a complex loop of cognition and cognitive perception has been established, one that is repeatable and builds upon itself.

The path of this cognitive loop is…

Sensorium > Consciousness > cognitorium > Consciousness > Cognitorium > Consciousness…ad infinitum.

This progressive cycle of cognitive manipulation and perception is an emergent phenomenon of great portent in the evolution of life. It constitutes the breaking away of the organism from dependence on the present sensory field, into the breathtaking heights of conjecture, abstraction, concept formation, imagination, and time, i.e., present/future. It coevolved a quantum leap in the cognitive potential of the brain, and the structure of the cerebral cortex. It is thought, or more precisely reflection!

DEPARTING FROM THE SENSORY FIELD

As the cognitorium is an extension to the sensorium, cognitive perception is an extension of sensory perception. Cognitive perception becomes active when the perceiver departs in any way from the sensory field. Whenever someone remembers, recognizes, categorizes, symbolizes (in any sensory modality) or imagines, they are departing from the sensory field and the cognitorium is at work.

Cognition evolved from its beginnings in simple learning to more sophisticated states, which include the ability to learn, represent, and cognitively manipulate these representations.

Cognitive manipulations have their evolutionary and developmental origins in sensory-motor manipulations. Therefore it is natural that they begin, both evolutionarily and developmentally, by mimicking them. Gradually however, cognition becomes free of the understood limitations of physical manipulation and becomes more flexible, abstract, and able to merge with other schemas that supplement or run counter to the sensory-motor, such as logic, or the premises of alternative geometries. Thus reversibility, conservation, and ultimately conjecture emerge, so that, for instance, one can imagine an object changing shape but retaining the same volume one of Piaget's developmental stages, or one can conceive of the transformation of matter into energy.

COGNITIVE PERCEPTION OR THE PERCEPTION OF COGNITIVE PROCESS

Consciousness (in its meaning as consciousness of or experience) functions as a clearinghouse for perceptual information. It registers inputs from both the cognitorium and the sensorium; then these inputs are reperceived from it by both. The only end point of this process is forgetting.

Consciousness understands the "common language" of *meaning*, i.e., self-referent and comprehensible qualities or percepts that the sensorium creates and the cognitorium both understands and speaks. When percepts are picked up by the cognitorium, they can be processed, the results experienced in consciousness, and, in turn, reperceived by the sensorium (as well as reacted to holistically [by both body and mind] to the degree that the person perceives they have relevance).

When conscious experiences are picked up again by the sensorium, the sensorium is open to the possibility that something may be happening that could require a somatic response. However, the sensorium does not have sophisticated discriminatory capacities, and it can easily be deceived that something is happening that warrants a somatic response, when in fact it does not (as in the case of known threats that are best answered by a nonsomatic response).

The somatic reactions of the organism to consciousness are similar regardless of whether the conscious contents have their source in the sensorium or the cognitorium. (With the exception of reflexes and conditioned reflexes, which may bypass consciousness completely.) For instance, a loud sound, an unfamiliar sight, a scary thought, and the hallucination of a ghost can all produce fright and an adrenaline reaction. The fact that this is so supports the above analysis and explains the psychosomatic illnesses that bedevil modern man, where he is not only acting but somatically reacting as if environmental circumstances exist that, in fact, do not. However problematic this bidirectional sensitivity of the sensorium may be on occasion, it is necessary to effect an adequate level of responsiveness to cognitively perceived situations. Otherwise one might decide to run or fight from a cognitively perceived threat, but would lack the motivation, emotional drive, and adrenaline response to maximize the body's ability to do so.

HAZARDS OF COGNITIVE PERCEPTION

In abstract thinking, the cognitive continuum may be only a distant analogy to a sensory quality, and the reference point may bear no relationship to the point of consciousness of oneself. When the reference point clearly doesn't refer to the perceiver, it remains a cognitive convention for dualizing things, which is the only way most of us can think about them. It is by maintaining the illusory quality and dualistic structure of sensory perception, but substituting an arbitrary point or concept for the perceiver's point of consciousness, that abstraction takes on its powers. Of course, it also creates numerous problems due to the concretization of perceptual illusion and duality and their projection into all human expressions and endeavors.

The abstract reference point in cognitive perception plays a large role in the evolution of many higher cognitive functions. For instance, quantification and measurement are enabled by abstract reference points such as zero or some other mathematical value.

When the reference point is clearly an abstraction, things stay relatively simple, but when the reference point is in lieu of, or an extension of the point of consciousness and mistaken by the perceiver for his point of consciousness, conceptual (cognitive-perceptual) errors begin to occur, and things start to get interesting.

Simple but significant errors occur when the perceiver mistakes an abstract reference point for his point of consciousness, or vice versa, say, when he mistakes something as cool when it is cooler than it used to be but unfortunately still too hot to safely touch, or when he perceives something as a bargain when it is half-price, although it is still unaffordable.

Far more significant consequences ensue when the perceiver mistakes his self-concept for his self and uses it as his point of consciousness, therefore systematically misperceiving or perceiving from a false center. A paranoid personality, for instance, projects the dividing point between friendly and hostile far lower than a secure personality and therefore suspects almost everyone. A powerful, successful person, on the other hand, may err in the opposite direction and consequently greatly underestimate risk.

Paranoid Friendly --- X---Hostile
Powerful Friendly--- X---Hostile

This universal phenomenon of using one's self-concept for one's point of consciousness is the key to personality development and is one of the most significant explanatory concepts for understanding human behavior. The identification and correction of this phenomenon is a key to successful psychotherapy and furthermore is at the heart of all valid spiritual and mystical traditions.

All self-concepts are definitionally mistaken to some extent as well as completely illusory. If one mistakes his self-concepts for his core or Oneness Self (which is his real point of consciousness) and then projects those self-concepts into the world, he is not only dualizing Oneness, but dualizing around a false fulcrum, thus skewing his experiential data. So he is twice removed from reality, laboring under the double jeopardy of perceptual illusion and a false center. In science, this is roughly the equivalent of heaping a measurement mistake on a fundamental mistake in theory or classification. Yet it is how we all function!

COGNITIVE PERCEPTION AND THE MULTIPLICATION OF PHENOMENA

In dualistic perception, a thing, any individual thing, is a focus of an infinite number of possible referent points. Location, velocity, acceleration, temperature, color, hardness, weight, shape, stickiness, intelligence, friendliness, sociability, etc. Any way we find to describe or qualify the perceiver can be found to be a potential quality of the perceived as well. Of course, it goes both ways. Any quality that can be applied to the perceived object must also be applicable to the perceiver.

This principle is directly related to the multiplication of phenomena in general, and probably to the multiplication of fundamental particles that physics is finding and which are confounding the search for the basic nature of the universe.

5. THE SECOND REALM

Oneness has no appearance.
Appearance has reality,
But it is not the reality of oneness.
Appearance is a second realm of reality.

THE SECOND REALM

Qualities are the appearances or perceptions of things rather than their reality. Appearances are the terms in which an organism knows and thinks. Appearances are all that noncognitive organisms are guided by. Cognitive organisms are guided by appearances as well as representations of appearances and manipulations of these representations.

Perceptual experience is not the same as the object of perception, but is an emergent phenomenon. It is illusory with regard to that which is ostensibly being experienced, but seems fully real in itself. By and large, it is all that we've got. The emergent *reality* of perceptual experience, if you choose to call it reality, I call the Second Realm of reality or just the *Second Realm*.

COGNITIVE PERCEPTION

As we have seen in the last chapter, perceptual self-reference may be purely sensory (for example, something may be hot or cold depending on the temperature of the perceiver), or it may be more or less abstract, involving boundaries (self/other, mine/yours), location (front/behind, nearer/further), self-concept (honest/dishonest), etc. The purely sensory level is sensory perception. The more abstract level is cognitive perception.

Humans, and to a limited extent other higher animals, are capable of cognitive as well as sensory perception. Cognitive perception, by my definition, takes place any time consciousness goes beyond the limits of an immediate sensory field. The moment an animal represents something to itself, cognitive perception ensues. An imaginary image or symbol such as a word is a form of representation, but so is a memory.

Cognition usually involves further manipulation and conservation of the representation. A cat, seeing a rat run into a pipe and going around to head it off at the other end, is involved in a complex cognitive act. It includes representation in image, conservation of the image, and manipulation of that image in order to figure out where the rat is going to reappear. Even if the cat just chased a rat down a hole and waited for him to come out, those functions of representation, conservation, and manipulation would, of necessity, have taken place.

Human perception can be cognitively extended to accommodate other reference points, say the freezing point of water or the location of the sun. To say runny ice cream is warm because it is not hard even though it is still cold to the touch, or that the moon is close because we know it is nearer than the sun, these are a perceptual abstractions...cognitive extensions of perception.

In addition, higher forms of life cognitively extend *organic relevance* to such relatively nonorganic modalities as social structures (of course, in presumably noncognitive, social species such as ants, social structures may be really of organic relevance), while with the evolution of culture and technology humans gradually are perceiving that nonsensory categories (radiation, pollution, anarchy, etc.) also have bearing on human survival. They are starting to cognitively perceive them, put them on continuums, and to quantify them with either arbitrary reference points or zero points on those continuums.

Cognitive perception is a metaphor. Something…an idea, concept, symbol, memory, abstraction, etc., is like or stands for a sensory perception, and furthermore the representation can be manipulated and conserved though logical transformations that recapitulate the sensory motor manipulation of an object (Piaget).

Radioactivity is a clear example. We understand it as being sort of like light, but different. It is invisible and can penetrate opaque substances, for instance. Of course, we cannot know it directly, but we can know about it, understand it, and, to a degree, imagine it. It is like unseen light. It is a cognition. It is a perceptual metaphor.

In summary, cognitive perception is an extension of sensory perception, i.e., it, too, puts qualities on a continuum with a reference point. But there are significant differences. The qualities are not sensed but cognitively represented, symbolized, in the central nervous system, and the reference point is not the sensory/organic point of consciousness of the perceiver, but an abstraction of the point of consciousness.

THE MULTIPLICATION OF QUALITIES IN THE SECOND REALM

When one goes beyond purely sensory perception to cognitive perception, both the perceiver (as a qualified point of consciousness) and the object of perception (correspondingly qualified) have an infinite possible number of corresponding reference points, i.e., location, movement, weight, friendliness, reliability, goodness, wealth, ad infinitum. Certain reference points become relevant to the perceiving organism, and form the basis of a cognitive perception of self.

In sensory perception, the organism projects upon the environment the qualities of the interpreted stimulation of its own boundary membranes. For instance, in sight, the seer projects onto the environment the interpreted stimulation of electromagnetic energy striking his eyes. Similarly, in cognitive perception, the perceiver, when perceiving others, projects onto them the illusory qualities of its self-perception as constructed from all relevant reference points in its history.

In "quantifying" the qualities of the other in relationship to itself, the perceiver engenders a whole new set of relational qualities. These "qualities" like space, time, color, stickiness, and hostility may be accurately thought of as modes of description or quantified experience. Or more accurately as linear, anthropomorphized abstractions of nonlinear reality. They also may be thought of as dimensions. (If you analyze them, the presumably basic dimensions of reality like time and space have little or no intrinsic difference from what would ordinarily be thought of as simple qualities, e.g., stickiness, hostility. All are illusory, dualistic qualities projected by the act of perception.)

Furthermore, the perceiver, perceiving itself, perceives even itself as an other (there is no other option) and thereby engenders in itself the same illusory qualities of dualistic perception. This is the case with ourselves even though we do not consciously consider ourselves as "other." This is where considerable confusion sets into the question of identity and the process of personality development. (There are numerous ways one can perceive one's physical or tangible self. However, there is no way that one can perceive the self, the "I," the eye that one is perceiving from. This distinction, which might seem an unnecessary splitting of hairs here, will become important in later chapters.)

DIFFERENTIATION

The effect of perception in creating qualities with reference to a perceiver and a perceived is called differentiation. Thus, differentiation and dualism are simultaneous aspects of perception. Because there are an infinite number of qualities that can be created by perception, differentiation itself is infinite.

Differentiation creates all the apparent but illusory qualities of the perceived world, all the properties of reality as human perception would have them. On the illusory level, differentiation is the action of perception, materializing the endless appearances of illusion out of the nonappearance of Oneness. On the real level, differentiation is the action of the evolutionary dialectic, yin and yang, the dance of organism and environment, evolving the thousand and one things, the endless forms of being, out of the no-thingness of Oneness. (We will address this second aspect of differentiation in the chapters on evolution.)

Differentiation is a primary law of creation.

ALL QUALITIES ARE RELATIONAL

All qualities are relational. That is, they are statements about the relationship of the perceived to the perceiver, e.g., cold, near, sticky, friendly, blue.

ALL DIMENSIONS ARE RELATIONAL

Like a quality, a dimension is a relationship between things. Usually, what we consider to be a dimension, e.g., space or time, is related to abstract coordinates. One-dimensional space, a point or unity is defined by one coordinate; it is only in relationship to itself. (Therefore, the concept of location is meaningless when talking about a point, unity, or Oneness. Every point is its own center.) Two-dimensional space is the relationship of two coordinates. Three-dimensional space is the relationship of three coordinates. Location is a point located in relationship to two or more coordinates. Time is a real point, i.e., the present, located on an imaginary continuum defined by two other imaginary continuums, i.e., the past and the future. Space-time requires five coordinates, i.e., the addition of past and future.

However, the things that we think of as sensory qualities are structurally identical to dimensions. The only difference is that the coordinates, the relationships that qualities are defined by, are between perceiver and perceived, and these are relations between sensations and their analogs rather than between abstract or mathematically defined coordinates. Categories like space and time are really both sensory qualities and abstract dimensions. That is, space, and arguably time, have a direct, sensory presence, i.e., they are experienced, but they also have abstract definitions in terms of coordinates which do not relate to a perceiving organism.

> All qualities are relational.
> All dimensions are relational.
> Qualities and dimensions are equivalent.

WHAT IS ILLUSORY ABOUT THE PERCEIVED WORLD?

The two interrelated aspects of perception, duality, and differentiation constitute the illusory reality in which mystics claim non-enlightened people are trapped. It is what meditators refer to when they claim that ordinary reality is not real. Although subject and object, cause and effect, better and worse, hotter and colder, faster and slower spring up instantly the moment the world is perceived from a fixed point of view, in reality no such properties exist. They are all artifacts of perception.

Imagine a beautiful day at the beach. Now consider that everything we perceive has some reality component, but that the quality of the reality component is entirely different from the perceived quality.

First, let us consider the temperature...a balmy 84...just hot enough to make a swim a pleasure. *Organic self-reference: just enough below our body temperature to make homeostasis easy to maintain. If our normal temperature were 0, we would literally die of the heat at 84; if our normal temperature were 120, we would need a winter coat at 84.*

Light blue skies, white clouds, tan sands, deep blue water, green palms...*Organic self-reference: a coding of light frequencies in the spectrum of light visible to humans into experientially different qualities to better aid figure ground differentiation.*

A delicious breeze…*Self-reference: one more aid to homeostasis of normal body temperature.* An ice-cold gin and tonic…*Homeostasis, rehydration, self-medication to reduce anxiety.*

An attractive man or woman in a bathing suit…*Self-reference: studies have shown average features for each race are perceived as the most beautiful.*

Peaceful day…*Self-reference: rapacious schools of bluefish are driving bait fish to the surface where they are being preyed on by gulls, thus being locked into a life-and-death battle on two fronts mere yards from where we swim, but fortunately we aren't bait.*

It's important to be aware that each of these more fundamental qualities that I have reduced "a day at the beach" to, heat, homeostasis, light, rehydration, etc., are not aperceptual reality either but just more fundamental levels of perceptual illusion!

THE SECOND REALM IS SEPARATE FROM THE REALITY OF THE FIRST REALM

The first realm is real but unknowable *(in the sense we know percepts).* The second realm is illusory but known. That is, it is already formulated in the language of perception. But is the second realm more than that? Is the second realm really a separate reality from the first realm or just a semantic category?

Is there a second realm reality out there, other than or beyond that constructed within the individual's perception, a reality other than Oneness? Does it have separate, independent existence? Furthermore, is the realm of the *knowable and the known* a reality that can be accessed by the individual directly, without perceiving Oneness and rendering it illusory? That is, is illusion a primary, and parallel reality with Oneness?

A second level of the same question is this. Is there a repository of second realm reality out there with the potential to be directly (psychically) accessed by a human with enough faith, LSD, or time served in the lotus posture to sufficiently alter his consciousness? If there were, it would follow that it could be accessed directly in a coherent sensible form, because the second realm is in perceptual, experiential terms already.

If the second realm is real and really a realm, if it is more than the functioning of one man's perception, it makes sense to look for some sort of collective phenomenon, a collective unconscious, a second realm universal. There might be a realm composed of the collective perceptions of the human race, or perhaps a wider collective than that, mammals, the animal kingdom, even all life.

The next question is "what might it contain?" Is it a pool of all the current perceptions of all men, or of all life? Does it contain a memory of the past, even a total memory of the past, as some people contend? Are there really such things as the collective unconscious, the Akashic records, and perhaps even records of past incarnations, and does the second realm contain them?

The proposition of a second realm universal, directly accessible through extrasensory means, is pretty hard for some of us to entertain, much less accept, and once entertained, it is even harder to rationalize. But it also has a tremendous amount of explanatory potential, enough so that one is tempted to accept it as inexplicable but true.

In one elegant stroke it can account for many varieties of psychic experience, channeling, past life experiences, access to the Akashic records and the like, where the individual seems to be accessing a bank of extrapersonal information that is already in illusory form (perceptual or even linguistic). Now, of course, these are phenomena most scientists and laymen alike, including myself at times, are predisposed to deny, minimize, or explain away, but unfortunately for our neat universes, they won't stay away. The proposition of a second realm universal helps rationalize all these claims. It doesn't say how the second realm universal is either held or accessed, but it it least posits its existence.

REAL ILLUSION

Is illusion a real part of Oneness?
Or is illusion no part of Oneness
and only the creations of illusion part of Oneness?

But how could something unreal create?
Illusion is real.
That is, it's real illusion,
but it is not part of Oneness.

If illusion is real, but not part of Oneness
Does this mean there is a reality other than Oneness
perhaps running parallel to it?
Twoness?
Duality?

Perhaps there are further realities parallel to Oneness.
Threeness?
Fourness?
Are there nonparallel realities as well?
Is something wrong with this thinking?

SECTION TWO

UNDERPINNINGS OF THE PHYSICAL WORLD

6. TIME, SPACE, AND EXISTENCE

Those illusions of time, space, and matter that the West reifies and affirms, the East deifies and destroys.

ILLUSORY TIME

Perceived time in the common view is like looking through the rear window of a moving car. The window frames the present and time passes from future to past, only becoming accessible to a consciousness as it becomes visible though the window. The instant time passes into the frame of the present, it starts receding into the past. The past is clearly there, although only discernible though memory or artifact. The future is unknown and indeterminate, and only becomes knowable as it passes through the window of the present to the past but it is clearly there as well, just out of sight. The present, peculiarly enough, is timeless time, one-dimensional, durationless, an infinitely brief instant through which events pass.

In this model, the past is all that can be known. The future, while it comes as surely as death and taxes, is unknown and unknowable, a probable line of regression, or a trajectory from the past. The present passes more quickly than it can be registered, although perception conveniently stretches it into something that has apparent duration, so that it can be savored and acted in.

The perception of time is subject to the same dualistic illusions as all other perceptual modalities. Past and future is one set of illusions. Beginning and end, now and then, are others. If we consider the matter dispassionately, we realize that there is no past and future, they simply don't exist. The past is no more: the future never was. They are cognitive perceptions, illusions, concepts, metaphors for spatial perceptions, memories, and anticipations, perceptual qualities. As perceptual qualities they are relevant, comprehensible, and extremely useful, but like all qualities they are illusory and ultimately misleading.

REAL TIME

Tantric time

Tantra visualizes time perpetually spewing from the mouth of the present, like flame perpetually spewing from the mouth of a dragon. That means that all that is, is perpetually creating itself in the present. At first this viewpoint seems extreme. After all, what about those things that were created yesterday, or twenty million years ago; aren't some of these things still with us?

This objection makes sense only in the illusory world. What are these traces of the past after all? If traces remain, they are present in the present. They are nested patterns continually recreating themselves on successively lower energy levels until finally they disappear. Even fossils are just time shadows cast in stone. And what about ourselves? Our memories are not our past either. We continually perpetrate and re-create ourselves out of our own present.

The present and the present only holds the past. The past is not a place or an entity. It is just the past present, the present that was but is not any longer. In the same way the future is just the future present. A projected, hypothetical generality that the present will never specifically fulfill. Henceforth, when we use or encounter the words past and future, we might understand them as past present and future present, no longer present and will be present. This alone will clear up a lot of the confusion about time.

(The images of the rear window and the flaming dragon's mouth were gotten from the excellent book *Tantra,* by Philip Rawson, although the exposition of these images is mostly my own.)

THE ETERNAL PRESENT

From the perceptual point of view, the present is just an infinitely brief moment, unperceivable, without duration, the one-dimensional now. From the aperceptual point of view, the present is infinite, always here. It is not a point on the two-dimensional procession of time. It is omnidimensional, infinitely expanded, the whole of time. It is the temporality of Oneness.

Two-dimensional time, a line from past to the future drawn from the viewpoint of the present, is an illusion. The past is a memory or inference, the future a projection. They are both constructs, belonging to the conjectural world of cognitive perception. They are both illusions, and time is an imaginary vector connecting two illusions.

What then is the reality of time, time unperceived. It is the eternal present. No matter what time it is, it is always the present. The present is all there is. In illusory time, the present is a point, a durationless transition between future and past. But in real time the present is infinite, always here, always present, an infinitely long time.

One naturally assumes that infinite time is the theoretical asymptote (the curve that approaches more and more closely but never quite arrives) of duration, the ideal longest time. But it is more complicated than that. The present is durationless in perceived time, but has infinite duration in real time. If you ignore the transition from perceived time to real time, you will stumble into the paradox that when you are in the present, the asymptote of brevity, you are also in eternity, the asymptote of duration.

Thus, eternity intersects (perceived) time at the point where reality intersects illusion, the present.

Eternity intersects time at the present.

To ignore the transition from perceived time to real time would be a "mobius," my term for the error in logic in argument of crossing from one meaning to another by unwittingly using the same word or concept in two different ways (named after the Möbius strip, the ribbon of paper twisted and joined into a loop so that the outside edge runs imperceptibly into the inside edge and back again). The transition would be a linguistic "mobius" if I didn't recognize that the words *present* and *time* can be used in two ways; it would be a perceptual möbius if I didn't recognize that one of the ways they can be used assumes that they exist in the realm of aperceptual reality, the other that they are perceptual phenomena. The planes of aperceptual and perceptual reality are very different and an entirely different logic rules them.

ILLUSORY SPACE

Space and the time illusion

When we perceive a distant destination, we think of the time it will take to get from where we are to where it is. We project our arrival as an event in the future and visualize it as a point in space-time. However, if the future is an illusion, the event in the future is an illusion, the distance between them is an illusion, and the space separating them is an illusion.

> No more water in the bucket
> No more moon in the water
> The distance already traveled is the past
> The distance to come is the future
> Space is the medium time travels in
> None exist

We measure space by the time it will take to traverse a distance in it (moving at the speed of light).

However, if (two-dimensional) time is an illusion, distance and space (by this definition) are dependent illusions.

>If there is no time, there is no distance,
>If there is no distance, there is no space,
>If there is no space, there is only here,
>Everywhere!

Suspicious reasoning to a self-evident conclusion.

>No time, no space!
>Why does it take me so long to get anyplace?

If, in Oneness, the illusion of time collapses into the infinite present, the illusion of space collapses into ever-present hereness.

>Time collapses into the now; space collapses into the here.

THE ILLUSION OF SPACE AND THE FRAME OF REFERENCE

Another way (aside from the nonexistence of time) to establish the illusoriness of distance and through it space is via frames of reference.

(Is the notion of space dependent on distance? It seems clear that locality is dependent on distance plus arbitrary reference points, but perhaps we could have another more global concept of space which is independent of distance or locality?)

Let us begin by taking ourselves as the frame of reference. We can discern approximately how far we are from the sun, Omaha, or even the refrigerator. But how far are we from our left foot. If you think that question is answerable, you are thinking not of your entire body as the frame of reference but of a point on your body like your eyes or your brain. The question of how far your entire body is from your foot is nonsense. You have to specify a point, an infinitely small locus of perception apart, as the frame of reference from which to measure.

Now let's think on a bigger scale. How far are you from the sun? This is approximately answerable. How far is the earth, a Venusian moon, or Pluto from the sun? Again, this is approximately answerable. But now ask yourself how far is our solar system from our sun? You can't answer that one. Our sun is part of our solar system. It is not a specific distance from the entirety of our solar system. You would have to specify an arbitrary point, a locus of perception in it, for this question to be answerable. However, as soon as you specify an arbitrary locus of perception you get into the realm of perceptual illusion. Distance and its dependent variable space only exist from a specific perceptual point of view.

Now let's enlarge our scope a little more. Consider any two solar systems in our galaxy. You can tell approximately how far they are from one another, but how far are they from our galaxy as a whole? Another nonsense question. Without a locus of perception apart from the system being perceived, you can't ask that question, and distance and space are illusory.

Now, how far is the earth from the cosmos, from existence, from Oneness?

Distance is dependent on a point of perception. Therefore, it is an illusion, and space is a dependent illusion!

LOSING LOCALITY

Locality is a special case of distance. As we have discussed, to conceive of distance, you need two arbitrary points or loci of perception, perceiver and perceived. To conceive of locality you need three, a perceiver, a perception, and a referent which may be either another perceiver or another perception. Then, you can triangulate the point you want to locate between the other two points. If you can't do this, location is impossible to determine.

There are two additional problems as well, quite large ones. First, if you consider those three points as a system, there is no way of locating this system except in relationship to two other arbitrary points outside of the system. Then, of course, if you take these five points as a system, there is no way of locating this system in space except in relation to two other arbitrary points, and so on.

The other problem is that the reference points would have to be motionless in order to locate something exactly, and, of course, there is nothing still in this whirling, expanding cosmos. So exact location is an impossibility, there is only location with reference to moving referents. In lieu of absolute stillness we have relative stillness, that is, referents that are synchronized with a coordinate system. So the best we can do is locate something perceptually in a moving coordinate system, but we can't locate the coordinate system (except in terms of another coordinate system, and on and on until we run out of coordinate systems and are just floating in space).

> Location is dependent on locatable points of perception,
> and there are none.

This, again, points to the fact that, like distance, location is an arbitrary artifact of perception. Without discernible location, locality seems an empty construct.

Without recourse to arbitrary points of reference, tell me where earth is located in space, in existence, in Oneness.

> Distance is an illusion!
> Locality is an illusion!
> Space is an illusion!

PERCEIVED SPACE AND REAL SPACE

Like perceived, two-dimensional time, perceived three-dimensional space is clearly illusory. But since there is nondimensional real time, (i.e., the ever-present present), there must be nondimensional real space as well. What could this be if not the here that is everywhere?

We can approach this intuitively. If we visualize ourselves from an arbitrary other, we can think of ourselves as lost in space. But in fact, we don't feel ourselves as lost in space, we just feel ourselves as here wherever in space we are, and we sense our piece of the earth as home, wherever in space it is.

Home is the singular of here. It is a taste of Oneness in a perceptualized world. That's why it's so special to us.

> When we look outward,
> We see space stretching endlessly everywhere.
> But we ourselves,
> Are we lost in space?
> Or are we here?

DIMENSIONALITY IS ILLUSORY

All dimensionality is qualitative and in the realm of perceptual illusion. The perceiver, i.e., (point of perception) and the perceived are equally illusory and equally perceptual artifacts. Moreover, it is the dimensionality of the perceiver that determines the dimensionality of the perceived.

SEQUENTIALITY

There a distinction between the present and now. The present is eternal and everlasting, but there is a sequential aspect to it. Things happened in the previous present and things will happen in the future present. "Now" refers to the things that are happening in the instant of observation!

However, even sequence is a function of perception, i.e., it refers to events passing (temporally) by a fixed point of perception. If there is no point of perception, there is no sequence, just change. There is, however, relative repositioning (of all things in relationship to each other) which might serve as an alternate definition of motion. If all of Oneness is engaged in a cosmic meteorology, infinite whirling change, becoming, transforming, and disappearing, any assignable place in it would be part of the process and not fixed.

You cannot even say there is a sequence to the entire system, because there is no fixed point outside the system to observe it from. Indeed, there is no possibility of such a point. The system is infinite, is all there is. There is no outside of it. Even if there were an outside, what could there be to fix a point to? What possible coordinates could there be to fix it by?

If we ask ourselves what real, or nonperceptual, sequentiality could be, the closest I can come is this cosmic meteorology of becoming, transforming, disappearing, and becoming again, without any perceptual standard by which to abstract and measure it.

Once again we have arrived, though long torturous reasoning, at a point the meditative philosophers have occupied so long, it has been reduced to a cliché.

Be here now!
Actually, you have no choice in the matter.

PRESENCE

Following our discussion, when you talk about something existing, you are making reference, at the minimum, to two simultaneous, interrelated, and irrefutable qualities, its hereness and its nowness. These can be referred to as its present hereness, but I prefer that wonderful word that combines both qualities, its presence!

Let us call present hereness "presence."

Oneness has presence,
Existence has presence,
Isness has presence.

THE MEANING OF NOW

Is there a difference between now and the present?

Equating the present with now is another möbius (see definition on p. 46). Even the present, as a universally relative now (i.e., as in, it's always the present everywhere) is illusory. When we posit a universal present, we are ignoring the fact that simultaneity doesn't exist, or rather only exists from an equidistant point of perception, and thus is a perceptual illusion itself. If simultaneity is illusory,* the universal present must follow suit. There is no universal present apart from perception.

> Everything exists in its own here and now.
> Every here and now makes its own individual present.
> Every individual present is inseparable from that place's hereness.

Hereness and nowness are aspects of the same thing. They are presence.

This suggests that the individual present is real, but the universal present is an illusion. Can this be right? If it is, not only is two-dimensional time (i.e., the present as a point on the march from past to future) illusory, the universal present as a frozen instant that can occur everywhere simultaneously is equally illusory.

If everything, every here and now, every presence, exists in its own present, does this also mean there is no universal presence, only individual presences? It seems to!

---

*Einstein in his formulation of relativity noted that the time of ocurrence of any event was related to the location of the observer. Two observers at different distances from the same event would invariably observe it occurring at a different time. He deduced from that that absolute simultaneity did not exist, but that it was a function of observation, of the relative distance between the observers and the event, the velocity of the information that communicated the event to the observers, and the nature of that information, e.g., the sound of an event lags considerably behind the sight of an event.

Presence and Oneness

If this is so, it implies a picture of the universe, of Oneness composed of infinite presences, each one an infinitely small point. This picture of infinite, separate presences contradicts the very concept of Oneness!

Is this picture right or wrong, and if it is wrong, where did we go wrong? Examination reveals a very subtle Möbius, a concealed Möbius of confounding the perceptual and aperceptual realms. You only have individual presences when you have individuals. An individual is a special case in Oneness, implying separateness, and, of course, a point of perception. Thus, the statement that every individual presence exists in its own present is a statement of the perceptual realm, and doesn't apply to the aperceptual realm.

An individual presence occurs when a living gestalt arises and identifies with or is attached to its place in Oneness. Individuals create a separate presence in Oneness, one which is also a point of perception. Individuals perceptually divide Oneness into separate presences.

Thus it all comes down to perception again. Oneness has one presence. However, some parts of Oneness have evolved into living gestalts that perceive themselves as self and everything else as other, with all that follows. In the perceptual universe, these then constitute individual presences. However, individual presences come down to nothing more than illusory perceptual points of separateness in the omnipresent One.

THERENESS AND SPACE

> Everything is in its own place,
> Everything is in its own space.

How can it be that there is no space, only hereness everywhere, when things are so evidently over there?

It all comes back to perception again. Everything which is there from an objective viewpoint is here from its subjective viewpoint and vice versa. Anything which is over there to you, the perceiver of it, is here to itself. Each point, each center, each nucleus, each perceiver that exists, exists in its own hereness. Everything exists in its own hereness. Thereness is only a perceptual artifact, a cognate of nonself in the duality self/nonself.

What is more, since something can exist only in the present, everything exists in its own present.

(However, there is only one present, and only one hereness. So that really (aperceptually), everything exists in the infinite present and the omnipresent hereness of the One.

>Oneness has presence, existence has presence.
>Presence is infinite and omnipresent.

Everything is its own Center of Perception.

If everything exists in its own hereness and nowness, it means that everything, every point, nucleus, gestalt, and perceiver is its own frame of reference. Everything is a self-perceived center to its own self-perceived universe. Neither hereness and thereness have meaning except in relationship to a perceiver, a frame of reference.

Space and time come into existence upon perception and around a perceiver to whom they are relevant though illusory. When perception ceases, they disappear just as suddenly.

Which means that the entire universe (as we know it) is an illusion that blinks into existence upon perception and extinguishes when perception is done. This does not mean that there is nothing real out there, only that it is not the universe as we know it.

What is the aperceptual universe?

THE COLLAPSE OF SPACE-TIME

What is the implication of presence for the construct of the space-time dimension that figures so prominently in modern relativity physics, as well as for the ideas that space and time are interdependent rather than independent continuums, and that it is meaningless to locate something in space without simultaneously locating it in time.

Presence both corroborates and contradicts space-time. It says that something can only be here in the present, which corroborates that space and time are interdependent, that where something is is inseparable from when it is. Yet, it denies that space, time, or location are real, completely nullifying the reality of the space-time dimension. Instead, it says that the space-time continuum, like space and time taken separately, is an illusion, a cognitive perception. It also says that where and when are empty words, lacking independent existence or reference to real existence, that there really exist only hereness and nowness (without reference to location in space or time), only presence.

This further implies that when physicists discuss relativity and the space-time continuum, they are only talking about the realm of perceptual illusion. They are, in fact, perpetrating a physics of illusion, whose relationship to the realm of reality or Oneness is unknown and perhap unknowable.

Real Space-Time

The space-time continuum is illusory because space and time are illusory. That does not mean, however, that apparent space and apparent time are independent, or that there are no real phenomena underlying apparent space and time. Oneness seems to support an infinite set of potential, individual presences in the perceptual realm, all of which are here and now to themselves, and there and then to one another.

THE NONEXISTENCE OF NONEXISTENCE

The ultimate mystery, the most fundamental of questions, is this. Where does existence, the existence that we all partake of, the ground of being itself, come from? Why do we exist? Why does anything exist? Why does existence exist? Was there a time before existence? If so why? Even more important, how did anything come out of nothing. King Lear's maxim, "from nothing, nothing comes," seems self-evident. But if this is so, where does existence come from?

Before trying to answer these questions, I would like to point out the distinction between not existing and nonexistence. Nonexistence the word, is often an insidious Mobius, an invisible splice that unnoticeably shifts the subject from apples to pears. Unicorns and good nickel cigars don't exist, but this has nothing to do with nonexistence. We can't argue that because these things don't exist, that nonexistence is an ontological possibility. After all, some things exist, impalas and good sawbuck cigars do exist. Everything, every form, every phenomenon does not exist in the present but existence does not imply the simultaneous existence of everything. There is evolution and extinction of forms but they all come out of the ground of existence, they all continually generate and transform themselves in the present. Nonexistence as an ontological category is different than a thing not existing.

Can existence exist without anything existing in it. If you understand that a thing is merely a perceptual category, the answer is clearly yes. So to get back to our consideration, we know there is existence in the present. Some things may not exist, but there surely is existence. It is impossible that the present could exist without existence itself existing. Is there also nonexistence in the present? Not in the absolute sense, i.e., we see that some things, some forms in Oneness, may be absent in the present, but nonexistence does not exist in the present. (Remember, I am using "nonexistence" in the sense of that which theoretically antedated existence, and therefore creates the mystery of the origins of existence). In the perceptual, dualistic world of separate things, some things can exist and others not, but in the aperceptual reality of Oneness this is impossible. Nonexistence would cancel out existence. (Nonexistence logically could not exist.)

Did nonexistence exist in the past present, that is, did it ever exist? It really seems unlikely. Existence seems inextricably tied to the present. (It may even be definitional, i.e., The present is existence.) As I have already said, the future and the past do not exist. Since they do not, it is nonsense to posit that something can exist in the future or the past. The retrospective "did exist" and the speculative "will exist" do not satisfy the standards for present existence. If the future and past do not exist, i.e., are not real, nonexistence does not exist in them.

For nonexistence to exist then, would be the ultimate contradiction of terms, the ultimate paradox. Nonexistence is a construct, a cognitive perceptual duality, an illusion, a metaphor of empty space. Existence is always here in the present. It is another name, an equivalence, for presence itself.

This then arrives us at the ultimate solution of the mystery of the origin of it all. The answer to the questions "Where does existence come from?" and "Why does existence exist?" is this: it is impossible, logically impossible, for nonexistence to exist. Existence is simply the only alternative.

Nonexistence does not exist, it never existed, it could never exist. Thus, it is pointless to ask where existence came from, much less who created it. The very ground of being, the ground of the universe, is tautological. It is that it is. We have been asking the wrong question, thus engendering a whole string of subsequent wrong questions and, of course, wrong answers.

What is the right question?

7. EMERGENT PHENOMENA AND THE NATURE OF THE UNIVERSE

A FUNDAMENTAL FALLACY?

First metaphysics and then physics have been looking for the fundamental stuff, the building blocks of the universe, for thousands of years. But perhaps the pursuit of fundamental stuff is a wild goose chase. The very concept of stuff feels suspiciously like an analog to physical matter, a cognitive perceptual illusion.

Perhaps the idea of fundamental stuff is a fundamental fallacy and the entire reductionist strategy a mistake. What if at bottom there is nothing, that is no material thing, and the universe consists of something like hierarchical gestalts of interrelationships of emergent phenomena that have no underlying, fixed identity or form. What if the universe consists of the appearances of existence, motion, change, form, creation, and destruction, etc., without anything moving, changing, forming, creating, and destroying except appearance itself.

Perhaps that which is undergoing formation, change, and destruction is itself forming, changing, and being destroyed and there is no material form or nature of it. On the deepest level, everything just is what it is; it just exists; it just is existence. By subdividing, splitting, or dissolving something you simply get to another form or appearance of existence, finding no more of its basic nature than if you combined it!

Furthermore, what if by trying to get at the basic stuff of the manifest, phenomenal universe, we are getting below the level of its reality. It's like trying to get at the basic stuff of life by reducing a person to chemicals and water, or reducing a CD of a Bach partita to digital commands. Instead of getting to a thing's fundamental reality, we are getting to where it ceases to exist.*

If everything comes down to appearances, organizations, or forms of existence, we could represent existence by E. Then perhaps science could talk about E. and its manifestation or appearance, A. Science can be freed to discuss phenomena in terms of its organizations, forms, and transformations, without any pretense that the nature of E. can ever be known, or indeed that it even has a nature.

Then life and nonlife, energy and matter, the strong and weak nuclear forces, electromagnetic energy and gravity can all be nominally unified as manifestations of E., or appearance, A.

$$E = \text{Existence} \qquad A = \text{Appearance}$$

---

*A good test of this is whether or not you can reconstruct what you have reduced from what you have reduced it to. If you cannot, that indicates you have discarded something essential, be it material or informational, and thus are below the level of its reality. As, for instance, if you reduce genetic material to simpler chemicals and lose the sequence of genes, or sum the digital commands in a CD and lose their sequence. [Is it just coincidental that sequences are the repository of the intelligence in both examples?]

This phenomenon of lost information makes the hypothesized phenomenon of the backward flow of time questionable. If the backward flow of time is just conceived as a cinematic trick, running the film backward, lost information, of course, presents no difficulties. But we must observe that this is hardly a good analogy. For one thing, that which the film depicts is not reality, just an image of reality. For another, running a film backward is an event that really takes place in a forward sequence. For instance, the film could break while rewinding it, this new thing demonstrating that it is not a reversal in time. Real backward time presents real theoretical difficulties, not the least of which is the above problem of regaining lost information. [For instance, in death and decay, information is lost that makes returning to life in the same form improbable. Even the genie in Aladdin's lamp can't do it.]

EMERGENT PHENOMENA

An emergent phenomenon is one that appears at a certain level of organization (of E). It is implicit or potential in the nature of the things that are being interrelated and the way they are being interrelated, but the phenomenon in no way exists except on the pertinent levels of organization. It appears on one level and disappears on another. A crude example is a mirror. Neither the silver nor the glass in any other form or combination or way constitute a mirror. But plate a sheet of polished glass with silver and voilà…an emergent phenomenon.

So much for simple examples. Life itself is an emergent phenomenon. Science doesn't know too much about the necessary conditions for its emergence. At least, we haven't yet been able to reproduce them. But it is clear to all but the religious theocracy that when organic structures reached a certain level of organization, they went into business for themselves, life emerged, and the rest is evolution.

When energy and matter collapse, they are supposed to form a black hole from which light can't escape. This is called a singularity. Singularities then are emergent phenomena. When a singularity expands again, energy and matter come back into existence. Energy and matter can therefore be thought of as emergent phenomena as well. They come to exist at a certain point of expansion, at certain pertinent states of organization.

The standard for emergence is forward sequence. Forward sequence is an aspect of the eternal present. The key word is "next." Even apparently "de-emergent" phenomena (the recollapse of energy and matter into black holes, for instance) are really emergent and necessitate a forward sequence. The inviolably forward sequence of emergent phenomena is another argument against the hypothesized backward flow of time. Every imaginable change in the flow of time, even reversal, would emerge, would of necessity come next. (Time is a perceptual or dualistic quality, forward sequence, the inescapable fact that every new thing comes next, is tautological, part of the tautological nature of the aperceptual universe.)

> Reversibility, like the backward flow of time, is exclusively a cognitive function!

All emergent phenomena are dependent on the conditions from which they emerged. Life emerged from a certain constellation of instructions, energies, and organic chemicals. Death emerged from life. Energy and matter emerged from the expansion of a singularity. A singularity emerged from the collapse of energy and matter.

If we take the viewpoint that absolutely everything is an emergent phenomenon of Existence, a form of E, we have an elegant and parsimonious theory. Clearly, everything seems to have emerged from antecedent conditions. It is, however, unclear whether there was a fundamental starting point. Even if there were, it is unlikely that its quality would be qualitatively different from other qualities and so constitute the primal stuff of the universe. It is more likely that it would just be an earlier form.

IS REALITY REAL?

All emergent phenomena, indeed all phenomena, are perceptual. They belong to the world of appearances. Even if we reduce perceived phenomena to more fundamental forms, we are at best reducing them to other appearances, and these appearances are also emergent phenomena. This truth holds, whether we arrive at it through chemistry or reason. Thus, if we reduce water first to molecules, then atoms, and then subparticles, we are just reducing it to *other* appearances, other sensory and cognitve perceptions. All of these levels of reduction are emergent phenomena!

If all things are emergent phenomena of E, what does this say about the reality of things? Or more to the point, what does this say about the reality of reality? We in the West have certain expectations about reality. These are rooted in a marriage of sensory modalities and the perceptual illusion of solid matter. Even if we know better, our expectations point us in materialistic directions, and they are responsible for a great deal of the difficulty we experience in making sense out of the universe. We expect that reality has to be substantial, and made out of a basic and irreducible substance, and that everything is mechanistically assembled from this basic substance.

We persist in holding on to these expectations despite the fact that all the evidence is leading us the other way.

The emergent phenomena of existence, however, are ultimately insubstantial and irreducible except to other emergent phenomena. Not only that, but in most cases they are not a structure assembled out of what preceded them but the birth of a new thing. Even when they are identical to what preceded them, they are not what preceded them, but a new thing that is identical.

This paradigm suggests that subparticles that physicists create when smashing atoms are not the primal building blocks they are mistaken to be, but emergent phenomena (which perhaps have never existed before) that have been born out of the unique conditions supplied by a particle accelerator. This alternate paradigm must be kept in mind whenever a gestalt is disassembled into its component parts.

NATURE AND THE UNIFIED FIELD

The unified field, the stuff of the universe, has two guises. On the one hand, it is E, existence, universality, Oneness. Perhaps it can never be cut finer than that. On the other hand, it is the nature of emergent phenomena, of things, of beings. It is the specificity of what is.

This is not a tautology, though it veers precariously close to being so. The nature of things is itself a two-headed idea. On the one hand, everything has *a nature*, has properties, has ways of interacting. This nature is a concept, a cognitive perception, an abstraction generalized from the things whose nature we are talking about. If we were talking about nature in this abstract sense, our statement could indeed be reduced to the tautology: the nature of the universe is the nature of the universe.

However, there is another sense to nature. Everything has its *own nature*, own properties, own ways of interacting. Every emergent phenomenon has an emergent nature. On this level the stuff of the universe is as infinitely varied as the individual natures of everything in the universe. There is no one stuff because everything does not share one nature. A dog has dog nature, a quark has quark nature.

Both are emergent phenomena.

That things have their own specific individual nature is universal; this is where we are pointing when we say that it is the nature of things, of emergent phenomena, that comprises the stuff of the universe on the perceptual level. On the aperceptual level, E, existence, Oneness itself forms the unified field. This self-evident and unremarkable observation might be almost as close as we are going to get to the ultimate secret of the universe.

The nature of things is implicit and only becomes explicit upon relationship with other things, i.e., the implicate order (of David Bohm) becomes explicate upon relationship (or upon perception, which, of course, is relationship reified). Not only that, but the explicit forms that things take are dependent on the things they relate to, even perception, (a relationship between perceiver and perceived) is a projection of the qualities of the perceiver onto the perceived.

EMERGENT PHENOMENA, EXISTENCE, AND PHYSICS

Quantum physics is in some ways still a prerelativistic, Newtonian metaphor. If it doesn't reduce everything to particles, waves, or energy packets, it reduces them to concepts, like probability waves. However, according to perceptual field theory, physical things and concepts are very similar. One is a perceptual category and the other a conceptual category, but both are categories, both are things; ontologically, they are similar.

Quantum physics is also, in some ways, still a pre-Copernican metaphor. That is, it assumes a false center. It is a description of things as they appear from a false center, as if it were the true one. Before Copernicus, the solar system was seen as if the earth was the center. In the case of quantum physics, physical reality is seen as if sensory perception (perceptual appearance, and by extension the observer) is its center.

False centers can be made to work, but since they assume perspectives that are not really central, they need many tortuous and illogical corrections in order to do so. The numerous particles that quantum physics spawns may be one consequence of its peripheral perspective. The problem of false centers is reminiscent of a monograph by the Gestalt psychologist Wolfgang Köhler, entitled "A Girl Describes Her Office." In it he recounts the tale of a secretary who describes the large corporation in which she works as if she is the center of it. Vast complications arise from this. In fact, it is almost impossible to figure out the corporate organization from her account. Once the correct perspective is taken, however, namely that the center of the corporation is not herself but the president, it reveals itself as a simple hierarchical structure. The problem is that quantum theory, like the pre-Copernican solar system, is a peripheral rather than a central metaphor.

Of course, the assertion that quantum physics takes perceptual appearance as its center can be argued against. After all, isn't it quantum physics that gave us an indeterminate world where nothing can be known before it is observed or measured, where light can be particle or wave, depending on the experiment, where things are simultaneously present everywhere, and an action taken on one thing can affect another instantaneously, faster than the speed of light; and where matter doesn't exist except as a wave of probability, again to be become determined only at the instant of observation. These qualities—simultaneity, nonlocality, the uncertainty principle, the observer effect, and nonmateriality—characterize an alternate universe, a through-the-looking-glass *quantum world* where everything runs contrary to expectations. With that in mind, who can accuse quantum physics of being perceptual-centric.

However, despite the looking glass world, the false center persists. With all that it is discovering or positing, quantum physics still struggles to know all things in perceptual terms, to fix things, to determine indeterminacy, to find a level of description where things will be things again, or at least concepts, which we know are much the same thing. The shortcoming of quantum physics, and for that matter relativistic physics as well, is nonrecognition that in all cases, one is simultaneously working with metaphors and viewpoints. Because things can be perceived but not known, all things and all theories are metaphors. *Everything is a metaphor for everything else!*

Because every metaphor is in perceptual terms, all metaphors, all theories of reality are perceptual-centric, that is, they start from the false center of human perception. If it is not one man's perception, then it is the collective perception of the scientists and the measurement instruments. This collective human center is certainly broader and more multifaceted than an individual's perception, but it is still no broader than a fly's eye whirling though the cosmos.

Thus, not only is perception illusory as to quality, as previously discussed, it is also illusory as to viewpoint, which, of course, determines the organization that is perceived. Indeed, quality and viewpoint/organization are two allied although separate guises of illusion. Quality is the appearance that emerges as a function of the duality encoded in sensory perception. Organization is the structure that emerges as a function of the location of the perceiver relative to the perceived. For example, if the perceiver is located on earth, the apparent structure of our solar system consists of things revolving around the earth, whereas if the observer is at the edge of the solar system, the apparent structure of the solar system consists of things revolving around the sun. The real organization of things is constant, even though the apparent structure or organization is radically altered when the perceiver's location shifts.

Every metaphor or theory of reality (including the theory by which human beings negotiate their world, namely, that things are what they seem) is illusory both in the viewpoint from which it comes (perceptual-centric) and the quality and the qualitative guise in which it appears. Both these forms of illusion are inescapable in ordinary perception.

The aperceptual viewpoint, in contradistinction, completely abandons the effort to reduce to perceptual terms, to dualize, quantify, or thingify. Instead, it recognizes that there are two parallel realms of reality, the perceptual and the aperceptual, and that each realm is subject to different "natural" laws. Any description, any explanation of reality, has to take both realms, the perceptual and the aperceptual, the illusory and the unknowable, into account. (This is the principle of 2X, i.e., the necessity of two simultaneous levels of explanation.)

The above analysis and the ensuing principle of 2X has tremen-

dous potential to clarify and explain all sorts of scientific phenomena, particularly the apparent paradoxes of the quantum world. Let
us take the collapse of the wave function as a particularly significant
example. The notion of wave function, as it pertains to state or location, says that the state or location of any particle exists solely as a
wave of probability; it is indeterminate. The indeterminacy collapses, that is, becomes fixed or knowable at the instant of observation
or measurement. The rigid application of this principle leads to in-
digestible conclusions, such as are embodied in the thought experiment of Shrodinger's cat. In this experiment a cat concealed in an
opaque cage is either executed or not, according to a random process
of execution unknowable by the experimenter, who only learns the
outcome after the cage is opened, that is, after observation. According to indeterminacy theory, the cat has to be simultaneously alive
and dead (or even worse, neither alive or dead) until the cage is
opened, even after it has been gassed! No amount of respect, even
awe of science, can make common sense accept that one.

How did quantum physics trap itself into this box of indeterminacy? To answer this, let's go back to a six-year debate between Einstein and Niels Bohr on the Heisenberg indeterminacy principle and
the nature of reality. Einstein agreed with the uncertainty principle
insofar as to agree that the position and momentum of an elementary particle cannot be measured simultaneously, but he denied the
implication that since they cannot be measured, they do not *have* a
definite position and location. Instead, he argued that the problem
lies in the measurement or observation, not in what is happening in
reality. He did not accept the position that observation has an effect
upon and maybe even creates physical reality. Bohr, on the other
hand, in the pursuit of a consistently rigorous position, maintained
not only that a particle could not have a definite trajectory, *i.e., location plus momentum, but further that the particle could not even be
said to exist on its own until observed.*

They both had part of the truth, but by taking their individual
viewpoints as the whole truth both went awry. Einstein was right that
observation determines the knowing of what happened, but not what
actually happens. However, Bohr was also right in his refusal to cor-

relate what was eventually perceived with what really happened, to confound "perceptual phenomena" with aperceptual reality.

For starters, both men failed to distinguish observation from perception. Strictly speaking, there is no observation. The whole concept of observation entails the illusion of objectivity. Observation means objective perception. But perception can never be objective. Perception is the inescapable epitome of subjectivity. An occurrence or phenomenon can never be observed—that is, never in the objective sense, therefore what is the use of discussing observation and its effects. Since perception is all there is, it is the only thing you can fruitfully discuss. Therefore the first thing that has to be changed, both semantically and conceptually, is the word observation. If we substitute for observation, perception and the meaning that it has taken on, all of the paradoxes of indeterminacy become clear. Mere observation, should there be such a thing, changes or creates nothing, however, perception is another matter entirely. Perception changes or creates appearance. So in the instance of Shrodinger's cat, since there is in reality no possible observation, nothing happens upon observation. However, something does happen upon perception. However, it does not happen in the realm of reality, but only in the realm of appearance. Perception does not alter reality it just brings reality into appearance. Even more to the point, perception does not work retroactively, it works when it is taking place. Therefore it does not change or manifest that which did or did not happen to the cat in past time. It just brings about the experience of what has happened to the cat, at the very moment that the box is opened and the contents perceived.

In overlooking the distinction between observation and perception, both men also overlooked the position that there exist two parallel realms, perceptual and aperceptual. Reality does not depend upon perception, but perception does depend on an underlying reality. According to the principle of 2X, a particle is whatever it is in the aperceptual realm. It is not really created or even necessarily affected by perception. Whether a particle has either absolute momentum or location is another issue beyond the scope of this discussion. On the other hand, the particle becomes known and therefore "determined" through observation or perception. Its location and momentum are determined through perception because absolute momentum and location are perceptual qualities. They are apparent phenomena, dualistic illusions, or viewpoints. The act of perception creates appearance, and determinacy is a function of appearance, not of reality. The pivotal mistake shared by most physicists, indeed most scientists, is in not recognizing that determinacy itself is exclusively a property of perceptual appearance, not a property of (aperceptual) reality at all. Determinacy is a function of (perceptual) knowing, not being. The collapse of the wave function takes place when the aperceptual is perceived. It is a function of perception, of perceiving the aperceptual. The reason it is instantaneous is because it does not take place on the physical plane, just in the mind. (Actually, there is no such thing a probability wave. The probability wave is just a hypothesis to explain the puzzling failure of the aperceptual realm to satisfy perceptual expectations for behavior of "particles.")

Observation, perception, does not determine when, where, and how something occurs, just when, where, and how it is known!! Knowing, in both the ordinary and the scientific sense of the word (but not the aperceptual sense), pertains exclusively to the world of perception. The only way it bears on the aperceptual world is by interpreting it.

The diagnosis of perceptual-centrism even applies to Einstein's conception of the universe. Like the conceptions of Copernicus and Galileo, Einstein's conception of the earth as a concentrated space-time body, taking the path of least resistance (or shortest path) through space-time around a more concentrated space-time body, was a major conceptual advance. In it he found equivalences between energy, matter, space, and time, among other things. But while the connectedness he envisioned was revolutionary and profound, even it did not go far enough. As we have seen, even space and time are illusions. They depend on a perceiver. They are aspects or viewpoints of Oneness, not the lowest common denominators of reality that they are commonly held to be.

Einstein was perceptual-centric in the sense that he was also working with the apparent universe, and thus unwittingly placing his human perception at the center of things. While he was not Newtonian, he was Einsteinian, i.e., he didn't fall into the trap of trying to reduce everything to things, particles, and waves, but he did fall into the subtler trap of reifying dimensions into things like space-time, energy, and matter, as if they were the irreducible phenomena of which the universe was composed. Equivalencies, Einstein demonstrated, invariably point to a common root or underlying unity, but even the master of relativity didn't go far enough. He looked for unity at the level of intermediate illusions like space, time, matter, and energy. Who knows how far his genius would have taken him had he recognized that all phenomena, even dimension, were appearances or guises of something else, and that the unity he sought lay beyond phenomena!

We need to remember that whatever this unified stuff of the universe is, it is not what is disclosed by human perception, which means that in an absolute sense, it is not anything. Or alternatively, that the question is not valid as asked. Beyond that, unlike the solar system conceived by Copernicus and more correctly reconceived by Galileo, what we are dealing with might have no one center, either phenomenologically or ontologically. That is to say, not only is the center not the way things appear to human perception (phenomenologically), it may be that in reality there isn't any center (except the perceiver) (ontologically). In the perceptual realm, every perceiver is the center of the universe, whereas in the aperceptual realm center might be a meaningless concept, a projection, along with the notions of materiality and fundamental stuff.

BELOW THE LEVEL OF SEPARATION AND THE OBSERVER EFFECT

The basic tenets of the aperceptual field theory proposed by this book are the following:

> 1. There exist two realms of existence, the realm of Oneness and the "perceptual" realm of separate things.

The realm of Oneness is unperceived, unknowable (in the perceptual sense), has no qualities, and does not follow the Newtonian laws of physics that govern the realm of separate things. The realm of separate things is knowable, tangible, qualitative, and is governed by the Newtonian laws of physics, yet it is in some profound sense illusory. All of its qualities are created by perception, either self-perception or perception by other perceivers.

> 2. Everything exists and functions simultaneously in both of these realms.

This is the basis for the rule of simultaneous or dual explanation, abbreviated as "two ex," or "2X." This rule states that, in perception, there always exist two levels of existence, Oneness and duality.

> 3. To be adequate, every explanation has to take both levels of existence into account simultaneously, the aperceptual realm of Oneness and the dual realm of perception.

Nothing can be adequately accounted for on only one level of explanation. This principle resolves most apparent paradoxes!

> 4. Everything is a separate thing when, and to the degree to which, it perceives or conceives itself as separate.

Separation is fundamentally a matter of self-perception! It is a matter of identity! This principle of self-perceived identity holds equally for almost all levels of existence, from the atomic level to the "I concept" of you and I. In fact, it is the key to enlightenment!

Quantum Phenomena and 2x

When you get to the level of quantum phenomena, you get below the level of separate things. You get below the level of aggregation at which self-perception or self-conception emerges. Therefore you get below the level at which there exist two realms. There remains only Oneness. There remains only the unknowable, aperceptual, nonqualitative realm of primary, undifferentiated existence. This is why the "laws" of physics do not apply at the quantum level, and instead nonlocality, indeterminacy, the observer effect, and other seeming paradoxes and anomalies appear.

Observer effect

At the quantum level, any differentiation into "things" is solely the creation of an external perceiver. It is the creation of the observer. This accounts for the observer effect, whereby the observer changes that being observed. The observer doesn't merely change that being perceived, in a sense he creates it. Not into what it is in the realm of Oneness but into which it appears to be in the realm of perception. He separates out, thingifies, that which does not thingify itself. He conceptualizes a thing, when and where there is no thing to conceive itself. Then, he further applies his (Newtonian) expectations of a thing to his concept. He expects his concept to behave like a thing. When his concept does not conform to his expectations, he attributes its failure to behave predictably to the observer effect as well as to other paradoxes and anomalies.

THE PROBLEM OF FINELY TUNED CONSTANTS

Aperceptual field theory has implications for the cosmological problem of finely tuned constants. This problem (as usually stated) exists exclusively in the context of some perceptual errors of a probabilistic, ecological, and evolutionary nature.

The problem of finely tuned constants, posits that life and indeed the present form of the universe can only exist as the result of a fine tuning of separate constants and their interrelationships, one so improbable as to be virtually impossible to achieve by chance. This problem leads some cosmologists in the direction of teleological solutions like an intelligent or living universe, a universal design, a direction toward life, or a divine creator. I don't propose to examine these theories, but rather the erroneous suppositions which necessitate them.

The first error inherent in the problem of finely tuned constants is the probabilistic one. Ordinary probability theory is perceptual or Newtonian. It assumes a closed system containing a finite and knowable set of things, then presumes to apply methodology based on these assumptions to open systems containing infinite and unknowable quantities of variables. Aperceptual probability, on the other hand, were there such a thing, would begin by assuming an open system with infinite and unknowable variables. In such a system, the probability of any predetermined outcome eventuating before the fact approaches one divided by infinity, in other words, a virtual impossibility. On the other hand, the probability of any outcome occurring after it has occurred is one, an inevitability. This implies that every outcome, every constant, and every system of constants, including the universe in its present form, was equally improbable, virtually impossible before the fact, yet inevitable after it. Taking into account both the viewpoints of before and after, it is equally as improbable for the universe not to exist in its present form (after) as it is for it to have come into existence (before). Impossibility and inevitability are equivalent statements from different temporal viewpoints.

The second perceptual error is a little more complex. This error comes out of a worldview comprising separate things varying randomly in isolation, a view that is an almost inevitable outcome of the normal "thingification" of the everyday perception. The error of separation engenders a cascade of derivative errors. The first of these is overlooking of the "possibility" that seemingly separate things are not really separate, but merely separate perceptions (from different viewpoints) of the same thing. If they are not separate things but part of one thing, the circumstance that they are finally attuned to one another is not astounding but rather inevitable.

The second derivative of the error of separation is ecological-evolutionary. Our universe did not occur as the sum of different unrelated probabilities. Rather, it evolved in a complex lockstep where every "next step" of the whole in all of its infinite complexity and diversity could only have eventuated from its preceding conditions. Indeed, if you take the system as a whole, the next step has to eventuate from the preceding steps.

Evolution is not something that occurs only to an organism in relationship to its immediate environment. It is something that happens simultaneously to the universe as a whole. The identification of separate, individual parts is a perceptual illusion, as is the narrowing of focus down to an individual organism or species and its immediate niche. Every part is really a simultaneously coevolving aspect of the whole.

The universe, then, is an evolving whole, an infinitely complex ecology in which every aspect from the weak nuclear force to life itself is a complementary part. The question of how the constants of the universe became so finely tuned as to support life is simply not a valid question. In a whole, which is what any ecological system is, aspects or perceptible parts of the whole are always precisely tuned to one another, for they coevolve that way. If one or another part was varied, the outcome, or whatever you chose to designate as the outcome, would, of course, vary as well. In every case, however, the constants would always be precisely coattuned.

To summarize, there are multiple perceptual errors concealed in the formulation of the problem of finely tuned constants. The first is ignoring the difference between the assumed system and the actual system. The second is ignoring the temporal viewpoints of before and after, and the fact that the prediction before the fact is diametrically opposed to "prediction" after it. The third lies in the realization that in aperceptuality, there is no viewpoint, therefore, no before and after. The fourth is the error of separation. The fifth is ignoring that it is the whole which is coevolving, not any isolated part.

THE LIMITATIONS OF THEORY

Nonmathematical proofs

Everything is a metaphor for everything else. Every scientific theory, every description, every communication, every perception is a metaphor. The thing in itself cannot be known, let alone perceived, explained, described, and communicated, because the thing in itself does not exist. Every known thing is partial, a perceptual category abstracted from the unknowable whole.

Because everything is a metaphor and no metaphor can hold the whole, we eventually reach the limits of any metaphor. We can only extend a metaphor so far, even a brilliant metaphor, before we get to the point where it no longer applies.

The implication for science then, is that it is logically impossible to have a complete theory of anything.

HOW MUST SCIENCE PROCEED?

The proper starting point of basic science is genesis. Non-dual or aperceptual science needs to begin by studying the basic processes by which something emerges from no thing. It must study genesis at all levels: how duality arises out of Oneness, how phenomena arises out of noumena or materiality arises out of it immateriality, how experience arises out of the void, how life arises out of nonlife. They are all closely related if not the same thing and must embody common principles. These *first principles* need to be understood before we can be on solid ground.

This is the paradigm shift that is needed in order to move from an illusion-based science to one based in reality. Most if not all of the correlations that today's science is finding, reveal not linear causation but rather an underlying unity. Even the basic relationships of physics, like those Einstein uncovered between space and time, point to an underlying unity. Einstein called it the space-time continuum; however, even the space-time continuum is not the fundamental level of reality. Beneath that is the fundamental unity of Oneness Itself.

Basic science needs to refocus its attention. It has been looking at phenomena and it's tempting to say that it needs to start looking at noumena instead. But noumena presents itself as the void, and how can we look at the void? No matter how closely we look, there's nothing there. However, we can look at the processes by which things emerge from the void. We can study the basic processes of emergence by which the world as we know it self-creates. These are the processes fundamental to the emergence of the cosmos, the evolution of life, the development of an organism, the synthesis of qualitative experience by perception and the way all of these processes interplay to create ecological hierarchies. Once these processes of emergence are understood science will be better able to understand the much smaller but infinitely more complicated questions that it now pursues.

Science, far more than it is accustomed to, needs to take philosophy into account. Moreover, when it does, it should hold to the same rigorous standards in philosophy that it applies to its methodology, however much that challenges its comfortable ways of seeing the world. Sloppy philosophy in science is no less reprehensible than sloppy methodology. They are both bad science and lead to invalid conclusions. A science that does not acknowledge the role of perception in creating phenomena from noumena, for instance, is philosophically naive and its findings cannot help but be limited and circumscribed by illusion.

EVOLUTION AND ORIGINS

8.   LIFE

BIG DEAL
If Oneness contains death
And everything in Oneness is one
Then everything is dead.
If Oneness contains life
And everything in Oneness is one
Then everything is alive.

DEAD...ALIVE...What's the difference?
You think you know it when you're alive
And it's a big deal.
You won't know it when you're dead
And you won't care!

PERCEPTION AND SELF-IDENTIFICATION

All units of life, from the simplest to the most complex, have their own perceptions of self and of other.

The self/other perceptions of all units of life tend to be determined their boundary levels of organization. The boundary of a unit of life is at least partly a matter of self-perception.

Characteristics of life

For something to be alive it has to have the following characteristics:

- It has to be a gestalt or have organization.
- It has to have a boundary, someplace where it starts and leaves off.
- More important, it has to know where it starts and leaves off. (Boundaries, however, differ widely in definiteness.)
- It has to perceive.

Units of life can be as simple as an amoeba, as elementary as the components of a cell (nucleus, mitochondria, genes) or as complex as a human being. They can be symbiotic (lichen, Portuguese man-of-war), semiautonomous and subordinate (animal or plant cell), semi-autonomous and superordinate (central nervous system), or autonomous (plant or animal, i.e., tree, human).

An amoeba may know everything in and including its cellular walls as self, and the fluid in which it swims as other. A cell, similarly, may perceive everything in and including its walls as self and the organism that it is part of as other. (Perhaps even some of the component parts of the cell perceive themselves as self and the surrounding cell as other.) Similarly, a body organ perceives more or less everything within and including its walls as self, and the body that it is part of as other.

Higher autonomous forms tend to perceive everything outside of their skin as other. However, they also tend to perceive subordinate levels of organization, their cells, organs, etc., as other as well. Ironically, their sense data, their thoughts, and self-concepts (or ego) are usually perceived as self, even when they have their origin in other.

ACTIVE SELF-INTEREST

When I use the words "perceive self and other," I am not asserting that the quality of perception of a cell is the same as the quality of perception of a human, that they have the same notion of self and other, or that they have a self-concept. That would be absurd, (although I suspect that all units of life have a quality more akin to human consciousness (not thought) than most of us suspect). I am positing a more operational concept of perception. Something can be held to perceive that acts like it perceives. This entails a bounded gestalt acting or reacting as a whole in relation to that outside of its boundaries. It also entails that bounded gestalt acting in a lawful manner in a lawful environment with self-interest.

This formulation introduces two additional concepts that are essential to aperceptual field theory, "lawfulness" and "self-interest." All living things act with self-interest (with certain instructive exceptions), that is, they act to further their survival and reproduction. This entails identifying one's own level of organization and perceiving from it, then acting in accordance with the primal illusion and in contradistinction to Oneness. To use the most general example, living things act against the entropy to gain personal energy and organization.

If things are totally incapable of action on any level, it is impossible to tell whether or not they are perceiving. Therefore, "action" in the specific form of "active self interest" qualifies not only as a test of perception, but as a criterion or even definition of it. This standard of "active self interest" might serve as a criterion for aliveness as well. (I broadly interpret action not only as the external action of an autonomous being, but including all action, even the internal changes of a subordinate unit of life. That is, changes in the internal chemistry or boundary permeability of a cell in response to the perception of changes in its environment should be considered an action. Even when an animal is sleeping, its bodily functions, particularly respiration, qualify as active self-interest. Likewise, the many functions of a plant, photosynthesis, phototropism, collecting nutrients from the soil, dispersing its seeds, etc., constitute active self-interest).

active self interest = perception = aliveness

LAWFULNESS

Lawfulness is an equally important if more abstract consideration. In fact, if you cannot assume something is acting lawfully, you cannot tell if it is acting with self-interest and thus cannot tell if it is perceiving at all. For instance, if a drop of fluid had a substance poisonous to amoebae concentrated at one end, and an amoeba swam toward it instead of away from it, you would have a conceptual problem. If the amoeba were acting in a lawful manner (evading destruction), the principle of active self-interest would be violated and doubt would be cast on whether the amoeba was perceiving. (Of course, you would have to assume the same lawfulness for the environment.) On the other hand, if the amoeba was broken, i.e., not acting in a lawful but in a random manner, you couldn't tell anything about the event at all. (You might also, of course, have a mutant amoeba, but this is quibbling.)

My concept of lawfulness is similar to the Taoist concept of nature, rather than to the laws of physics you learn in school. Things act according to their nature in a universe acting according to its nature. Things do not *obey* laws, they embody the dynamics of their own identities. What we ordinarily think of as laws are, excuse me for harping on this, just another perceptual artifact, an abstraction of the behavior from the behaver. While this reductionistic approach is valuable for predicting and controlling phenomena, and even has utility as an intermediate stage in the understanding of the way things work, it is illusory and as such confounds our ultimate understanding. This concept of the nature of things is very important, and I will return to it later in this chapter.

SELF-PERCEPTION*

Every form, every unit of life, is just consciousness identifying with and perceiving from its level of organization. Every unit of life, because it is a separate locus of perception, has its own self-perception, its own awareness of being what it is. Individual consciousness originates when lives originate, develops as lives develop, and dies when lives die. Consciousness tracks life because consciousness is just another aspect of life. Consciousness become the self-perception of a life's Isness. It is as much a part of life as is the physical body. Life is a form of consciousness. We are unused to thinking that all life has consciousness inextricably associated with it. However, any other conclusion is inelegant and indefensible. (This presents some moral issues with regard to the subjugation and eating of animals, which the Buddhists among others have eschewed. But I am not convinced that consciousness can be attributed to animals and denied to plants, which leaves people of strict conscience without anything to eat. Nor is the distinction between higher and lower orders of consciousness worth anything to my mind. About the only thing you can say about the higher orders of consciousness is that they reify the illusion of the individual self. It doesn't seem much more of a sin to kill the illusion than to eat the meat!)

To ask where this consciousness came from is once again to fall into the fallacy that consciousness is a thing apart from life. It is not. Consciousness is inseparable from life, the whole, the part, and the part within the whole.

Just as I am not asserting that the quality of perception of a cell is the same as the quality of perception of a human, I am not asserting that the experience of consciousness of a cell is the same as the experience of consciousness of a human. I have never consciously

*In this chapter I talk about units of life perceiving themselves and perceiving others. Strictly speaking, perception can only be of "other", while "self" can only be *known*. This knowing of self is unconscious and there is no thing, quality or concept there, while the perceiving of other creates dimensions and tangible qualities. However, by perceiving other and knowing itself to be *not* that, the self can implicitly perceive itself. Consequently, there is a sense of perceiving self that is useful for the moment. In later chapters, I maintain this distinction more strictly.

experienced the consciousness of a cell, but I have experienced my human consciousness and I know it is complex and inextricably mixed with sensory impressions, thoughts, and self-reflection. It is unreasonable to think that simpler life forms replicate this. They have neither the sensoriums nor the cognitoriums. Nevertheless, I suspect that the consciousness of all life shares a fundamental quality of sentience and that the primary difference between the consciousness of an amoeba, a tree, and a human is in what its sensorium and cognitorium present it to be conscious of.

Simple units of life may or may not experience consciousness the way we do; however, they all act as if they are conscious. The objective criterion for consciousness is the same as the objective criterion for perception, namely, active self-interest. Again, let me point out that this is one criterion for life itself.

THE EQUIVALENCE OF CONSCIOUSNESS, PERCEPTION, AND LIFE

Now something interesting is emerging. This same criterion, active self-interest, seems to be equally applicable to the determination of perception, consciousness, and life. Now in physics, two guidelines apply. If it is theoretically impossible to get information about something, it is assumed not to exist. If it is theoretically impossible to tell the difference between two things, they are assumed to be equivalent. For instance, since it is theoretically impossible to get information about the universe before the big bang, the "before" is assumed not to exist and the big bang is viewed as the origin of the universe. Since it is theoretically impossible to tell the difference between gravity and acceleration, Einstein considered them equivalent and based his general theory of relativity on this equivalence.

> Active self-interest = perception = aliveness = *consciousness*

We have seen that it is impossible to tell whether something is alive or perceives unless it displays active self-interest. Now we add consciousness as well. If it displays active self-interest it can be said to be perceiving, alive, and conscious; if it does not display active self-interest, it cannot be said to be any of these. (It may or may not be.) Furthermore, one cannot discriminate between perception, consciousness, and life on the basis of active self-interest. According to the logic of physics, this would justify three remarkable conclusions. One, if something does not display active self-interest it cannot be said to have either life, consciousness,* or perception. Two, if it does display active self-interest it can be said to have all of them. Three, life, consciousness, and perception are equivalent. That is, they are three appearances, three disparate perceptual qualities of what in reality is the same thing. There are no defensible differences between them.

This answers, or at least makes irrelevant, a lot of elementary questions. What is life? What is consciousness? Is such and such alive? Does so and so have consciousness? Perception, consciousness, and aliveness are separate perceptual guises of the same thing, and one test, operational standard, or criterion suffices to determine all of them, active self-interest.

This criterion clarifies the boundary between life and nonlife in certain rudimentary gestalts such as viruses. If something acts in its own self-interest, it can be assumed to be alive, conscious, and perceiving, regardless of its structure. If it does not, it is not.

That suggests another question, namely, the difference if any between activity and reactivity. All sorts of nonbiological things react to external conditions. Does that mean they are alive? Again, I refer to the criterion of active self-interest, remembering that self interest in my definition includes survival and reproduction. All sorts of nonbiological things react. However, I don't know of any where survival and reproduction are the consequences of that reaction. If I was informed of any, I would be hard pressed not to think they were alive.

Animate

Because of the equivalence of life, perception, and consciousness,

---

*I am using consciousness in the limited sense of awareness, as in the awareness of an "I" of something. There is another broader sense of the word which is as "an aspect of existence."

it would be well to have a term that means all three simultaneously, implicitly recognizing the equivalence, and stating so to the reader. I nominate the word ANIMATE for this very important position. Henceforth, when I refer to something as animate I am referring to it as alive, possessing consciousness, perceiving, and acting in its self-interest.

GESTALTS

A gestalt is any boundaried system or organization that functions as a whole. An atom, a molecule, a crystal, a cell, a virus, a bacterium, a plant, or animal, or any boundaried subsystem like a seed or an organ are gestalts. They have organizational integrity. On the other hand, mud, aggregate rock, hamburger, a river are not gestalts, but aggregates of gestalts. For the most part, they do not function as an organized whole within their boundaries (although, of course, their boundaries may organize them, e.g., a river). Blood cells are gestalts. Blood is probably not a gestalt but an aggregate of gestalts organized by the circulatory system, which may be considered a gestalt.

Living gestalts

Some gestalts are living organisms and some are not. Then there are some gestalts that occupy a questionable transition zone between the two. It is axiomatic that living gestalts have consciousness. That is the way they know that they are, where they are, and how to organize and function.

Gestalt and perception

Living gestalts also perceive. It is because they have consciousness that they can perceive. However, perception and consciousness are not quite the same. Perception is a special case of consciousness.

Every living gestalt has the power of perception to one degree or another. Even membrane irritability in a single-celled organism can be construed as perception, particularly if it leads to some action on the part of the cell.

A perceiving gestalt is any gestalt that responds to its environment in the pursuit of its self-interest! A perceiving gestalt is, of course, a living gestalt.

A SELF APART

A perceiving gestalt, any perceiving gestalt, is operationally conscious of itself apart from the rest of Oneness. (That is, it operates as if it is conscious of itself as apart from Oneness and unconscious that it is part of Oneness!) It identifies with itself on its own level of organization. It has its own awareness, and subordinates, as well as ignores or forgets its identity with the whole of Oneness. (Then it turns around and selectively interprets biologically relevant aspects of this selfsame Oneness through its sensorium.)

How does the Isness of a gestalt in Oneness evolve to know itself as separate from the totality of Oneness (which practically comes down to asking how gestalts arise and function as islands of increasing organization and energy in an entropic surround.) Why is it evolutionarily advantageous for living gestalts to perceive and act separately from the rest of Oneness? Why are there no living gestalts that know themselves and act as if they were part of Oneness (with the possible partial exceptions of enlightened beings).

The answers to these questions are mostly tautological and self-evident. First, enduring, living gestalts evolved to perceive in their best interests, otherwise they couldn't act in their best interests. Perceiving as a gestalt is simultaneous with acting as a gestalt. Second, they have to act in their self-interests, the self-interests of individual survival and reproduction, because those that don't won't.

Still, the question arises, why do perceiving gestalts know themselves but tend to remain oblivious of their identity with Oneness? Any perceiving gestalt, insofar as it is a perceiver, is by necessity in illusion. This means, of course, that sensed aspects of Oneness are not experienced in real form (there is no such thing), but rather perceived in a dual and illusory form. The one thing that cannot ever be perceived is Oneness in its wholeness. (Wholeness and perception are a contradiction in terms.) The self-interests of individual survival and reproduction, of necessity, set perceiving gestalts apart from the universal community of Oneness and instead compel them to be consumers of it.

Perceiving gestalts, to the extent that they know their Oneness, know it not as qualities but just as a sense of pregnant voidness.

(Problems arise when a subsystem in Oneness overidentifies with itself and forgets that it is a part of all Oneness, or even part of a dominant gestalt, as when an individual cell forgets that it is part of a body and becomes cancerous, or when humanity forgets it is part of the earth and destroys the ecological balance! Problems also arise when a superordinate system forgets its subordinate systems and acts in a way that endangers them, as when a person undermines his health by smoking, or when a superordinate system fails to regulate its subordinates.)

THE CORPORATE ORGANISM

Every living gestalt has its own organization, its own limited autonomy. Most gestalts are subsumed or regulated by higher systems like the endocrine system and the peripheral nervous system, which have regulatory functions. These regulatory systems in turn are regulated by involuntary brain systems, which also have their own organization, their own limited autonomy. These systems exist in an organization matrix, a hierarchy where every system does its job, being more or less responsible for its own survival and reproduction (within its niche in the whole organism), at the same time being at the bidding of one or more superordinate regulatory systems.

As you go up in the hierarchy of systems, you get to higher levels of generality. However, whether you get to higher levels of consciousness is a matter of opinion. For example, a blood cell is perfectly conscious in itself; it is just from the point of view of the ego that it is not. There are yogis who can voluntarily slow their heart, but less likely any who can slow their cellular processes.

The hierarchization of semiautonomous selves frees the regulating or executive selves to concentrate on larger tasks. They in turn free the ego to concentrate on survival, defensive, and social behaviors, confident that inner processes will go on more or less smoothly without their attention. It is similar to a large corporation. There are workers of every sort from factory workers to salesmen to maintenance personnel, then there are middle managers, and finally there is the CEO whose only functions are to integrate feedback data and make decisions. Though all of these corporate employees differ in the level of organization of their jobs within the corporate structure, they all have lives of their own, selves if you will. They are all more or less responsible for their own survival, although the survival of the corporate habitat is essential to that survival.

9.　EVOLUTION

Duality is illusion.
Illusion is the intelligence that guides evolution.
Therefore, illusion is the principle that unifies the biofield.

All there is in reality is oneness.
Therefore, oneness must be the (primal) perceiver,
Perceiving itself to create duality and illusion.
Thus, begins the never-ending march of evolution.

THE TWO FACES OF GOD

Oneness, the God within, voidness, Isness, Self, Buddha nature, is one face of God.

Oneness is the invisible face of God, that which can never be known. It is the potential from which all things spring, to which all things return, which all things eternally are.

Duality, oneness perceived, illusion, is the visible face of God, the face that takes on an infinity of appearances. It is the organism living in the illusory world of its perception, living in a cosmos that exists only from its point of view, and living in it as if its survival is paramount.

Oneness is the ultimate yin, infinite potential, the passive principle. It is real, monolithic, mysterious, and unknowable. Oneness perceived, duality, is the ultimate yang, active principle. It is manifest, illusory, experienced, knowable.

The God principle cycles from passive to active to passive again as it cycles endlessly from Oneness to duality to Oneness. Oneness begins as whole, yin and passive. Upon perception Oneness manifest, becomes dual, yang, illusory, creative, and differentiated. The forms it evolves, however, exist once more in Oneness, real, unknowable, and eternal in potential. Therefore the circle turns, the cycle endlessly progresses, yin to yang, yang to yin.

Thus, God creates and the world evolves.

Oneness awakening, reaching around and looking itself in the face...that is the ultimate mystery and the ultimate answer. It is the God principle. It is the creative principle. It is the evolutionary principle.

For if God is not the evolutionary principle, what is left for it to be?

EVOLUTION OF ONENESS

(The God process)

> Evolution is the evolution of Oneness.
> The cycle from Oneness to duality and back, endlessly,
> is the evolutionary dynamic.
> Oneness is the clay that duality sculpts.

The people who protest evolutionary theory and believe only God could create life are not entirely mistaken, more misled. Their error is to anthropomorphize the God principle.

On the other hand, evolutionists may make the mistake of seeing a mechanistic universe at work instead of the God principle at play.

Everything that works has to work somehow, but that does not mean it is a machine.

God must be the evolutionary principle. All other roles are beneath it.

LESS KNOWABLE THAN ONENESS

If anything is less knowable than Oneness (and nothing is)
It is the dance between Oneness and illusion
Not real
Not illusory
Neither perceived nor there to be perceived
No wonder it has neither name nor form
God, creation, evolution
Mouthfuls of nothing

LIFE

Life is self-created
Because it and only it perceives, strives, and evolves.

THE PRIMAL ILLUSION!

The primal illusion is an individual organism behaving as if its survival is crucial. Yet, if all organisms didn't behave that way, the entirety of life would become extinct. Therefore, it is not only illusion but the primal illusion that drives evolution.

EVOLUTION AND THE TAO

The great Buddhist and Taoist masters have demonstrated that one can fathom the way things work by pure contemplation, without the assistance of experimentation. The reason they can do this is that, at bottom, everything is pure process. The way everything works is the way all things work and all things work the same way because this is the only way things can work. All other explanations are wish fulfillment, magical thinking, or just plain confusion. (Although the greatest Taoist and Buddhist masters have demonstrated that you can figure out the principles underlying reality by pure contemplation, countless numbers of accomplished and revered sages and mystics have shown just how wrong you can go following the same route.)

Evolution is the process by which life organizes. It is a process inherent in all life on all levels, from subsystems of life forms, cells, and perhaps even cellular components to the most compex organisms. (Perhaps even some reactive chemical compounds undergo evolution-like processes. How else would you account for the emergence of life from nonlife?) The evolutionary process is the same on any level, be it microbe or man. On the upper reaches of the evolutionary tree, meta-evolutionary or stochastic processes, processes that combine randomicity, natural selection, and other sources of information and variation shape individual psyches and cultures. (Both evolution and meta-evolution are perceptual.)

Evolution proceeds according to a law so ancient it is axiomatic of existence itself. Twenty-five hundred years ago in China, a master of reality called Lao-tzu described this evolutionary principle and called it "Tao" (pronounced "dow"). Lao-tzu and other Taoist philosophers saw the Tao as the organizing principle behind all existence, and didn't particularly concentrate on the evolution of life. Contemplative minds like Darwin, Hegel, and Piaget have been rediscovering and renaming the principle of Tao in their own areas of inquiry ever since.

The Tao is commonly translated as "the way." People with a need to give up self-responsibility and seek divine guidance take this to mean the way to live, but the real meaning is both simpler and subtler. The Tao refers to the way things are: the way things work, the way that things that have come to be came to be, the way that things have to be because there is no other way. It refers at base to the way

Oneness manifests in perception, enters the creative process, and returns to Oneness again. It is the process inherent in existence. It is a principle as primary as cause and effect, but realer and considerably more profound. It starts with the evolutionary principle!

THE EVOLUTIONARY PRINCIPLE

The Taoist perception of reality is that nothing is hot or cold, friend or foe, cause and effect. These distinctions are all arbitrary, properties of the world of appearance or illusion. Instead, everything is part of a vast continuum of Isness, totally devoid of perceptual qualities.

The illusion or dimensionality of the apparent world is engendered by the act of perception. The act of perception differentiates perceiver from perceived whereas the relation between any two corresponding reference points on the perceiver and perceived, on one level of discourse, differentiates the properties of the perceiver from the properties of the perceived, and creates a perceptual quality.

The perceiver is a simultaneous focus of a potentially limitless array of reference points ranging from body temperature to self image. Differentiation takes on as many guises as there are points in question. Things in the perceived world are either hot or cold, near or far, friendly or threatening in relationship to these subjective referents, while in the real world they just have relatively valueless characteristics like molecular activity, and waveform, which in themselves are just cognitive metaphors for perceptual illusions.

In Taoism and other Chinese philosophical systems, the poles of duality are abstracted into two forces, yin and yang. These are variously translated as feminine and masculine, dark and light, inner and outer. A lot of specifics have been written about the specific characters of yin and yang, but I think they can be best understood as polar opposites. The most basic example is differentiation around a fixed reference point, like close and far. Other oppositions might be along the lines of passive and active, directionality, and charge. I think intuitive distinctions, e.g., characterizing various foods or bodily energies as yin or yang, tend to confound the principle. On the other hand, even if yin and yang are purely reversible qualities like polarity, directionality, or charge, these differences probably do have specific effects on humans or other life forms.

THE PRIMAL YIN/YANG IS ONENESS/ILLUSION

The primal yin yang is that of Oneness/duality, reality/illusion, or aperception/perception. These are, of course, different ways of saying the same thing. This level of discourse between realms is not actually the workings of duality but the meta-evolutionary principle. The meta-evolutionary principle occurs simultaneously and concomitantly with the evolutionary principle. The evolutionary principle, the ordinary yin/yang, is the interaction between the poles of a duality that drive the stream of changing form in both poles. The dynamic of the evolutionary principle is played out solely in the perceptual realm, but the resulting changes are in both realms

OTHER NAMES FOR THE EVOLUTIONARY PRINCIPLE

Evolutionary systems other than Taoism have their own names for the poles of duality: In Darwinian evolution they are thought of, rather statically, as organism and environment, or as the somewhat more process-oriented survival and extinction. But it is clear Darwin is talking about the reciprocal actions of organism on environment and environment on organism.

In the psychology of Jean Piaget (who, by the way, started his career as an evolutionary biologist), stages in the development of the child's intellectual structures are also seen to proceed though the "evolutionary principle." Piaget describes cognitive growth as successive levels of adaptation achieved through the alternation of assimilation and accommodation. In assimilation the mind assimilates the environment, and in accommodation it accommodates itself to the environment, or something like that. Few have ever gotten it completely straight, but it is clear that their difficulty is that they are trying to specify the alternating poles of duality, between which there are no inherent or nonrelational distinctions. Piaget is getting at the same evolutionary principle.

In Hegelian dialectics, ideas are what is evolving. The poles of duality are called thesis and antithesis, and the evolved new idea or form is the synthesis. Thus, the evolutionary principle is applied to the development of thought or the idea.

The dynamic common to all of these evolutionary systems is that yin and yang, organism and environment, assimilation and accommodation, thesis and antithesis, interact, alternate, and act on one another. In this way form is evolved, be that form the species of Darwin, the idea of Hegel, the developing intellect of Piaget, or the thousand and one things of Taoism. The unseen evolution of Oneness is taking place at the same time that appearance is evolving. The evolutionary principle or Tao is responsible for the synthesis of all of the forms of existence, life, species, culture, thought, illusion, and individual psyches.

MODERN DARWINIAN EVOLUTION

The basics of Darwinian evolution can be summarized simply. (I ask the reader to forgive me if I inadvertently attribute to Darwin a later sophistication of the theory.)

Evolution takes place in populations of organisms. Of course, Darwin was talking about species, but he recognized that a population within a species could become isolated from the whole and then evolve separately.

All populations contain variation. First, there is an existing variation of all identifiable characteristics, roughly distributed according to a bell-shaped curve, even in seemingly homogeneous populations of organisms (species). Second, reproduction, with its division and recombination of genetic material, introduces variation. Thirdly, genetic material mutates introducing variation.

Organisms have a will to survive and reproduce, and act in this regard according to the best of their ability. There are exceptions to this rule, both in the case of social organisms that subjugate their individual well-being to the good of the social unit (bees), or components of composite organisms that subjugate their well-being to the good of the composite organism (lymphocytes). However, if you consider the determining level of organization (hive, mammal) to be the organism, the rule holds good.

Some genetic variations are advantageous to the specific efforts of an organism to survive and reproduce in a specific environment, others are deleterious.

The organisms that have advantageous traits tend to survive and reproduce more successfully (to and in a given environment). Disadvantageous traits, of course, have the opposite effect.

Variable success in the cycle of weaning and reproducing is known as natural selection. Over time natural selection culls an isolated gene pool into a more or less homogeneous form, or in other words, shapes a species. This process is called Darwinian evolution.

In the years since Darwin first wrote, the theory has been worked out in much greater detail, and a lot of refinements have been added to it. I will mention only two of these.

The first is that what evolves, i.e., changes from one relatively stable, reproducible form to another, is neither the individual nor the species, but the genetic makeup of the individual and the gene pool of the species.

Second, the environment in which an individual or population strives to survive is not fixed. It is everchanging. Some of those changes are more or less independent of the individual or species (like climatic changes), but many more are brought about by the adaptive efforts of the organism itself. Relocation, nest building, tunnel building, grazing, pollination, fruit eating and seed dispersal, proliferation, and countless others are all ways that species change their effective environment. This changed environment then, in turn, is effective in changing the species in a perpetual and progressive

cycle or spiral of accommodation and assimilation.

EVOLUTION AND APERCEPTUAL FIELD THEORY

Aperceptual field theory gives a wider theoretical context to Darwinian evolution, just as unified field theory with its convertibility between energy and matter gave a wider context to Newtonian physics. The first thing to look at is the role of illusion.

> Perception disinforms consciousness into illusion.
> However perception is the intelligence that guides
> evolution.
> Therefore, illusion guides evolution.

Organisms have a will to survive and reproduce, and act in this regard according to the best of their ability. Whenever they do so, however, they are acting according to their perception (with all that implies). That is, they are acting not in the real world of Oneness, but in the perceived world of duality or illusion. This means that an illusory worldview, with the perceiver as the center of an imaginary universe composed of other, and apprehended dualistically in the language of the senses, is the intelligence that informs the evolving organism and guides its evolution.

Or conversely and more simply, as an organism acts according to its illusions (perceptions), evolution progresses. It all comes down the the same principle: illusion guides evolution.

PARALLEL REALITIES

> Although illusion is not part of oneness
> Its offspring instantly return there
> Once again to be perceived as illusion.
> Thus, the two parallel realities
> Illusion and reality
> Constantly fertilize one another.
> Evolution
> Creation

Aperceptual field theory redefines evolution, not only in the emphasis it gives to perceptual illusion, but in pointing out that the interaction of the realms of Oneness and duality, or reality and illusion, is the primary evolutionary dialectic, far more basic than the interaction of organism and environment.

The one irreducible constant that drives the world is not the speed of light, it is illusion. Illusion is that which we can't get away from, it is our constant companion, that which simultaneously gives meaning to experience and ultimately renders it meaningless. Illusion is the inescapable artifact of perception's otherness. The field of illusion is consciousness.

THE PROBLEM OF ORIGINS AND THE RELATIONSHIP BETWEEN DUALITY AND THE CREATION OF LIFE

It is self-evident and tautological that all things survive better in an environment favorable to their survival. Yet, that simple insight is the starting point for the evolution of life.

There probably are nonliving substances that react in a way that is quasi-perceptual. In order to qualify for this, they would have to be more stable or enduring in one kind of environment than another, form more complex compounds in a favorable environment, and perhaps even change their environment to a more favorable one or migrate to a more favorable environment. It also follows that if there were variations in these substances, the variations that accomplish these operations most successfully would endure the best.

These compounds then could be said to "operationally perceive." That is, they would react as if they perceived the world in terms of self and other, and act in their own narrow best interest. Thus, even though they are not alive, they would be on the first rung of the evolutionary ladder, operationally self-interested, and one can imagine them fumbling toward life through higher and higher levels of self-organization. Even though they are not conscious, they react in some rudimentary way as if they were.

Thus, we can imagine something akin to self-referential self-interest, not only guiding the evolution and development of life forms, but also playing a role in the transition of matter from the inanimate to the animate.

INSIGHTS

Life evolves. That is a fundamental condition.
All that is alive by its own striving evolves.
Change without striving is not evolution.
The poles of duality are the wellsprings of cosmic creativity,
Not in themselves but in the interaction between them.

COGNITIVE EVOLUTION

The direction of evolution is a clear, if stochastic progression, from the physical to the sensory, from the sensory to the cognitive, from the biological to the cultural, from the concrete to the abstract. (A stochastic sequence is one that combines randomness and selectivity.)

From the very first, physical bodies and sensoriums coevolved of necessity. However, the proportions to which they did so differed greatly. Early in evolutionary history, before the clear differentiation of flora and fauna, evolution clearly favored the physical form. The sensorium was relatively simple and unchanging, and responses were relatively localized rather than communicated through a nervous system. Later, as flora and fauna differentiated, the evolutionary emphasis diverged. In flora, the balance stayed greatly in favor of physical evolution. We saw a great profusion of forms with a relatively limited range of behavior. In fauna, however, the hemoglobin metabolism, with its far greater possibilities of behavior and locomotion, necessitated that the evolution of the sensorium and central nervous system take on a bigger role.

At first, evolution was primarily the evolution of the first realm, of Oneness. That is, the things that evolved were organic forms, bodies. However, as fauna emerged, the realm of illusion (perception and percept) evolved more complexity and started coevolving increasingly with the realm of Oneness. As the sensorium and brain evolved, the way it perceived and conceived changed, and the environment became increasingly a cultural-informational one, thus further accelerating the evolution of illusion.

As the brain, particularly the human brain, became increasingly capable of cognition and cognitive perception, the field of evolution gradually shifted not only from the first realm to the second, but ever further, from the sensorium to the cognitorium.

Increasingly, cognitive structures subsumed bigger and bigger bites of sensory experience. They also played progressively larger roles in the intelligence that guides adaptive behavior, and ultimately determines the course of evolution.

Animals have always (cognitively) changed their environment, and then evolved physically to accommodate their changed environment. Burrows and nests as well as skyscrapers are cognitive structures. Humans, however, have shifted the principal focus of evolution from their bodies to their cognitive structures, hammers, telephones, computers, and civilizations (which, like nests, are extensions of themselves). This shift has put an exponentially increasing adaptive stress on the organism, challenging the new brain and stimulating a corresponding surge in its evolution. However, the trend we see in humans, of shifting the evolutionary focus from the organism to its cognitive structures, is ancient. Increasingly, this trend first changes the way people live, the environment in which they live, their technology, culture, and tools. Only as a last resort does it change them biologically!

THE PRIMAL ILLUSION AND THE SUPERIORITY/INFERIORITY SPLIT

The primitive self-concept, as an extension of the primary duality of self and other, perceives in exclusionary categories. The world is the negative of itself, or what itself is not. In other words, the self image sees itself as the embodiment of qualities the world lacks. This is the paradigm for the superiority-inferiority split, a basic duality, which in turn motivates the development of personality, or the evolution of personas.

However, there is a transitional variable between the primary duality of self-other, and the superiority-inferiority split. This has to do with survival and is what I call the primal illusion.

All organisms behave as if their individual survival is both crucial and paramount. This is totally an illusion on their part! Yet, if individual organisms didn't act that way, they would die. If species didn't behave that way, they would become extinct. If no organisms functioned that way, all life would become extinguished. This is why it is called the primal illusion. (So much for "spiritual agendas which call for the protection of all sentient beings." Their success would bring about the total extinction of life more quickly and surely than any nuclear catastrophe.)

This, of course, is simply to say that if life in the individual did not strive to survive, it wouldn't, and life in the collective would cease.

(There are some exceptions for social and gestalt organisms that form an extended self and act as if the survival of this extended self, hive, colony, gestalt, or symbiotic organism is crucial.)

Obviously, survival and reproduction begin with the identification (at least operationally) of those things that further it and threaten it. Once you identify positive and negative qualities, you have values. Some things are good, some things are bad. Some things are better, some things worse.

Social animals tend to form hierarchies or pecking orders according what qualities are advantageous in their particular species: strength, speed, intelligence, cooperativeness, social skills, whatever. Those animals higher up the hierarchy tend to eat better, mate more, etc. It is interesting that in apes, social ties are more important than physical prowess in determining and solidifying rank, thus heralding the evolutionary emergence of social prowess as a primary survival skill.

Humans (and any other animals that have the ability to form

self-concepts) have self/other, or self-concept/other-concept perceptions, relevant to these issues of survival and procreation. So they
start perceiving themselves as stronger or weaker, faster or slower,
more or less intelligent, popular, attractive, sexy, rich, and so on.

As we have said, these qualities are valued. Some, like strength,
speed, intelligence, are primary values with a directly discernible
link to survival and reproduction. Others, like fashionableness, sophistication, wit, popularity, etc., are more derivative, but a little
thought will readily reveal, if not their direct survival advantage, at
least how they got linked in perception to survival.

These valued perceptions of self and other always contain a self-
judgment, whether implicit or explicit. I'm stronger, you're better
looking, she's sexier, etc. Even when the self-judgment is positive,
i.e., "I'm stronger than him," it also contains or implies its opposite
in some form, i.e., "I'm weaker than someone," "I'm weak so I must
become strong," "I'm in danger of being weak," "I must do so and
so; otherwise I will be weak," etc. Of course, when the self-judgment is negative, i.e., "I'm weak," the implication of stronger others
is apparent.

The stated and implied aspects of this judgment, in aggregate,
add up to the superiority-inferiority split. That is, whenever there
is self-judgment, whether positive or negative, its opposite always
exists. Furthermore, it exists in the same person's self-concept, if
not as a conviction, then as a possibility or a memory to be guarded
against or compensated for. For we all start out as infants, tiny and
helpless.

The superiority-inferiority split, however, is more than just a
qualitative distinction. It is a distinction that matters, a distinction
that moves people from elation to despair, a distinction that motivates heroic acts and destructive ones. Without the primal illusion,
these perceptions of self and other would not take on their compelling force, and the superiority-inferiority split, a force that forms
people's personalities and motivates their deeds, would never arise.

EVOLUTION AS A MULTIPLE DIALECTIC

In evolution we see the simultaneous confluence of multiple dualities. Three of the principal ones are illusion and oneness, organism and environment, and self and other. (There exist innumerable other potential dualities as well.) Thus, we can describe evolution in dialectical terms. One pole of the duality is the thesis, the other the antithesis, while evolution is the ongoing synthesis that in turn perpetually provides fresh theses and antitheses.

In the adaptive duality of organism and environment, the co-evolving organism/environment is the ongoing synthesis. It would be more in keeping with traditional evolutionary thought to refer to the evolving organism as the synthesis, but further consideration will reveal that what evolves is not only the organism. The environmental niche coevolves. In cases where the environmental niche is not concrete and easily perceived, it's easy to make the mistake that it's only the organism evolving. However, in cases where the environmental niche is stable and concrete, as in the habitats of ants and bees, it becomes apparent that that which is coevolving is the organism/environment whole...their relationship.

In the case of ants and bees, not only is it apparent that the hive and the anthill are coevolving, but it is also clear that they have evolved to such an extent that it is unclear whether they are best considered environment or organism. It is all how you look at it. If the hive and hill are considered the organism, what are the specialized insects to be called? Are they individual organisms or highly evolved, specialized cells? Are soldier ants and drones warriors, or are they cells in an immune system. Is the queen a mother or an ovary? Of course, it doesn't make any difference what you consider them to be, they are what they are. I only use these examples to highlight the arbitrariness of the organism/environment duality and reinforce my point that what evolves is neither organism nor environment, but both together.

The ongoing synthesis of the coevolving organism/environment then provides fresh theses and antitheses in the form of new forms for the organism and new modifications of the environment. (Which is thesis and which is antithesis is wholly dependent of viewpoint.)

The next duality, illusion and Oneness, is even more important than organism and environment, for it is perception and illusion that creates or determines how the organism sees and responds to the environment. The duality of illusion and Oneness is not fully independent of organism and environment, but rather an additional variable. It modifies and enriches the picture of what is happening in evolution. Not only is illusion a function of the organism's perception of the environment, but it is also a function of those aspects of the environment, fauna and flora, that are alive and reciprocally perceiving the organism we are studying. (Definitionally, all life perceives and acts and reacts in self-interest. Even plants generate toxins in the leaves and seeds to prevent them from being eaten, which, in turn, has an evolutionary effect on their would-be consumers.) The illusion-driven evolution of both organism and environment then takes place on the Oneness level (to be again perceived in illusion).

The level of illusion is not simple, but itself multivariate. To start with, there is the primal illusion of being apart, which gives rise to the conviction that individual survival and procreation are of paramount importance. Without this illusion and its derivative convictions, life would not do do what it needs to do in order to survive, procreate, and evolve. Then there is the primary illusion of sensory perception, perceiving Oneness from a point apart and dualizing it into dimensions. Next, there is the secondary illusion of cognitive perception, projecting qualities of self onto perceptions and creating qualities. And sometimes there is the further cognitive illusion of thinking (in quasi-perceptual qualities) and responding to the products of thought or conclusions as if they were perceptual presentations.

The third duality, self and other, is a derivative of both the duality of illusion and Oneness, and the duality of organism and environment. If we graph illusion and Oneness and organism and environment as vectors intersecting one another, the vector of self and other might bisect the angle between them.

At first glance the self would seem to be synonymous with the organism, and other with the environment, but a little thought will show you that this is only sometimes the case. Consider not only the individual but the flock, the pack, the school, the hive, the family, the species, and the tribe. All of these combinations and more, which seem to provide numerous examples of altruism when taken from the point of view of the individual, really reveal nothing more or less than the changeable boundary between self and other. Sometimes the individual is self and all other individuals, even within the same species or group, are other. At other times, larger groupings such as the pack or tribe or even the species are perceived as self and evolve together. Variation in the boundary between self and other not only alters the course of evolution, but changes that which is evolved.

What we have now is a six-pointed star, three vectors intersecting at a point. The point is the sum of three simultaneous theses and antitheses combining to yield an ever-evolving synthesis, which, in turn, is furnishing fresh theses and antitheses for further dialectics on all three vectors. This point of intersection yields a more complete picture of evolution than the mere interplay of organism and environment or for that matter, any of these dualities taken singly. However, this is more an example or a model of a new way of approaching evolution than an exposition. For there are not only these three dualities at work, there are many others, mind/body, exterior/interior, energy/matter, past/future, hot/cold, near/far, ad infinitum, and each one adds complexity, explanatory, and predictive power and wholeness to the evolving picture of evolution.

SELF/PSYCHE

10. THINGNESS AND THE PERCEIVED SELF

NOTHING REAL

Is nothing real?
Yes
no thing is real!

THINGNESS

Thingness is the universal category. We live in a world of things. They surround us, live things and dead things. An object is a thing. An empty pitcher is a thing and so is a full one. Elbows and shoulders are separate things, but an arm is one thing. A clod of earth containing sand, decayed vegetable matter, worm excrement, and millions of microorganisms is one thing, a crystal is another. Molecules, atoms, muons, and quarks are things. Broadly speaking, everything that exists, in all of its combinations, is a thing. Nothing knowable is not a thing. What is a thing? What is the thing in something? What is absent in nothing? Where does one thing stop and the next thing begin? Some things seem clearly defined, but for most the boundaries are unclear. Aspects of different things overlap and everything blends into everything else. Things are rarely as clearly defined as their names are.

Yet, what is a thing? To try to find thingness in reality is a doomed quest. Thingness is an arbritrary, perceptual category. A thing is only a thing relative to something else. The laws governing the perception of thingness are quite lax. All that is required is that in some way the thing in question can be distinguished from something else. Things can be figure and ground, they can lie alongside one another, they can be separated by other things, they can be features of something else like the nose on a face and the pimple on a nose. They can contain other things. It helps if some other thing can be seen as separate from a thing, but this is not necessary. It helps if a thing is named, but that is not necessary either.

It is interesting that even admittedly mental constructs, ideas, emotions, and events are frequently called things. Most of us would readily agree that calling these things *things* is a metaphor for *physical* things, but it is more than that. It is evidence that we both perceive and conceive in terms of thingness.

What are these physical things we model our thoughts and feelings on? They all are no more real than ideas, emotions, and events. They are all figments of our perception. They are the category of the nameable, the seeable, the identifiable, the locateable, the pointable, the referable, the separable. They are the ever-shifting boundaries of the thousand and one things that perception projects and evolution creates. This tendency to perceive and conceive in terms of thingness, separate, stable, isolated, nonrelated, uncommunicating, *physical* things, is what has led all of human thought and human endeavor, particularly in the physical sciences, on such a wild goose chase all these years.

So what is a thing? First and finally, it is a perceptual illusion, a category, sensory or cognitive. It is the perception of separateness, of something, anything, that can be distinguished in any way whatsoever from anything else, and in perception everything can. I realize this definition, by using the word defined, violates the first rule of lexicography, but I can't do a thing about it.

Nothing that can be distinguished from anything else is not a thing.

THINGNESS AND SELF

If thingness is just a perceptual category, and anything that can be separated from anything else, whatever the anything else is, is a thing, this raises the question, what is the thing that we perceive our self from? If every perceiving gestalt, part and whole, in every combination, has consciousness, what is the point of origin of the perception, the thing from which we perceive our self? In our body we have innumerable, almost infinite points of potential perception. At the very least every cell, nerve, organ, gland, system, muscle, muscle group, and brain structure, in every possible combination, is a perceiving gestalt, a potential separate point of perception. Contrast this staggering multiplicity with our experience of perceiving as a single unified self.

While we are at it, let's consider the corollary question, what is the thing that we perceive as our self? Again, we are faced with a staggering multiplicity of things (objects of perception) in a multitude of combinations, from body parts to our bodies, from appearances to abilities, from feelings to behaviors, from memories to plans, from feelings to thoughts, all of which could be seen in part or whole as ourselves, or selves within selves.

The question of what is a thing turns out to be a question that gets to the very heart of perception. Very near that heart is the question of what is a self. The answer to the first is the generic form of the answer to the second. The self perceived is also a thing, that is a perceptual category. It is anything that can be perceptually distinguished from anything else. Only it has to meet one additional criterion: we have to identify it in some way with "ourself," or a projection of it. Once again the definition is circular, using the word defined in the definition. Fortunately, although we might be hazy on the concept of self, we all know what an "ourself" is, so we can intuitively understand the definition.

There is one significant difference between the perceptual category that is a thing, and the perceptual category that is a self. You can only perceive a thing, but you can perceive from or at least through the thing that is a self! This fact is so extraordinary that it provides an auxiliary definition of a self. A self is a thing that provides a perspective for perception.

So what is a self? First and foremost, it is a thing, anything, that you perceive as a self or self-perceive as yourself. Second, it is any perceiving gestalt!

IS THERE A SELF?

Self and self

At this point we have to make the distinction between the perceived self as an object of perception and the Self, which is the perceiver itSelf. It's very difficult in discussing what is a self to keep these two selves separate because they commingle in experience and reality. The self that we experience ourselves to be and the self that we experience in others are an admixture of Self-the-perceiver and self-the-object-of-perception. A complicating difficulty is that the Self perceives through the self, thus dualizing, interpreting, and distorting the object of perception into specific forms of illusion.

In the following discussion I am going to touch on the mix of the two as they occur in nature, whereas in forthcoming discussions I will concentrate on their separate aspects. However, I will endeavor to keep to the convention of designating the perceived self with a small "s" and the Self as perceiver with a large "S."

I have postulated that the consciousness of every cell, nerve, organ, gland, system, muscle, muscle group, and brain structure, in every possible combination, qualifies as a self. However, intuitively, this formulation seems much too reductionistic. Try looking in the eyes of someone you love and try to apply this formulation. It won't ring true. It seems that there is some center, some essence, some soul from which people come. (It also seems that sometimes they are closer to it than at other times. Also, we have the impression that some people are more grounded or centered in their Self than others.)

If, according to the previous definition, the self is just the consciousness of any living gestalt, a perceiving thing, and all units of life large and small, in nested biological systems, have this consciousness, what is this self that looks at you from your child's eyes and melts your heart? Is it just an illusion?

Furthermore, how can anyone function as an organized whole, giving their attention to one thing at a time, focusing, intending, directing their energies toward goals? How can anyone have a consistent character if they are not one self but a multitude?

The answer is complex. First of all, we have to admit that there is much that is illusory in our perception of a unitary, integrated self, whether it be the self in others, the self in ourselves, or the self as a concept. The unity of the perceived self is largely a perceptual construction, an artifact of the integrating function of perception. (The integrating function of perception will be discussed further in the chapter on the evolving self.)

Another part of the answer is organization. Unlike every thing, which only has to have a perceived organization and perceived boundaries every living, perceiving gestalt, every self, has an intrinsic organization and real though not absolute or exclusive boundaries, (as well as a self-perceived separateness or thingness). As I have said, most living gestalts are organizations within organizations which, in turn, have organizations functioning within them. However, every gestalt has its own organization as well, an organization that functions within its boundaries, and defines it. I call this the determining level of organization. The determining level of organization defines the identity of a gestalt. To a cell the determining level of organization is the entirety of that which goes on within its cell walls. To an organ like a liver it is roughly that which takes place within the membrane of the organ. The blood cells circulating within them, though they each have their own organization, their own perception, and their own self, are organized en masse by the organ that directs their flow and used by that organ for a number of purposes. The self that is the liver is organizing and utilizing the selves that are the blood cells. Thus, in a sense the self of every living entity can be said to be its determining level of organization.

With regard to humans and other higher animals, there seems to be a self that is a determining level of organization, subsuming all suborganizations. It is difficult to determine precisely what this is, and the subordination of suborganisms is far from complete. If it was, we would all forget to breathe. Certainly high on the hierarchy of dominance is the brain. But even that remarkable organ seems to be merely the domain and not the substance of the self. If anything, it seems to be the idea, the self-perception, the self-concept, the perceived identity, that evanescent partnership of information and neurons in which the determining level of organization is found, and in which the pattern of the self generates and evolves.

The self as an emergent phenomenon

The other thing to be said about the self in this regard is that it is an emergent phenomenon. It comes into being as an entity organizes, changes as the organization changes, and disappears when the organization disintegrates. Whatever the determining level of organization of a being is, there is its self.

11. THE EVOLVING SELF, ONENESS PERCEIVING

ORIGINAL PERCEPTION

The metaprocess for the evolution of personality parallels the model for the evolution of life itself. Oneness forms an organization or gestalt in itself, i.e., an individuation of body, mind, and consciousness, thus forming an individuated, or real Self. This real Self, which is still in the realm of Oneness, perceives itself, thus forming a self-concept. This self-concept, then, is a perception, the primal perception, the first illusion. In sum Oneness organizes itself into an individuated Self and this Self perceives itself forming a self-concept. Thus, Oneness perceives itself, creating illusion. (I don't really know how this is done. I only know that logically, it must occur for what exists to exist.)

A note on Self and self

The uncapitalized self is usually used to denote something like the self-concept, personality, or ego, and the implication is that it is a limited conception of self or even a false self. The capitalized self is usually used to denote the Vedantic concepts of Brahma or Atman, and usually interchangeably. In Vendantic thought Brahma stands for universal consciousness while Atman stands for universal consciousness embodied in and functioning as an individual, with the further nuance of being self-recognized as such by the individual in question.

After the individuated Self in Oneness perceives itself, creating an initial self-concept, this initial self-concept perceives itself, forming another self-concept. Inevitably, this new self-concept perceives itself, forming another and yet another self-concept, each one encasing its predecessor like Chinese boxes.

Self-concept perceiving self-concept is fundamental to the dynamic by which illusion, further self-concepts, and ultimately personality evolve. The first act of perception, wherein a *gestalt in Oneness* perceives itself as self in a field of nonself, rendering itself dual and illusory, is original perception. The self pole of this duality becomes the seed of self-concept. That is, it develops into self-concept through successive acts of perception. The other pole, nonself, becomes the world or world concept. This act of original perception has been committed countless times and will be committed countless more until life extinguishes. It is repeated every time a life is organized in Oneness.

The self is "that which is not other."

More precisely, following the principle that an eye cannot see itself, by extension neither can an "I" perceive itself. The real or individuated Self, the gestalt in Oneness, only can perceive other or notself. This means that, like Oneness itself, the real Self is an inference, a negative implication, that which is not other. No wonder it cannot be experienced directly, only experienced through. However, this initial limitation is soon overcome. As the Self is bifurcated and multiple separate subselves arise, each an other to each other, those selves start perceiving one another and the combined result approximates the self perceiving itself (but the Self never perceives itSelf directly).

The original or primal perception* is the forbidden fruit, whose taste catapulted man out of the paradise of innocence (Oneness) into

---

*I am also calling the original perception *primal perception* to distinguish it from a related but different sense in which I use the term *original perception* in later chapters.

the realm of illusion, in which resides duality and differentiation, represented by good and evil. Original sin is a misconception. It is the original perception that started it all, that started perception, illusion, duality, distinction between Self and other, knowledge of good and evil, judgment, sin. It is the original perception for which man is trying vainly to atone in his yearning for the purity of the unperceived Self. According to Taoist philosophy, the perception of distinctions is of itself the source of good and evil.

> When the people of Earth all know beauty as beauty
> There arises (the recognition of) ugliness
> When the people of Earth all know good as good
> There arises (the recognition of) evil

> —*The Wisdom of Lao-tzu, Lin Yutang,*
> *Modern Library Edition, 1948*

SELF-CONCEPT

The self-concept (Self perceived by itSelf) is unique in that it, and only it, can replace a real Self as the loci from which perception originates. The ontological implications of this are puzzling! How is it possible for a self-concept to replace a real Self, for an idea or illusion to replace something real? Does this suggest an equivalency between a real Self and a self-concept, between matter and idea? Does it imply that both are real, or alternatively, that both are illusory? Does it call into question the distinction between real and illusory? Does it imply that the organization of a gestalt in Oneness is itself a conceptual process? Does it further imply that all that is physical in nature is at the same time conceptual in nature? Or, taking it from the other end, does a conceptual construct on the part of an organism automatically take place on a physical dimension?

This phenomenon, the self-concept taking over from the real Self as the locus of perception, is one of those cracks in the cosmic egg. If we pry it open, we will fall into the abyss of an altogether different reality and we will have no choice but to try to make a home in that reality.

The answer lies in the nature of the Self. If you conceive of a self-concept as a Self, that is, if you make it real, make it a thing, and then think of it as a locus of perception, that it can play that role is indeed mysterious, even miraculous. However, if you resist the impulse to reify a self-concept into a Self and just be content with the idea that in perception self-concepts operate as if they are selves, everything becomes clear. Self-concepts are conceptual filters to perception. Perceptual knowing is not from self-concepts; it is merely through them. The self that you experience, the self that you experience yourself as, the self that you know as your self, is merely an assemblage of self-concepts and has no reality in itself. It is as the Buddhists say, a form empty of spirit. This said, understood, and accepted, for simplicity's sake, I sometimes discuss the self and self-concepts as if they are, and function as, loci of perception.

How does self-concept occlude the real self?

On a more practical level, how does self-concept occlude perception from the real Self? How does illusion seize control? In the hierarchical accretion of memory, self-concept is erected upon the Self. This is why drugs that disrupt memory free people from self-concept and more or less reestablish original perception, i.e., perception from Self. Self continues to be the primary locus of perception, but it perceives through an overlay of self-concept which disinforms it.

CONSCIOUSNESS, MENTAL AND PHYSICAL

One thinks of consciousness as mental but, of course, it is also physiological. Separation of the two realms is indefensible. The consciousness is the experience of the physiology; the physiology is the substance of the consciousness. All neurophysiology, in fact, all biology has a conscious component; and all thoughts have a physiological counterpart. (That all consciousness has a biological component is far less certain.)

Self-referent thoughts have both physiological and motivational consequences. As a self-concept develops, it serves as a template that evolves, determines, and guides physiological development and the behavior of the organism (within genetically determined limits, of course) and vice versa. The different self-concepts or personas of a person have not only different psychological profiles, but surprisingly also different physiological profiles, with all sorts of metabolic distinctions. We know this from multiple personality studies.

Every Self, the organizational integrity of every individuated consciousness, even the Self of a cell, is in some way a self-concept. That is, it comes out of and holds to its location, its form, its quality of separateness. This further implies that every Self is shadowed by a self, a perceptual illusion. But what does this mean? A self being an illusion on the part of Self implies that all life is self-reflexive, starting and ending in self-perception! Either there is no real Self, no perceiving, physical, biological Self at all, or all selves are simultaneously biological and conceptual, real and illusory. Either way, all life is organized by its own self-concept. There is no life, however rudimentary, without both a real Self and its self-concept organizing one another in tandem. Every (individuated) Self is a self-concept, every self-concept a Self. Life originates with Self and self-concept, organizes with Self and self-concept, and evolves with Self and self-concept.

WHEN SELF-CONCEPT PERCEIVES ITSELF

So we are left with a picture where self-concept does not actually supersede the Self and act as a primary locus of perception, but simply acts as if or appears as if it does. However, as I said before, it is simpler and easier to follow if I talk about this apparent process as if it is real and speak of self or self-concept perceiving itself!

When self-concept (SC) perceives itself, we get a second self-concept (SC^2). This in turn yields another duality which we could designate as SC^2-world. SC^2 then supersedes SC as the loci of perception, and perceives this world from its new perspective which, of course, yields a new duality, SC^3-world. This process repeats innumerable times, self-concepts perceiving themselves to form new self-concepts, continually redefining the world as not SC^2 or not SC^3. In other words, the world is definitionally that which is other than the self (NOT SC), as well as vice versa.

Evolution of personality

This succession of self-concepts is the template for the evolution of personality and the development of multiple personas. Let us see how it works. The newborn, perceiving its world from its special viewpoint, comes to some very peculiar notions. For instance, it senses that the world is populated by huge beings, a distressing number of which seem to have dominion over him. It is small and helpless; yet, on the other hand, it is symbiotic with one of these huge beings, its mother, over which it is discovering it has some magic powers, i.e., crying gets attention. At the same time the infant is discovering it has some magic powers to control its own body. So it forms some ideas of itself and the world and the boundaries between them. These ideas are continually coalescing into new self-concepts as new experiences are had, which in turn, become new vantage points for perception. This process is the development of personality which involves the denial/compensation cycle, elegantly described by Roberto Assagioli and discussed below.

Modes of self-evolution

As the world of other begins to hold more people and a social context complete with acceptances, rejections, and rules develops, things get really tricky. Successive editions of the evolving self-concept define and redefine what the developing child is and is not. They do this by comparing self to what other people are, in relation to social mores and that insidious category of social mandates, the "shoulds."

As this progresses, self-definition begins progressing toward attitude. So now the child is viewing himself not only in terms of what he is and is not, but also in terms of what he should be and should not be, and by extension, what is good and bad.

As the child learns that some of the attributes of his perceived self are socially desirable and some undesirable, self-rejection and compensatory self-inflation ensue. With them the evolution of personality and the development of personas begins in earnest.

The advent of self-rejection/compensation complicates things considerably. What happens is that self-concepts begin to multiply. Instead of only one self-concept superseding the previous one as a point of perception, multiple self-concepts arise which either alternate or are present simultaneously. These all perceive their own distinct worlds from their own distinct vantage points and form their own versions of reality. The way these multiple self-concepts form is distinctive and important. Every time a self-concept is rejected, the person tries to fashion a compensatory self-concept out of self-percepts and behaviors he can feel good about. This is a gradual process. Sometimes it can be quite positive, sometimes quite negative. It can enhance survival and achievement or start a neurotic or even psychotic process.

(Success at forming a compensatory self-concept depends on two factors. The first is the nature of the self-concept rejected, and the validity of the reasons for its rejection. The second consists of the person's resources and success at fashioning a positive self-concept out of reality materials, or at least elements he can corroborate socially. People who can't corroborate a positive self-image in reality or society tend to synthesize positive self-concepts through such self-deceptions as social manipulation, fantasy, delusion, and even hallucination, thus becoming neurotic or even psychotic. The depth of the disturbance depends on how desperately the person needs to deny the judged self-concept and how far he is from being able to craft a compensatory self-concept out of reality materials.)

The multiplication of self-concepts

How self-concepts multiply is quite interesting and adds another level of paradox to a picture already amply supplied in this respect. Upon internalizing the judgment that part or all of his personality or his being is unacceptable or unlovable, the child denies the judged personality or fragment, i.e., the persona, and then crafts a compensatory persona. The child forms a social perception of self-other, then holds the other pole as a model, and in striving to become it, rejects himself.

Now what happens? As much as its possessor might desire it, the denied self-concept, and the behaviors that it spawns, does not cease to exist. Instead, it falls into a kind of limbo. It is shut into the closet like a defective child one is ashamed of, and since it gets little or no additional experience in the world, ceases to develop or mature (although it is always there providing a focus for the underlying sense of badness or inferiority which motivates the compensatory self).

As the person shifts all his energy into developing the compensatory self-concept, the compensatory self-concept, for all purposes, becomes the person, and of course, his point of perception. (If there are multiple self-concepts or personas present, and there usually are, what happens is that the one that is out or dominant is the principal persona. When there coexist multiple points of perception or personas, and a person is doing something that is unacceptable to a subordinate persona, he experiences considerable anxiety and sometimes the subordinate persona wrests control away from the previously dominant persona.)

A paradox is that the rejected self, for better or worse, is the original expression of that person. It is what they perceive themselves to be at the time they reject themselves and therefore could be held to be more authentic, more their real self. The compensatory self is an invention, modeled after what they perceive as other and better than themselves. Yet, it is this compensatory self, this aping of other, which becomes the main trunk of personality development while the prior, rejected self becomes stunted. In this way people become further and further alienated from their original natures.

This compensatory self goes on developing until it too gets judged, self-rejected, and replaced by another compensatory self. It is always the compensatory pole of the duality that becomes the main trunk of personality development and the prior self that is rejected and stunted.

As I have pointed out, however, denied self-concepts never go away (by being denied, that is). Rather, the process of denial is the ultimate confirmation of their reality; they forever remain as the motivating force behind compensatory self-concepts and rear their heads again when people get discouraged or defeated. (People tend to believe that their rejected selves are real and their compensatory selves are lies they are living. In fact, neither are real. This week's rejected self is just last week's compensatory self.)

We are arriving at a very peculiar picture of manifest human nature, one of multiple self-concepts developing through a flip-flop of denials and compensations, self-concepts progressing not through gradual maturation and change, but through revisionary cycles of rejection and compensation.

Of course, the reality is neither so simple nor so absolute as the theory. For simplicity I spoke of self-concepts being denied and replaced with their perceived opposites. In fact, the whole of a self-concept rarely is rejected, just some part of it, some trait or gestalt of traits, such as shyness or ingenuousness. Other aspects of the self-concept, the ones that have escaped condemnation, are preserved to develop and mature alongside the compensatory selves, for as long as they are perceived as successful. So it is more accurate to think of the self-concept being split into acceptable and unacceptable parts than being denied in its entirety. However, the split-off fragments of selves, by virtue of being split off and perceived as separate, metaphorize into whole personas.

The persona that ensues after the split, should it run into trouble itself, is not necessarily rejected whole cloth either. Parts can be rejected and parts retained, fragmenting it in the same way. So a personality is gradually built up of rejected selves, compensatory selves, and unrejected personality fragments. This view of personality is of considerable complexity, with all these autonomous and semiautonomous components functioning alongside one another. However, as we pay attention to our internal dynamics, it is an elegant description of the conflicts we find within ourselves, and it is well supported by the psychosynthesis work of Assagioli.

The evolution of the self summarized

Because there is so much complex material here, I would like to offer a summary. A personality or a self develops by an evolutionary process that follows many of the same principles that are characteristic of the evolution of life. To begin with, like the evolution of life, it is driven by perception or perceptual illusion. It starts with the individuation of Oneness, the embodiment of consciousness in a body, which creates a Self, a real Self. The individuation of Oneness is the seminal event in the origin of life.

The individuation of Oneness is itself a perceptual event, consisting of a level of organization, a gestalt of Oneness perceiving itself and perceiving itself as a part apart.

Next, Self perceiving itself yields a self-concept. This self-concept ostensibly replaces the real Self as a locus of perception, and appears to perceive itself, leading to an infinite succession of further self-concepts, $SC^{2'3'4}$ etc. This succession of self-concepts, all ostensibly perceiving themselves and all acting as new loci of perception, undergo an evolutionary development that parallels physical evolution. The self-concept or personality rather than the organism is that which is being evolved.

The parallels to physical evolution go further. Let's examine the workings of the evolutionary principle or evolutionary dialectic as it applies to the development of the personal Self.

To start, look at interactive duality. We have seen that physical evolution takes place via the mutual adaptation of organism and environment. The parallel to organism and environment in the development of the personal self is self and other, or self and world.* Just as there is an interaction between organism and environment, there is an interaction between self and world. In this case, the interaction is one of definition, distinction, and comparison.

The next evolutionary parallel is selection. Self-concepts organize into subpersonalities or personas. These resemble the per-

---

*Self is a misnomer and extremely misleading. For self really denotes the whole of self/ not-self or I/not-I. Self-perception is a perceiving of self and world. Self-concept implies a concept of not-self just as the concept of other (than self) implies a concept of self.

sonalities of multiple personality disorder except that they are not usually inaccessible to one another. The aggregate of these personas makes up the total personality. These personas form, extinguish, and reform by an evolutionary process of selection, or survival of the deemed fittest. Their success and failure, survival and extinction, lie entirely in the perceptual domain.

Briefly, personas come in pairs. There is a primary persona and a compensatory persona. Primary and compensatory personas form a second tier of dialectic (over self and other). At first there exists the primary persona or self-world concept. When, from the perspective of the world pole of the persona, the self pole is judged unsatisfactory for any reason, that part is rejected and a compensatory persona is erected. This tries to incorporate the desired but (judged to be) lacking qualities of the nonself. This compensatory persona then becomes the new primary persona until such time as some aspect of it too is judged lacking and subsequently rejected. This process of rejection, and revision is the selective evolution of the personality.

As long as a judgmental, comparative dynamic continues in play, the evolution of personality will continue. However, it is within the human potential to stop this dynamic of judgment, rejection and compensation, and instead move toward a synthesis of positive traits around the real or core Self. We will talk more about this.

TEMPERAMENT AND PERSONALITY

Self-concept and personality

What is the relationship between self-concept and character, how a person really is? We all know people whose self-concept is not in accord with their actions, who, for instance, think of themselves as pious while we observe them to be sanctimonious. Does this mean that self-concept has little or no bearing on the reality of character, that it is just a gloss on the hard reality of what we are? This is a difficult question. In the above example I would explain the discrepancy by the differing effects of multiple self-concepts, one viewing itself as pious, and another viewing itself as oppressed and deprived. However, in other examples I can think of, particularly those involving children, the picture is considerably murkier.

Certainly, research has indicated that people differ in temperament from infancy, and even animals of the same litter seem to have temperamental differences. This seems to indicate that there is a certain reality to character prior to self-concept formation. On the other hand, self-concepts form early on, how early it is difficult to say, but we are probably talking about infancy. There is nothing in character that cannot, with ingenuity, be explained by the guiding factors of multiple personas. However, to deny the role of constant influences like temperament and physical prowess seems reductionistic. Undoubtedly it is another issue like the nature-nurture controversy, and the answer is that both inheritance and self-concept are active in the formation of personality.

Who are we?

The account I have given of personality development as a series of compensatory revisions can be seen as progressive alienation from one's original nature, whatever that is. As such, it brings with it some disturbing questions. What then is the real self, the real me, the real personality beneath all these things. Indeed, is there such a thing? When we experience our self, what do we experience? When we know someone else, whom do we know? Is there even such a thing as a personality in the way we commonly think about it, as a unified, formed expression of an individual, or is it an illusion or construction born of wishful thinking and supported by perceptual illusion? What about character, nature, temperament? Is there anything real and solid behind this progression of fragmentation, denial, and compensation that develops our personality?

What is man? Who are we? Who are the family and friends who populate our intimate world and make us feel secure and real? The answer to these questions is complex. It is also deeply disturbing, in the sense that it disturbs our worldview. Perhaps it is as disturbing as the ideas of relativity, evolution, the dissolution of solid matter into particles and energy fields, and the realization that the earth is not the center of the universe. But like those great revolutions in understanding, it too confers power and wisdom.

My answer has three parts. The first two support our fears that the people we relate to and rely upon, indeed, our very ideas of what a person is, are essentially illusions, projections, anthropomorphizations. The third part looks at some redeeming factors that partially justify our ordinary views of one another.

Multiple personalities

In the first place we have to acknowledge the reality of multiplicity and change. People have multiple self-concepts or personas (multiple personalities if you will, but not in the pathological sense). No matter how internally consistent people appear to us or even to themselves, they are not. They exhibit markedly different personality constellations at different times. These shifts depend on which of their self-concepts they are perceiving from, and whether they are in the rejected or compensatory phase. Even the most uncritical observer has to admit that both they and the people around them go through distinct *moods* including periods "when they are not themselves," and also that the very traits that are most characteristic of them...honesty, forthrightness, cheerfulness, whatever...cannot always be relied upon.

Second, people change over time...sometimes markedly. The idealistic firebrand whose campaign you worked on ten years ago became another political hack. The girl that lived only for you when you married her has developed into a busy professional woman that hardly has time to fit you into her schedule. That nerd that sat across from you in high school has become president of the American Dental Association. Change, like the movement of the hour hand of a clock, is usually imperceptible as it happens, but striking when you look back and see how late it's gotten.

At the same time, there is a consistency in most people. In fact, this consistency is a prime indicator of mental stability. Even when people go in and out of different moods, different personas, it usually is clear that it is *they* that are doing it. They are seldom unrecognizable and when they are it shakes us up.

Perception and the illusion of an integrated personality

So what we have is a little bit of a paradox. On the one hand, we see a picture of people as composite beings, fragmented and changing. On the other hand, we experience people as constant, enduring, and indelibly themselves. We even experience them as containing some distinct essence of their own. It will help us make sense out of this paradox, if we acknowledge the function of our perceptual process in constructing this illusion of an integrated other. People's personalities, their manifest selves, are only known through our perceptions of them. In this respect, even the people we know are perceptual metaphors for underlying Selves that are in reality, unknowable!

One of the primary modalities of sensory illusion is continuance or connectedness of discontinuous phenomena. This is the way we connect visual samples to make a continuous visual field. Indeed, if the eye is prevented from scanning, vision quickly gives way to blindness and panic ensues. It is this propensity of perception for synthesis that visual media takes advantage of, as successive stills on a motion picture screen are connected into motion, and pixels or dots in three primary colors are connected into an unbroken image in the full range of hues. So the disparate parts of ourselves, our personas, are connected into the illusion of a whole by the synthesizing power of perception, be it self-perception or perception by others.

The quality of our perceptual illusions is immediately comprehensible. Perception is the ultimate, user-friendly interface. We instinctively know what almost every perception is, how it relates to us, and frequently how to respond to it. Nowhere does this friendly familiarity, this comprehensible illusoriness, count for more than in the illusion of person-ality. In fact, the perception of personality is the primary anthropomorphism (in the sense that we derive a conception of humanness from our experience of self as a monolith and then project that conception onto others).

Human perception is the anthropomorphic level of the organization of reality!

Unifying factors

The synthesizing and anthropomorphizing qualities of perception are crucial in establishing the impression of a unified personality, but they are assisted by four unifying variables. The first of these is that most people have a "core personality." This "core personality" is more or less shared by all of a person's personas. It contributes memories, language, common skills like reading, and primary drives and emotions to each and every persona.

The second unifying variable it that all personas share the same body.

The third unifying variable is that in most "normal" people, one, or at most a few personalities predominate. These predominant personalities are commonly perceived as the person's "normal self," while personalities that are less frequently "out" are perceived as moods, or aberrant states to be "gotten out of," or sometimes, depending on what they are, to be "gotten into." A little investigation, however, will reveal that these "moods" are the expression of alternate personas.

A fourth unifying variable is creative style. Every change the personality goes through, every compensatory self-concept, is an expression of the individual's creative style. This "creative style" is a sort of metafactor or common denominator in personality. It is a process variable. It influences how individuals will go about meeting their personality challenges. It is a combination of givens (from intelligence and inherited temperament to body type) and experiential factors. It is formed in early childhood and is largely set, though far from immutable, in early childhood. It is also a strategic constant that largely determines how a person will meet psychological challenges. For instance, one person may meet challenges by attempting to see the truth in every issue, while another may look for a way of denying it.

Creative style is a relatively stable factor which runs through all of a person's various personalities and creates consistency and even constancy. It helps us recognize the people we know as the people we know.

Despite the above unifying variables as well as others I have not mentioned, we are forced to conclude that there is no unitary personality, no one person, just a perceptually integrated complex of personas. However, this conclusion brings us back to a host of very emotional questions and objections. Why are some people charming, lovable, or dynamic while others are depressing, irritating, or just plain unlikable? Why are some people introverts and some extroverts. Above all, why do we love and believe in someone and not someone else. And more to the point…how can we?

There are two other contributions to the apparent unified personality: level of organization and consistency. While each persona is a separate gestalt, there is a level of organization where the entire personality comes together in one inclusive gestalt. The problem is that this is experienced sequentially; it is spread out over time, so that the perceiver experiences one facet, one persona at a time. This sequentiality is balanced by consistency, a consistent meeting of persona and situation. This consistency in turn lends a measure of predictability to people's responses. And this consistency and predictability go a long way to making the people we know who they are.

Self-realization

The last and far away the most important unifying factor in people is the Self and the possibility of Self-realization. The Self is that original nature that is the archetype of humanness. Anterior to the development of self-concept, ego, and personas, the Self is the bedrock of the person. All the archetypal functions that people recognize as humanity at its most human—love, compassion, parenting, mercy, justice, brotherhood, striving for excellence, artistic creation, etc.—are functions of the Self. What we see, recognize, respond to and love in people is not so much their "personalities," but their Self. That which they sometimes are in spite of themselves. We love people whose personalities are so transparent that the light of the Self shines through. Truly great humans, real saints, are those who are so integrated that they are one with their Self and act from it.

We will discuss the Self more in the next chapter on Self-realization.

12. SELF-REALIZATION

All knowing returns to the unknown knower and we are that!

THE ANTHROPOMORPHIZED SELF

That "Self" that we are in Oneness is utterly, unspeakably different from the "self" or "I" that we perceive ourselves to be. Since ordinarily we perceive ourselves as self and other, with the same dualism that is in all our perceptions, our self-perception is as illusory as all our other perceptions. The implication of this is that Man doesn't merely anthropomorphize reality; he anthropomorphizes himself. (By anthropomorphize I mean to perceive, interpret, and understand in human perceptual analogs, in terms of our projected experience.)

This raises the question again of what we are! What are we on a reality level? What is our real, nondifferentiated, aperceptual Self? Again it is impossible to know* since, as in all things, to perceive is

---

*In this chapter I am using the word "knowing" in the perceptual sense, that is, knowing the qualities and dimensions of something. I have introduced another sense of the word knowing which is aperceptual knowing, the sentience of pure consciousness; however, this knowing yields no qualities, dimensions or laws. Again, I propose to use the convention established earlier for referring to the self: the capital letter is used for the Self in reality, and the small letter for the personal self in perceptual illusion.

to change, appearance is never reality, and knowing is just a perceptual metaphor. The self that we perceive ourselves to be is a product of the same perceptual process we have been talking about all along. Perception of self is just as illusory as every other perception and in precisely the same way.

Since the perception of self is illusory, does this mean that self itself is illusory? We have seen that every thing is merely a perceptual category reified. Is the personal self merely another perceptual category? I don't see how, logically, this could be other than the case. However, if, as I firmly believe, the self is no more than self-perception, self-concept reified and anthropomorphized, we have to see that it is the granddaddy of all perceptual illusions and as such plays a seminal role in the formation of an enormous class of derivative illusions.

There are, however, some things we can say about the nature of the real Self. For one thing, it is devoid of anthropomorphisms. Those familiar "human" qualities that warm our hearts when we think about ourselves and others, when we think about humanity, don't exist on the level of the real Self. They are artifacts of self-referential self-perception and don't exist in aperceptual reality any more than, say, color does. In a perceptual reality, Madonna is no more sexy than an iguana in estrus.

For another thing, we don't exist exclusively, or even principally on that "personal" level of discourse that we experience ourselves on, the level that is defined, albeit tenuously and unevenly, by our social experience. We exist on a multitude of other levels as well: homeostatic, chemical, cellular, electric, atomic, energetic, genetic, etc., and even these levels are cognitive perceptions. We anthropomorphically perceive these levels in ourselves as tired, thirsty, hungry, cold, sick, or well, etc. (As a corollary to this, although we experience our personal self as unified, it is made up out of innumerable separate consciousnesses.)

In addition to our personal self we have experiences of a higher or spiritual Self. These come when, in altered states, we balance on the outer edge of self-reference and have an experience of ourselves as one with the cosmos, oceanic consciousness, omniscience, a continuum of energy. What do these experiences say about who we are? The question "who am I" has to account for those experiences as well.

There is a very strong temptation to think, perhaps to wish, that we can "know" aperceptual reality through meditation and other altered states, but the logic of aperceptual field theory predicts a paradox, the sort of paradox that we have grown familiar with through modern physics. In fact, it is almost a rephrasing of the uncertainty principle. It is the following: *The closer you come to knowing aperceptual reality, Oneness, the less you can know yourself. Although you can approach knowledge of aperceptual reality, at the very point you achieve that knowing, the you who is doing the knowing will disappear.* This is because you can only know reality by becoming part of it, and this entails giving up being apart from it which is, of course, giving up the illusion of your personal separated self.

This limitation on knowing aperceptual reality and the ensuing paradox also applies to the problem of knowing your real Self, because the real Self is in aperceptual reality, is an aspect of Oneness. The corollary paradox then would be: The closer you come to knowing your real Self, the less you can experience a self apart. (Knowing not in the sense of knowing perceptual qualities.)

Perhaps the best way to know reality (in the sense of understanding) is through abstract thought, logic, mathematical models, etc. Because perception is the stuff of illusion and anthropomorphism, the further we get away from models derived from sensory and perceptual experience to the abstract realms of logic and mathematical modeling, the more accurate we have a chance to be. The scientific geniuses of the modern age will be those individuals who are able to construct extraperceptual universes and move within them easily, to comprehend abstract models that have no analogs in experience whatsoever. "Knowing" in this way is a chilly prospect at best, unlikely to satisfy those who have a longing to know the qualities of themselves, reality, or God! However, trying it the other way leads to the anthropomorphic feelgoodism of popular mysticism.

Real knowing of the Self is a simple resting in the void. What is the void devoid of…simply of the products of perceptions, of qualities.

(What does this say for the science of psychology? Psychology's modes of operation are an indiscriminate grab bag. They include correlating anthropomorphisms (illusions) with one another, explaining anthropomorphisms in terms of other anthropomorphisms, and deriving anthropomorphisms from models that themselves occupy a continuum of anthropomorphism from completely experiential to mathematical. Psychology has yet to find a terra firma from which to operate. However, this can be turned to advantage, because unlike the physical and biological sciences, which are convinced they are based in physical reality, at least some branches of psychology have always known that they are dealing with perception and experience.)

ORDINARY PERCEPTION IS FROM OUR SELF-CONCEPT, NOT OUR SELF

Recall the propositions that duality is Oneness perceived and that the first duality derives from the actions of Oneness individuating and perceiving itself. These propositions would lead one to conclude that the nature of the perceived self would be always determined by the individuated Self perceiving itSelf. However, it is not so simple. Self-concept is an intervening variable, and from its onset is an ubiquitous one. (This ubiquity of self-concept as an intervening variable in perception is why we need psychologists and gurus.)

A unique situation is created and compounded by the fact that we do not continue to perceive the individuated Self from the point of view of itSelf but instead come to perceive it from the self-concept. (The perceived Self is a self-concept.) Of course, we also experience the world or nonself from this same viewpoint.

The process is something like this. First our real Self, an individuated locus in Oneness, perceives itSelf (as other than the rest of Oneness) creating a self-concept or illusory self. Then, when we next perceive our Self, we do it not from our individuated Self but from that illusory self. Thus our original subject-object perception becomes more and more an object-object perception. In short, we start perceiving both our real and our perceived selves or self-concepts from the viewpoint of other perceived selves.

This continual folding back of perception on itself develops a self-image that grows more derivative, layered, and convoluted with each cycle. As our self-image develops, the relatively real self-referent points (location, temperature, capacity, undifferentiated consciousness, etc.) become augmented and sometimes confounded by delusory, arbitrary, even imaginary self-reference points (worthlessness, talent, greatness, bad luck, unlovability, virtue, invulnerability, etc.). Soon we are operating in a world furnished not only by the unavoidable illusions of perceptual duality, but also by the reified ghosts of projection and comparison. The alternation of reality and self-image create a meta-evolutionary feedback loop that is ultimately responsible for the creation of personality, culture, and civilization itself, with all its accomplishments, absurdities, evils, and wonders. In the final analysis, self-concept or self-image plays a larger role in directing man's development and evolution than either the real Self or primary illusion.

THE UNKNOWN KNOWER

The logic of aperceptual field theory, my own meditative experiences, and the reports of master meditators all agree that we have two parallel selves. One is the aperceptual, unknowable Self which is attached to a perceiving gestalt in Oneness. This aperceptual Self, as it exists on an individual level, is also called the real Self, the core Self, or just the Self, as the context dictates. But the name I have given it that I like best is the unknown knower. The other is the perceived, known, illusory self which is a self-concept, a perception. This is the self of our experience, the self we know as our self. Furthermore, we can divide this experienced or perceived self into two subselves, the higher self and the personal self.

(The distinction between Self and self is very clear. If it is a perception, it is self. Every self that we know is self. On the other hand, all knowing is ultimately a function of Self that is unknown, that is we know the knowing but we don't know the Self that is knowing.)

The original perception of core self

A Self is differentiated consciousness, the consciousness of a differentiated gestalt, a living gestalt in Oneness. All real Selves have consciousness; however, this is not to imply that they are aware, that they know that they know. It is only to state that they behave and behave lawfully and intelligently in relationship to their environment. This intelligence or consciousness when it is not aware of itself, not known by itself, I refer to as sentience. The unknown knower is sentience.

Selves have the tendency, coming out of their ability to know, to know themselves. It is almost inevitable, given something that has the power of knowing, that it should know itself in some way. However, whenever something apart knows anything, it is a perception, with all that implies.

(I have stated previously that an eye can't see an eye, and an "I" can't see an "I." This implies the impossibility of Self-perception. However, when a Self perceives itself, it is really perceiving other and implying the existence of itSelf. Just as you can't have (the perceptual category of) hot without cold, you can't have a self without an other and vice versa. The perception of other necessarily implies—in a real sense is identical to—the perception of self. When a Self perceives self-OTHER, it creates something, a perceptual category, an idea, a reciprocal image of itself. I call this the implicit self. This self-concept then overlays the Self and the Self perceives through it. (However, for all intents and purposes, it is as if the idea, the self-concept replaces the Self as the locus of perception.)

When (the consciousness of) an individualized, real Self perceives the rest of Oneness as other or world and implies itSelf as self, that is Original Perception. This original perception yields the primal duality of self-other, which is the first self-concept. It is subject made into object, subject objectified.

The Self perceiving is the most direct level of perception and knowledge possible. It is looking without anyone (any self-concept) doing the looking. It is the end of the line, where the buck stops passing. It is perception free of the distortion of a self-concept. It is Self without self-awareness. It is Original Perception. It is also the deepest level of perception.

However, for all of that, what it perceives is illusory, is still perception. That which the Self perceives is the first level of illusion.

Although original perception is still illusory, it is not delusion, it is not self-deception. Illusion, qualification, duality is an inescapable artifact of perception, of observing Oneness from a single vantage point. This vantage point is real, it is a site of differentiated consciousness in Oneness. The act of perception dualizes, creates illusion. On the other hand, once a self-concept or self-image is formed, it functions as if it is the locus of perception. Because the self-concept is not real (i.e., it is a perception and therefore illusory), it distorts. Perception from an illusory self creates delusion, self-deception.

Perception from illusion = *Delusion*

In original perception the organism perceiving the world creates illusions like materiality, time, and space as well as qualities like color. At the same time it also perceives itself. (World or other contains within it its negative, which is the implication of self.) This creates self-concept or self-image which, because it is a perception, is illusory. The self-concept then becomes the locus of perception which, because it is illusory, creates distortion or delusion. For instance, the self-concept may be of itself as weak or strong. Either illusion distorts subsequent perception, misleads action, and may get the perceiving organism into trouble. A concept of oneself as weak may lead an organism to yield unnecessarily and then fail to get its rightful share. The opposite illusion may lead an organism to reckless challenge and consequent destruction.

ARCHETYPES?

What are archetypes? They are various images, symbols, legends, myths, ideal embodiments of universal roles. In content they are metaphors for the expression of real Self, not only of the individual, but also all humanity and its culture. The more primary archetypes, those that come first to one, convey the pure form of some aspect of humanness, some role like mother or warrior. However, advanced archetypes go beyond communicating humanness to communicating enlightenment. They become expressions of undifferentiated consciousness. As the ego or personal self lets itself be educated by the higher Self, it becomes better able to understand reality and the archetypes become more unitary and powerful. As the growth curve of the ego approaches reality, the archetypes approach the expression of Oneness.

Since archetypes are experienced, they too are perceptual metaphors, albeit of a special kind. They are saying that an aspect of primal human reality is like this dream or symbol, like that legend or myth. (For instance, the ideal of motherhood is like the Madonna-child relationship.) The metaphors of primary process (including archetypes) are formed by a quasi-perceptual process. They are qualities or illusions formed by the act of perceiving the human condition, just as colors are illusions formed by the act of perceiving wavelengths.

ARCHETYPES AND SELF REALIZATION

Primary process is the communication of the real Self with the ego.

Any investigation into what we are (on the aperceptual level) has to deal with what Freud called primary process (i.e., dreams and other unconscious constructions and communications) and with archetypes.

Archetypes and primary process provide glimpses into the real Self. There are two problems with experiencing our real Self. First, since the Self is Oneness rather than a percept, it is not in qualitative or perceptual form. Second, since it is interior there is no sensorium to qualify it, nor point in space from which it can be dualized. It can be known, but this knowing is different from perceptual knowing. It doesn't have any tangible qualities that can be appreciated. The way we get around this is by translating that which is known into quasi-perceptual qualities, qualities that are qualitative but have an unreal quality about them. This process is what I call dreaming. In dream sleep, the contents of the Self are experienced as an imaginary scenario complete with sound, form, movement, and color, character and plot. The same quasi-perceptual faculty is at work in our awake experiencing of the Self. Somehow, qualitative metaphors for the nonqualitative contents of the Oneness are furnished, so that the Self can be experienced in some tangible fashion.

A further problem with experiencing Self is that its consciousness is occluded by self-concepts or personas. These personas are strongly motivated by self-denial and compensation, which keeps them vying for control. (This is why psychological work is invaluable when following a spiritual path. The more the person gives up self-denial, the less need he has to compensate, and the more easily his ego can give up control to his Self.)

While the personal self is accruing more and more levels of distortion, the real Self continues to know things as they are. Its only problem is communicating back to the personal self, which becomes more and more immersed in its own, self-created reality and less apt to listen. The Self's ingenious solution to this problem is to intrude its communications when ego defenses are low, through sleep and other altered states of consciousness. These, then, are received in the form of dreams and other primary process.

Primary process contents, including archetypes, consist of the consciousness of the real Self intruding into personal consciousness in sleep and other altered states.

The communications of Self to self are the most mysterious and magical gifts to which humanity is heir. To those who choose to follow them intentionally, they represent sign posts to what Jung called individuation…a journey in which the archetypes point the way and the ego, gropingly, follows.

VARIETIES OF SPIRITUAL EXPERIENCE

There are many varieties of spiritual experience. One is original perception, self and world perceived directly from the consciousness of the Core Self though a psyche stripped of the distortions of self-concepts, attachments, emotions, and entrained memories. This is the primary second-realm phenomenon, perceptual and illusory but undistorted. Original perception is powerful, direct, objective, unadorned and devoid of symbolism and imagery. Its aesthetic is the uncluttered, spare, spontaneous, spacious, quintessential. Zen art always directs consciousness to inner space, quiet, and voidness. A garden of random rocks reverberating in framed space, the reverberation suggested by lines in the sand; A *sumi-e* painting of spare strokes reverberating form on rice paper; single notes of the flute reverberating in the silence. It is akin to the "empty mind" perception of Zen and brings to mind that well-known Zen teaching story where a disciple asks a master…

Tell me, what is Zen?
Have you finished your rice?
Yes.
Then wash out your bowl.

Another variety of spiritual experience is experiencing the higher Self, the world of primary process…dreams, archetypes, symbols, images, feelings, visions, voices, and visitations. A third variety is externalization, projecting the contents of the higher Self outward and then worshiping them. A fourth variety of spiritual experience is resting in the void, resting in One's real nature or Buddha mind.

Some people would take exception to my distinctions, holding that whether you look inward, look outward, or externalize makes no difference. It is all spiritual and all points in the same direction. On one level it is a matter of semantics; however, my distinction is very useful, and clarifies the difference between various traditions and various spiritual predilections. For instance, the Hindu tradition, looking to the higher Self, fills, virtually overwhelms inner space with its various gods, images, chants, and devotional emotions, all artifacts of primary process. The Christian tradition does much the same thing, although it goes about it differently, externalizing and projecting a God in heaven. The Zen tradition, looking outward from an empty mind, allows just enough seed in the void to highlight the absence of anything real. Other forms of Buddhism, most notably the Tibetan, combine or confound the Hindu and Zen traditions. Religious feelings, as most Westerners would identify them, feelings of faith, devotion, and appreciation of miracles as well as all forms of God-consciousness where God is a person, symbol, or thing, come from looking toward the higher Self, i.e., receiving messages from the higher Self.

The quality of the spiritual perception, whether looking inwards or outward, depends on the purity of the self doing the perceiving. If the core Self is doing the perceiving, the vision is clear and transparent as to its meaning, and wisdom results. If, however, the personal self is doing the perceiving, self-deception and ego distortion creep into the process. The distortion can be as mild as spiritual pride or as severe as religious fanaticism. The extent and kind of distortion that creeps in depends on which self is doing the perceiving. Some people are much freer from ego and social distortions than others, and it is the process of getting free of distortions that makes up the preponderance of what is called spiritual work.

GEO -CONSCIOUSNESS

Definitions:

> Geo: whole, opposite of ego, egoless.
> Geo-perception: the perception that one is not solely the center of a small self; rather taking the perspective of the universe in which one is contained, the perspective of Oneness.
> Geo-consciousness: the consciousness attained through Geo Perception; the awareness of Oneself as transcending self/ other, body/mind, organism/environment, etc.

Throughout the history of life, the perception that one is not the center of the universe, individually, collectively, or globally, has been counterproductive to the survival of the individual. In the history of social animals, particularly humans, it has been potentially detrimental to the survival of the particular social group, tribe, or society. This is one underlying reason why geo-consciousness or true spirituality has been seen as a threat, persecuted, and if possible eradicated by the ruling classes wherever it has arisen and begun to spread. (This throws an evolutionary light on religious persecution.)

Geo-consciousness arises by Original Perception, from perception of the personal self from the core Self. Geo-consciousness is a self-limiting mechanism. It controls individual and group aggressiveness and expansionism, potentially limits population growth, and regulates the impact of civilization on the earth.

This century has seen an explosion of technology. The rise of the West has simultaneously encompassed and co-opted the East as well as tribal and subsistence cultures everywhere. Humanity as a whole now threatens to overwhelm the global ecology. Geo-consciousness, once counterindicated for individual and group survival, has now become mandatory. Limiting rather than expanding has become essential as a survival strategy, not only to us as individuals and nations but for the entire human race. It is not coincidental that as global ecology has approached crisis, geo-consciousness and the techniques for attaining it have risen in popularity. In affluent societies, ecological and environmental perspectives have moved out of the university into the mass culture. Although only a minority of people and governments have come to realize it, conservation and protection of the earth has now become the primary and overriding concern of mankind and will stay so as long as we have an earth to protect. As the media is continually bombarding us with messages that our survival is threatened by atmospheric pollution, global warming, the ozone hole, radioactive waste, and the poisoning of the water, ego and geo-consciousnesses, personal and universal self-interest are converging, albeit slowly and erratically. Our sense of boundaries is fast expanding from our skin to our planet. Sometimes it eclipses narrow self-interests and regional, national, religious, and racial identities in the process. More often, it uncomfortably coexists with them.

INVISIBLE KNOWING

All appearance is constructed by perception and its extension, cognition. That which lies beneath appearance can be known only by inference, but once inferred, it needs to be grasped by an image, a symbol, a name, or a concept. These are all cognitive perceptual metaphors, things. Even a field, that *ultimate grasping at fundamentals* of modern physics, is a thing. Grasping perceptually, *perceptualization*, despite its manifold benefits, inescapably plunges us into the world of things, with its inescapable accompaniments of separateness, boundary, duality, and illusion.

The need for perceptualization delineates the limits of human knowing. Even psychic processes (should you be inclined to recognize their existence) have to be grasped to be communicated, even if only communicating them to oneself. And grasping knowing, knowing what we know, always gets us into the realm of perception. Granted, we know on some real level without the necessity of grasping what we know. Let us call this *invisible or aperceptual knowing*. Invisible knowing is the way, for instance, that our bodies function.

In fact, invisible knowing effortlessly accounts for most of human function. Some forms of Eastern thought, particularly Zen and Taoism, idealize it and seem to advocate its extension to the regulation of one's entire life. With their growing familiarity with this line of thought, a growing minority in the Western world is coming to share this bias, often confusing invisible knowing with enlightenment.

This confusion, the mistake of interpreting unexamined emotions and prejudices as invisible knowing (following gut feelings), and the anti-intellectualism that may follow these errors, make invisible knowing just as problematic as an over-reliance on perceptual appearances.

Furthermore, aperceptual knowing shares a fundamental problem with perceptual knowing. The problem is the error of separateness and self-centeredness. The act of perception separates the perceiver from the perceived, and places the perceiver at the center of knowing. Invisible knowing, too, is an understanding relative to oneself, a separate center `of knowing.

Indeed, all living organisms are built on the illusion of self-centeredness and are, in fact, embodiments of self-centeredness. The evolution of the organism is, in one sense, a materialization of a process of learning, genetic learning if you will. Furthermore, this learning has self-centeredness as its starting point, and that error has become the paradigm for all the subsequent learning that constitutes the evolution of life. (It is only an error from an "objective" viewpoint. From the viewpoint of the learning organism it is correct. As a matter of fact, self-centeredness is the viewpoint of the organism.)

Both aperceptual and perceptual knowing share this erroneous base in self-centered separateness and therefore share subsequent errors, although perceptual knowing expresses these errors differently. Unfortunately, invisible knowing is, in its own way, just as misleading as perception and cognition. Idealizing it and following it unconditionally can get you into just as much trouble.

The solution, the paradigm of real enlightenment, is not sacrificing perception and higher cognition for invisible knowing, anymore than it is a continuation of the uncritical Western embrace of the rational mind. Rather it is a perspective that includes and transcends both levels, that uses intellect to recognize and encompass intuition but follows neither blindly. Enlightenment is not the abandonment or even destruction of the thinking mind so that one is ruled by intuition. It is the transcendence of both by holding both in a vision that realizes their fundamental error and the subsequent limitations that follow from this error, then corrects them and goes beyond.

CONSCIOUSNESS

13. THE WAY THE UNIVERSE KNOWS ITSELF

Consciousness is the substance of reality.
Consciousness is the substance of illusion.
Consciousness is the unified biofield!

ISNESS PERCEIVED

We suspect consciousness does not exist in Oneness
just because we experience it dualistically.
Conscious / unconscious.
Oneness does have Isness,
that is, whatever it is, it is.
About that, at least, there can be no argument.
Perhaps consciousness is Isness perceived
Which would mean that
consciousness is the illusion of Isness.

What an illusion!

CONSCIOUSNESS

There is a wide degree of opinion about consciousness, from scientists who claim there is no evidence for it on the one hand, to mystics, philosophers, and a handful of scientists who claim that it is the fundamental stuff of the universe. I occupy a position somewhere between the two. I believe there is an active aspect to Oneness, call it being, which is the raw ingredient for that consciousness that integrates, animates, and sometimes makes aware all forms of life. This force of being is also responsible for interrelating and organizing nonliving gestalts. Therefore, in some sense I would agree with those who maintain that consciousness is the fundamental stuff of the universe, with the caveat that it is not consciousness as we experience it, or as it animates life. Rather, it is some force of being, which in the mysterious alchemy that creates life is transformed into what we experience as our consciousness. However, having recognized this underlying unity, it seems to me confusing to use the same word, consciousness, to point to what puts together an atom, a molecule, a crystal, algae, a tree, a mammal, a perception, a thought, and an intention. Later in this chapter I will propose a terminology that will diffuse the spectrum of consciousness into different hues, but for now I will reserve my use of the word for that which lives.

CONSCIOUSNESS AND ITS EXPERIENCE

Mystics, some philosophers, and even some scientists claim consciousness is the basic stuff of the universe, shared equally by people, cake, cars, and photons.

On the other hand, we all have the experiences of consciousness, and these experiences point in another direction. Sometimes we are conscious and sometimes unconscious. Sometimes when we are unconscious, we are conscious on another level, as in dreams or even anesthesia. Sometimes consciousness seems fuller or more intense than at other times, for instance, when we are scared. Other times consciousness may change focus; for instance, while eating something delicious we may forget about something that is troubling us. Furthermore, consciousness seems to constantly change location and boundaries. First, we are conscious of one thing and unconscious of another, and then it might reverse. These shifting, experiential guises of consciousness seem to contradict its universality. As a matter of fact, insofar as consciousness is an experience and a dualistic phenomenon, conscious/unconscious, it appears unlikely to be a universal aspect of Oneness and likely to be a perceptual one, which, of course, makes it illusory.

However, embracing the latter formulation is as uncomfortable for me as embracing the former! On the perceptual level, consciousness and unconsciousness are reciprocal illusions. We can't conceive of one without its opposite! On a deeper level, however, consciousness seems to be a fundamental, a constant. When we are conscious, what we are conscious of is an entire spectrum of things, perception, thought, feeling, memory, even the memory of unconsciousness. However, if we enter a deep meditative state in which none of these contents are present, consciousness is still there. In fact, we ask, how can we even know illusion, if the capacity for knowing is not a fundamental aspect of Oneness? And what could this capacity for knowing be, if not consciousness?

After meditating on the problem, I came up with the following model, which resolves at least some of the difficulties. It is a little tricky, so bear with me. The verb form of the noun Oneness is Being. Consciousness is an active aspect of Oneness, an aspect of Being! It is integral or equivalent to Being. This, of course, means that it is universal. In discussing Oneness, we are referring to the realm of Oneness, not duality. So there is not a perceiver and a perceived, a subject and an object, a knower and a known, there is just consciousness everywhere. Where there is not a knower and a known, there cannot be any experience of, and there cannot be any experiencer of...consciousness. Of course, without an experiencer, there can be no experience, as we normally think of experience.

No more water in the bucket
No more moon in the water!

So we are left with two forms of consciousness, dual or experienced consciousness and universal or inexperienced consciousness. This seems to be a contradiction in terms, but it needn't be, depending on how you look at it. Consciousness is commonly equated with our individual experience of it, but if you separate the consciousness and the experience of it, you arrive at a model where consciousness is an inexperienceable that enables you to experience.

The way the universe knows itself

But what is the medium that this experience of consciousness exists in, you quite rightly ask. Isn't it consciousness as well? Well, yes, but upon examination this, too, is not as contradictory as it seems at first. The problem of studying consciousness was elegantly summarized by the futurist Peter Russell as to trying to use a flashlight to try to find the source of its own light. That is…truly…the limitation, but what if you use two flashlights? Then you can shine the light of one on the other. After all, it's the same light, the same consciousness, no matter where you find it or from which source it is emanating.

Oneness is one flashlight, unexperienced consciousness. But when Oneness individuates, to the extent that the individuated parts perceive themselves as apart, the parts act as separate flashlights and they can shine their light on one another. This is the way consciousness experiences consciousness! This is the way the Universe knows itself!

Isn't this what nature does? Isn't this the universal solution of all creation, the two-flashlight solution, polarity, division, perception, duality? Before the flashlight divides, there is just consciousness without experiencer or experience, unexperienced consciousness. After the flashlight divides, you have experienced consciousness, knowing that you know. You have an experiencer and therefore you can have an experience. The moon is back in the water.

Consciousness as a metasense

The definition of consciousness as "an inexperienceable that enables you to experience" sounds very much like the description of a sense. All the senses—sight, hearing, touch, taste, and smell—fit the description of being impossible to experience in themselves, while enabling you to experience something. That is, you can see something, but you can't see sight. Yet paradoxically, all visual experience shares the quality of sight. This leads to two closely allied conclusions. One, consciousness is the raw material that is specialized into all of the senses, or the common denominator of the senses. Two, consciousness is a sense in itself.

The first conclusion is almost too self-evident to comment on. It seems clear that consciousness, the sentience of being, is a precursor that became specialized into the many, distinctive sensory modalities found throughout life.

On the other hand, what about the proposition that consciousness, naked consciousness, without a sense organ, is a sense in itself? Again, it's all in the way you look at it. On the one hand, it seems probable that when Being is organically embodied on the physical plane, consciousness functions primarily as a specialization of the irritability of cellular boundary membranes. On the other hand, there is evidence to suggest that every being apart can know itself without benefit of senses. Furthermore, gifted persons have the ability to know in an extrasensory sense that can only be explained by their ability to use pure consciousness as a sense, either by projecting or expanding their consciousness into another, or merging their consciousness with another. (I'm not sure that there is any real difference between these formulations.)

BY THE NAMES WE GET TO THE NATURE OF THE THING

Nowhere does inexact terminology and the failure to discriminate between the aperceptual and perceptual realms create more confusion than in thinking about consciousness. There are, of course, several meanings for most words, but when speaking precisely, one has to select one meaning for each term. To help keep the discussion conceptually straight, and so the reader doesn't invariably link experience with the word consciousness, I am going to use different words for the different guises of consciousness.

There are two basic distinctions to be made in consciousness, life/ nonlife and experienced/unexperienced. For now at least, I am not going to wrestle with the problem of whether there is consciousness without life, but will confine my discussion to the living. Within this realm I elect to call unexperienced, aperceptual consciousness "sentience," or "knowing," "sentience" being the passive or noun and "knowing" being the active or verb form. On the other hand, I will call experienced, perceptual consciousness, "awareness." The underlying phenomenon, whether or not it is experienced, is simply consciousness.

Definitionally, "sentience" and "knowing" do not imply a separate experiencer and an object of experience; therefore, they do not imply experience of. On the other hand, when there is individuation and two flashlights, then you have knower knowing, you have subject object, perceiver perceived, experiencer and experience. You have awareness!

Whatever terms we choose, *sentience, knowing, awareness,* or even *being,* we remember that we are dealing with the perceptual guises of Oneness. They are syntactical rather than real. They are illusory, representing the dualities of separateness and Oneness, passive and active, part and whole, living and dead. To discuss consciousness we must use dualistic language. However, to truly understand, we must see through language's necessary illusoriness.

KNOWING KNOWING

All we can say about awareness is that we have an experience of knowing. This is ourselves as knower, experiencing that we know. If all is reducible to sentience, we can abstract from this that we are pure sentience, sentient of pure sentience. Therefore, we say that awareness is the sentience of a part by another part. It is knowing knowing. In our experience the aware part is our self. In the experience of another, the aware part is their self. In the final analysis, the aware part is a living gestalt, a separate organization of identical consciousness perceiving and identifying with itself as self.

The apparent difficulty in accounting for awareness derives from the fact that everything is always happening simultaneously in two separate but parallel realms, perceptual and aperceptual. In order to make sense of things, we have to derive the perceptual or dual realm from the differentiation of the aperceptual, monadic realm of Oneness. That is, we have to derive the experiences of consciousness from Oneness, awareness from the sentience of being. In this way we come to the formulation that the experience of awareness in the perceptual realm is derived from the sentience of sentience or the knowing of knowing in the aperceptual realm, where subject and object are just identical consciousnesses, sentiences, or knowingnesses in a differentiated organization or embodiment.

Theoretically, you can have awareness, knowing of knowing, without perception. By that I mean, without the "known" being a perception. In this case an individuated self is knowing Oneness or knowing the sentience of another, but not as a perceptual process. This is what happens in pure meditation, but probably is also a state in which at least some animals and maybe even plants rest. When people meditate, they go through two stages, aware and merged. In the aware stage they are themselves observing sentience of another. In the merged state, they lose themselves to the whole and awareness ceases.

You can also have perception without awareness, in the sense that someone is perceiving and acting on its perception without knowing it, as in the case of a reflex. Perceptual processes are taking place, but there is no self separate from the process knowing the process.

Consciousness and nonlife

This again brings up the question of whether consciousness exists within the realm of nonlife. I see that all living gestalts, from single-celled plants to people, possess the quality of sentience or knowing, that is, they are sentient (know themselves) on whatever level of organization their self exists. (Note that I said living gestalts, units of life. I am not yet ready to extend the same quality of "knowing" or "sentience" to my old car, my mother's angel food cake, or a subatomic particle, and I suspect I never will be. However, I do recognize that nonliving gestalts are not dead, at least on the atomic level. They possess an organizational force or integrity of their own, probably a force even more fundamental than sentience. I just don't want to confound the inorganic and organic levels out of a sort of cosmic political correctness. I will discuss this subject further in the chapter on proto-evolution. Without at the moment further pursuing the question of whether nonlife is really conscious, let us just for now agree that in the inorganic realm, there seems to be either consciousness or some precursor to consciousness or some more fundamental presence of which consciousness is an aspect and further agree to call it something...say, "energetic relation."

If this is so, consciousness, whether awareness or sentience, whether experienced or not, is a universal.

CONSCIOUSNESS AND MATTER

There is an ongoing controversy taking place in the area of consciousness research. Let's call it the "mind/brain" or "consciousness/matter" controversy. Does the brain produce consciousness, or does it just present a home for it? Is matter or even life necessary for consciousness, or is consciousness a fundamental quality, which may inhabit, inform, and/or energize life or even matter, but doesn't need it to exist? The answer to this problem has wide implications for a theory of consciousness and perception.

When I was going to graduate school, psychologists were seriously exploring the nature/nurture problem. The problem, classically stated, was the following: is X phenomenon an expression of the nature of the organism, inborn and inevitably expressed with maturation, or is there some experiential or learning process shaping it? Experiments were devised to answer this question with regard to the visual perception of depth and shape. If, the experimenters reasoned, we could raise an animal without visual cues and then restore these cues in adulthood, we could determine whether shape perception was inborn or learned. So they made goggles out of halved Ping-Pong balls and raised cats wearing them. At adulthood they took the goggles off the cats and what do you think they found?

The cats were essentially blind!

The conclusion then to the nature/nurture controversy was ultimately that both are needed for normal development.

I think the ultimate answer to the mind/brain or consciousness/matter controversy is that, like nature and nurture, you need both. The reason you can't separate matter and consciousness is that at base there is no separation. The separation is only apparent, perceptual. All perceptions, including the perception or experience of consciousness, are illusions, viewpoints. The experience of consciousness is another perception of Oneness. All experience is rooted in perceptions of Oneness. Oneness is indivisible except in perception. Except in perception, there is no difference between matter and Consciousness, being and knowing.

PERCEPTION AS A SPECIAL CASE OF CONSCIOUSNESS

Perception is a special and complex case of consciousness. In terms of the structure or system of consciousness, it has three parts. (Physiologically, of course, it is much more complex.) The first of them is sensory activity. The senses are specialized boundary membranes and like all living gestalts, they are sentient. The second is the percept, the encoded sensory data residing in its neuronal network (however that happens). This network, of course, is also sentient. (Note that the percept is not perception. Perception is the organism's knowing of and response to the percept.) Finally, there are the parts of the nervous system responding to the percept. These also are sentient but part of their sentience is <u>of</u> the percept, i.e., knowing the percept. This is knowing knowing. However, this does not necessarily imply an aware self in the sense that you and I experience conscious perception. For that to take place the percept must be known by that special case of a self, an "I."

While consciousness is a universal, it appears to have a very different quality and behave according to different laws, depending on whether it is aperceptual or perceptual (that is, on whether its sentience is the sentience of undifferentiated Oneness or the sentience of a percept). Aperceptual consciousness behaves exactly as you would expect it to do *as an aspect of Oneness*. It is simultaneous, instantaneous, and devoid of qualities and dimensions (time, space, etc.). On the other hand, experienced, perceptual consciousness behaves exactly as you would expect a perception to do. It has tangible qualities and dimensions, and roughly follows the laws of Newtonian physics. It is tempting to attribute these differences to a variation in the nature of consciousness itself, but it makes much more sense to look to the contents of consciousness, and see that it is these contents that differ in nature and in the laws they follow. Perceptual consciousness has the nature of perception: dualistic, qualitative, relative, dimensional, and Newtonian. Aperceptual consciousness is entirely devoid of qualities, dimensions, or any tangible content whatsoever.

EXPERIENCING NOTHING

People are always experiencing
but they are usually not aware of it unless they are
experiencing something.
That experiencing of something is perception, dualistic and
sadly illusory.
Whereas that experiencing of no thing is the experience of
Oneness.
Therefore in order to get a glimmer of Oneness,
we have to be experiencing nothing
but with awareness!

Meditation

TRULY CONSCIOUS

We are conscious of Oneness only when we are
unconscious,
Or we are truly conscious only when we are unconscious.

The reality of consciousness is nothing like our experience.
It is not uniquely ours,
It is not uniquely human or even uniquely animal!
Every living thing, even plants and cells have it.

That consciousness is not unique is very interesting,
since it is our most cherished possession.
In fact, it is what makes us keep this stranglehold on our
individual lives.

CONSCIOUSNESS IS

When subject and object are the same
consciousness is…
When subject and object are not the same
consciousness is of…

14. CONSCIOUSNESS AND THE STRUCTURE OF SELVES

The brain is a development of the nervous system, which in turn is a development of the senses; this means that the brain evolved to handle perceptual information both externally and internally.

BEING IS KNOWING.
BEING SEPARATE IS PERCEIVING.

A SELF IS THAT WHICH KNOWS ITSELF AND PERCEIVES OTHER

Now we are going to go beyond gestalts and the nature of consciousness to further consider what a self is, how it is structured, and most of all, how a self knows and perceives.

Definition: A self is that which knows itself and perceives other.

This strikes me as an excellent definition, for what it says but even more for what it does not say. It makes no assertions about the quality or nature of self, except what it does. It is completely operational. The only thing we might add is this: a self is a unit of, or organization within, consciousness.

The domain of life consists of selves. In this domain every self is itself to itself, and *an*other to all others.

KNOWING AND PERCEIVING

When we speak of the whole, of course we are speaking about Oneness. On the other hand, when we speak of the part, we are speaking about a part of Oneness. If all is One, then, how can there be a part? Is not the part Oneness as well? This problem forms the background for the following discussion.

All selves are simultaneously wholes in themselves and parts of greater wholes. Consider ourselves. Our whole organism is a whole. Our individual organs and even our cells can also be considered wholes. At the same time they're all parts. We're parts of a species, and our organs and cells are parts of our bodies. When consciousness takes place within the (nominal) whole, that is "knowing." When the consciousness is communicated between (nominal) parts, separated by a boundary or space and mediated by some sensory excitation or neural transmission, that is "perception."

This is the distinction between knowing and perceiving. Knowing takes place within the whole or from the whole to itself. In this, it is an aspect of Oneness, of Being. It is sentience. Perceiving, which, of course, is only a special case of knowing, takes place from part to part. Although from the point of view of a knower and its experience they are completely different, from the point of view of real process this is the sole distinction. This principal is key to understanding the organization of consciousness and the relationship of consciousness to perception.

Because it takes place simultaneously within the whole, knowing does not entail any transmission from part to part. Therefore, it does not take any time, transmit over any space, nor undergo any transformation (dualization). On the other hand, in perception there is a necessary transmission of something from the part being perceived to the part perceiving. This separation makes knowing impossible and instead entails dualization from a fixed point engendering space, time and all other relational qualities or dimensions.

Reminder

All of these terms, "knowing," "perception," "sentience," precisely denote one or the other meanings of consciousness. I am using them because the word "consciousness," like "God" and "love," has taken on such expanded meanings and come to mean so many different things to different people that it is difficult to discuss with precision. To clarify this, I have nominated "sentience" and "knowing" to designate consciousness where there is no separate knower experiencing the first knowing, and "awareness" to refer to the experience of consciousness, knowing knowing. Perception is a special case of knowing, where what is known is a percept (encoded sensory data). Awareness yields a higher order of perception or knowing knowing, where the knower of the known is that construct known as an "I."

SELF KNOWING ITSELF

How does a boundaried, living gestalt know itself and know its boundaries? The answer is simple yet staggering in its implications. Every boundaried, living gestalt is a self. *Every self knows within its boundaries and perceives from its boundaries.* In this regard there are almost infinite selves, hierarchical trees of selves knowing themselves and perceiving others, fit into one another like Chinese boxes. The self associated with our experience of our self is just one of a multitude of selves constituting that being that is bounded by our physical body and energy field. Perhaps it is not even the self on top of the hierarchy.

One knows one's self and perceives other. This is the guiding principle, the distillation. However, since the boundaries between self and other are themselves a matter of self-definition (or self-perception) there are as many selves in an organism as there are possible gestalts of gestalts. In a complex organism this number is so great as to approach infinity, particularly if you get down to the cellular and subcellular levels. In this vast web of interrelated consciousnesses every living gestalt, every self, is possessed of self-knowing and other-perception.

Consequently, in complex life forms, self-knowledge is at once knowing and perception, within the whole and part to part. The part that knows is both a separate gestalt and part of a succession of larger and larger gestalts, eventuating in Oneness.

Can perception in the complex organism then be considered a special case of knowing? In other words, if knowing is always of reality and perception is always illusory, can perception be a process of knowing?

The answer is yes...when perception is taking place, the perceiving self is knowing the reality of itself. The percept is a real occurrence in its nervous system, even though that which has been perceived is illusory. That is why it can be said that a perceiver knows real illusion.

Perhaps because of this, people mostly experience their perceptions as part of their self, that is, they know their perceptions and through this aperceptual knowing "know" the world. However, there is a meditational practice sometimes referred to as disidentification, by which people systematically distance themselves from their bodies, senses, thoughts, and feelings, and try to identify solely with the pure consciousness of the observer. Through this process people know the knower as separate from the known. However, what do they know when they do this? A knower, turning away from its perceptions, can know itself but there will be no thing there. Or rather, what is there is something contentless and without referents, because the observer has turned away from all content and all reference. Instead, there is only a sense of presence, without form or content. There is sentience without anything to be sentient of but sentience itself, contentless awareness.

Ideally, one simultaneously should be self and Self, part and whole, perceiver and Oneness. One should be the observer and the observed. One should be one's own body and all life. One should walk on the earth and be the earth. One should be aware of Oneness and be Oneness. One should be and be being. One should be all of these at once, because in absolute truth, that is the absolute truth.

HOW IS THE SELF IN QUESTION DETERMINED?

If every self contains other selves and is contained in turn by still other selves, how is the boundary of the perceiving self determined? What decides, in all of these hierarchically enfolded and enfolding selves, what is the self that perceives other and knows itself. The answer to this question, which is almost too subtle to formulate, is this: every level of organization (regardless of how many other organizations are embedded in it or it iself is enfolded in) is a self, knowing itself to itself and perceiving others from itself.

THE DEFINED SELF

Nothing can perceive itself. An eye cannot see itself. An organization in Oneness, a Self, can know itself but it cannot perceive itself. By the same token it can perceive the rest of Oneness, but it cannot know it. That is to say, it cannot know all of Oneness while being a separate organization in it. It can only know all of Oneness while being one with it. It has to give up its (self-perceived) separation to know. (From the perspective of Oneness, nothing* qualifies as separate, while from the perspective of perception anything* can qualify as separate if it is perceived as separate.)

Any gestalt, to the extent that it is perceiving from any organizational boundaries that are less than and apart from the whole of Oneness, can be regarded as a self; whereas while, and to the extent

---

*It is important to maintain the awareness that whenever one refers to thingness (i.e., a thing, something, nothing, anything, everything) or any category that can be characterized as a thing, one is squarely in the territory of perceptual illusion. As you can see, this is quite an extensive territory, so extensive that one must make extraordinary and deliberate linguistic and conceptual efforts to get free of it.

that its consciousness is contiguous with the greater whole, any gestalt can also be regarded as Self. (I am using the convention whereby spelling "self" with a small "s" signifies it is the personal self, while spelling it with a capital "S" signifies it is the personal abode of the universal Self, i.e., the higher Self or, in Vedic terms, the Atman.) It is essential to the understanding of perception and reality to fully appreciate the extent to which self and Self are concomitant and the difference between the two only a matter of the self-definition of the perceiver, or to put it another way, only a matter of from what boundaries the perception is originating: truly a matter of perspective!

KNOWING THE WHOLE, REMAINING THE "I"

If every part is part of the whole, why can we not know ourselves as the whole? The answer again is that our self, our "I," is precisely defined by self-perception as a part, a separated, boundaried entity. If we extend ourselves to the whole in order to be sentient of it, we're no longer the part that we normally experience as ourselves and from which we can normally perceive. When we cease being ourselves which is apart, there's no separated self that can know.

This formulation suggests that there is no way of knowing beyond the boundaries of our defined "I." That implication, however, is contrary to experience, at least to the experience of meditators and mystics, who seem to be privy to information beyond the experience of the separated self. The explanation for this phenomenon resides in the structure of consciousness. Every separate consciousness, including your "I" consciousness, has a center and a boundary (see also Chapter XVI). The boundary of your "I" consciousness may be expanded or contracted at will, subsuming whatever part of Oneness is desired, and accessing information within that boundary. As long as the "I" center remains your center, the experience of knowing remains your experience. Then, it is possible, while keeping your center fixed, to expand your boundary to include the viewpoint of another.

Another possibility, however, would be to move your center to the center of another person, in which case you would be perceiving from his viewpoint. In doing this, one faces the possible danger of losing one's center to the center of the other person; you would no longer be aware of yourself experiencing him, but would just be him experiencing himself, with perhaps your self disappearing as a separate entity.

These considerations bring up the question of what qualifies your experience as your experience? What is responsible for your consciousness continuing to be your consciousness or your "I"? There are two answers. The first, which I find both self-evident and in some way inexplicable, is that it is yours; it is not somebody else's. It is yours because you are it. The question is sort of like asking why one apple on the tree is not another apple and vice versa.

The second answer yet again is that your "I" consciousness is a concept, a category of associations, physical and mental, that are associated with your bodymind. Even when people have "out-of-body" experiences, they don't lose their sense of being themselves, their "I" consciousness. They take the associations of their "I" concept with them, despite leaving the bodies behind that have done so much to engender these associations.

Why does the "I" concept stay intact over such radical transmutations? A possible answer can be found in the insight that the "I" concept is a defense mechanism. Ultimately, it is a defense against the threat of dissolution that accompanies the realization of Oneness. *In this sense, "I" or self is a defense against Self.* But it undoubtedly developed as a defense against perceived external threats, both physical (being eaten) or psychological. In that sense it is a defense against other, a self-perceived boundary against being other. As a defense it is very resistant to any dissolution.

WHEN A SELF KNOWS ITSELF

When one approaches his experience dualistically, it appears that there is always a knower and a known. However, there is a catch that reveals the erroneous nature of the logic of illusion. If there's really a knower, one can ask who knows that there is a knower. One has to posit another knower in answer. In that case the original knower becomes the known, but there appears a second knower who must also be known by another knower and so on. Sooner or later down the line there has to be some entity somewhere that knows itself. In the realm of Oneness what is one place is every place, so logic almost inescapably points to the conclusion that every living gestalt has the power of knowing itself.*

The condition that changed Isness from reality to illusion, is the same thing that changes Being to beings. It is separation from. Isness or Being knows itself and perceives other. When a life form perceives itself as separate from Oneness, it moves from knowing itself to perceiving other. When it gives up the perception of separation, it moves back from perceiving other to knowing itself once again. However, and this is the rub, there ceases to be any one (apart) to perceive Oneness.

THROUGH THE "I"S OF THE WORLD

Nothing can perceive itself. An eye cannot see itself. An organization in Oneness, a Self, can know itself, but it cannot perceive itself.

By the same token, a subself of a larger self (say a brain in a body) cannot know the state of another part of its body, say its stomach, while perceiving itself as separate from it. Hypothetically, when the brain gives up its self-perceived separation, it is not there to know itself as a separate entity. It ceases to be a perceiver. On the other hand, if it were to perceive itself as a separate entity, the brain would know itself, and as part of this knowing, its percepts (encoded sensory information) would also be known. In this sense it would "know" the proprioception of its stomach as a percept and could take something for heartburn.

If nothing can perceive itself, how is self-perception possible? The answer is, must be, that the self perceives itself through implication. It perceives the world, and anything that is not the world is the self. The world is not "not-self," rather the self is "not-world." Only the not-self can be perceived directly, the self is just a blind

---

*This progression follows the same path as a consideration of the question, "If there is a creator, who created the Creator?"

spot in the perception of the world. (While a Self cannot perceive itself directly, it can of course know itself.) Also, the self perceives how other perceivers in the world perceive it. Self sees itself through the eyes of the world. (The analogy of a flashlight looking for the source of its own light illustrates the problem.)

Of course, on a deeper level the perceived not-self determines a person's self-image, since the not-self is that which is seen and from which the self is inferred.

When children grow up, they alternate between Self knowing and seeing themselves though the eyes of the world. Self-concept can derive from self-knowledge, indirect self-perception, the eyes of others, or any amalgam of these views. Problems arise when seeing themselves through the eyes of the world occludes self-knowledge and people start rejecting who they are in search of more favorable comparisons with others.

KNOWING ONESELF

The literature of mysticism and psychology is full of references to knowing oneself. However, if you pursue this line of thought and entertain the possibility of knowing oneself, you get into very subtle issues. There are three interwoven questions. The first is whether it is possible to know oneself. The second is when you know yourself, what do you know? The third is what terms knowing oneself could possibly be experienced in.

Although I believe that self-knowledge is a reality, it is not what people expect, and certainly not what most people understand when they are exhorted to know themselves. Probably most cases of knowing oneself, upon examination, are really not knowledge but perception, or even worse conjecture and analysis. They are instances of a self perceiving another self to which it is related, as in the case of a person's brain perceiving its body. This is not true knowing because the self in question is constituting itself as one…apart…perceiving.

Addressing the second question, in cases where One does truly know one's Self, there is no one thing there to be known. Self-knowledge is empty, not full of qualities. You are in the observer while knowing the observer. There is no One outside of the observer to perceive the observer; therefore, there is no perceptual experience.

This brings us to the third question, the terms that the knowing of Self is experienced in. Perception is always in qualities, hot, far, fast, red, etc., which are either the illusions of the senses or cognitive metaphors for these illusions. What does it mean, what could it possibly mean, to know something without knowing qualities? It can't be light; it can't be sound; it can't have color, weight, size, velocity, location. It can't have words; it can't be pleasurable or painful; it can't even have emotion. Without qualities, what is there to know! However, in order for perceptual qualities to arise, there has to be a part apart, a point to perceive from. Since there is no point to perceive from, there can arise no perceptual qualities.

So we conclude that while it is possible to know one's Self, while Self knowledge is a very real potential, the Self that is known is not on the same level of discourse with selves that are perceived. Those selves that are perceived are, like all preconceptions, illusory and qualitative, while the Self that is known is real, empty, and devoid of qualities.

Then what does a person, a meditator, experience when sitting in their Self-knowing, their Isness, their sentience? No thing, or just perhaps a sense of clarity and presence.

SPIRIT

Self, that which knows itself and perceives other, may also be called spirit. As the word spirit implies, it is very fluid; it can change both its center and its boundaries instantly. Every consciousness, every continuous thread of awareness, every presence, every spirit, is able to move from one center to another, to expand and contract its boundaries, to change its shape, extending itself alternatively into its sight, its proprioception, its hearing, its environment, the consciousness of an other. It can even move from the material plane to the "spiritual plane," extending into the furthest realms of Oneness, the universe, energy, etc. The human spirit is attached to certain realms, body, mind, and thoughts, and moves more or less easily among them, but is resistant to moving beyond and encounters difficulty, even fear in the attempt. But it can be done. However, and this is important, wherever it extends itself to, it is and it knows, but it cannot perceive. Whatever it extends itself to become, its Self is no longer apart from it.

OCEAN KNOWING FISH

How, we ask, can one's Self be simultaneously one's central nervous system and the cosmos? Can the central nervous system know its percepts, at the same time that the greater Self is extended to the object of these percepts; neither separate nor conscious as a separate entity? So that one is perceiving as a human while at the same time, knowing like a God?

It is theoretically possible, but the experience of it would be like being a great Oneness Self, in which a discrete point of consciousness, knowing and aware of its perceptions, is embedded. Something like the ocean being simultaneously the ocean and one fish. The difficulty with, say, a single meditator doing it, is that when one is being the ocean, it is difficult to hold on to being the fish. When one returns to identifying with the fish, one loses the ocean. The trick is for the Ocean to center in itself, while retaining the separate knowing of the fish. *(This is inverted perception, from the whole to the part).* If one could avoid grasping one's fishness, one could do it and probably some mighty meditators have achieved the feat. If not, perhaps some mighty Oceans have!

A SELF CAN KNOW ITSELF AND PERCEIVE OTHER; A SELF-CONCEPT CAN ONLY PERCEIVE OTHER!

The reason it is so difficult to know yourself (in the sense of knowing the self-concept you are coming from) is the following: self-concepts, not being real (as is the Self) but only perceptions or concepts, cannot know themselves, they can only perceive other. When you rest in your self-concept, you function as your self-concept. You occupy that conceptual position. You are that point of view. You don't have anyplace to stand other than where you are. Only when you are in an alternate self-concept, can you can see the first one, even judge it. Only when you center into your Self can you see your self-concept, even revise it.

When one holds a self-concept, it usurps the vision of the whole person. It is a distorting lens imposed on the real Self of the person, through which the person cannot help but perceive. If you are familiar with computer software, it is like a shell program (in the sense that Windows is a graphic shell to DOS. DOS operates the computer, but Windows is the shell through which one operates DOS.) This is why a self-concept can function in lieu of a real Self as the place from which one perceives.

However, a self-concept is simply a cognitive perception. It is not real, not a Self. That it is not a Self is why it has no power to know itself. This is why you can progress from self-concept to self-concept, getting further and further from your real Self and eventually losing track of it. It is also why, in coming back to the nonconceptual, real Self in meditation, one returns to sanity. It further explains why people, as they get alienated from their real Selves, tend to get their sense of self from the peer groups and authorities in their lives, and why it is so important to balance those external sources with real, meditative Self-knowing.

IS PERCEPTUAL ILLUSION NECESSARY?

When you are identified with a percept, you are immersed in the illusory, relational qualities of space, time, matter, energy, etc., that give the percept its aspect of definiteness, tangibility, reality, etc. The unseparated Self is devoid of perceptual qualities. When you are aware of it, you sense a thereness but it is the presence of the absence. It is only when you know a percept that you know some thing. Self is devoid of thingness. What Self is has been variously described as Isness, Suchness, or Thereness, but this is just an attempt to find a word that does not imply thingness. Because of the tangibility of percepts, they tend to entrain our attention. We attend to them and neglect to pay attention to the far subtler aspects of nonqualitative Self, which is why we mostly live in the world of illusion.

How can we pay attention to aperceptual reality? We can't. The only way is to become it, in which case we dissolve the "I" that wants to know it, which is in some sense losing the whole point. Perception is the way the universe has solved this problem, and this solution in itself is the essence of life.

15. BEYOND PERCEPTION

Consciousness as a separate Isness is a given!
Consciousness of our separate Isness has to be discovered.

CONSCIOUSNESS AS A SENSORY MODALITY

Consciousness is both the way we know and the way we know that we know. In that, it is very akin to both our senses and our perception. Hypothetically, a single-celled, completely undifferentiated organism doesn't know it knows. It just knows and acts as a simultaneous occurrence. It is pure sentience. In order to know one knows, there must be boundaries, separation, multiplicity, a knower and a known. In complex, multicellular organisms, individual cells and cellular organizations (organs) know themselves within their perceived boundaries and perceive one another across their boundaries.

Perception is a complex, multilevel phenomenon. In single-celled organisms it is a matter of the whole organism being sentient of changes in the boundary membranes of its being and acting or reacting accordingly. In organisms of intermediate complexity it is

171

a nervous system communicating between sensory information and bodily functions and integrating them. In sophisticated organisms with complex brains it is a matter of a knower being aware of percepts and acting on them.

Is consciousness a sensory modality? Yes and no. No, it is not, in the sense that it does not separate, categorize, and dualize. It takes things as they are and grasps their reality whole cloth. Yes, it is, in the sense that it is the way organisms know, whether that knowing is sentience or awareness.

Ultimately, consciousness is not a sense, rather senses are specializations of consciousness. Although not actually a sense, it is interesting to talk about consciousness as if it is. It could be the legendary sixth sense!. It would, of course, be a proprioceptive sense, like pain perception. While the external senses have access (through the sensory organs) to the outside, consciousness only has access to inner events, to our minds. (At least in the ordinary view!)

It would also be a superordinate sense. We see, hear, smell, taste, and feel, and those are the primary senses. Then, we are conscious of these sense inputs, so consciousness is the superordinate sense that pulls the primary senses together.

Finally, it would be an integrative sense. We perceive our thoughts as well as our sensations with consciousness, and it is through the perceptual modality of consciousness that we integrate perception and cognition. Thus, we have a rough hierarchy of knowing which is proprioception, sensory perception, cognitive perception, extrasensory perception (perhaps), and integrative perception or consciousness. However, as I said, rather than considering consciousness a sense in itself, it is much more precise to think of it as that aspect of being called sentience, whereby all living gestalts know that they are, and in the process know the activity of their senses.

EXTRASENSORY PERCEPTION

Some people, myself included, believe or "experience" that consciousness can operate independently of the five senses and be a means of knowing external events directly, as in extrasensory or psychic perception. If consciousness knows the Isness of its own sensations and thoughts, is it so far-fetched to imagine that it could also directly perceive the Isness of the sensations and thoughts of others? Let's think about this.

First of all, how might it be accomplished? The only possibility I can think of requires challenging our common perception of the unit of human life, or for that matter the unit of life in general. That is, we commonly perceive the unit of human life as bounded by the skin boundary of the individual self, whatever that is. But suppose this is not accurate. Suppose each individual self is just the center of a continuum that stretches from individual human cells to the whole of the human race (and beyond). This continuum is structured like a graduated normal curve, with the individual its apex. What is more, the individual self is just the center of that curve from its own viewpoint. From another viewpoint, the viewpoint of either an individual cell or the entire race, the curve looks very different. Considered like this, the self as the unit of human life is not sharply bounded but a gradient.

This takes us no closer to an answer to how consciousness can perceive the perceptions of another person, but the question becomes different. Although we don't know how consciousness knows our own perceptions (nerves are the paths information takes, but do not account for the quality of consciousness), we can extrapolate that (if our individual selves are on a continuum with others) the way consciousness perceives the perceptions of others might be the same way it perceives our own perceptions. We don't know how knowing knows, but we know that it does, and if it knows inside the skin of an individual it might also happen inside the collective skin of the human race! Or, more simply put, consciousness might not be bounded by physical bodies.

If you think this is far-fetched, consider the case of bees and ants. In these cases the hive or colony is clearly the organism and the individual insects just specialized cells that are separated physically. Consciousness seems to be shared among all the individual insects with extraordinary rapidity and efficiency, although doubtless some kind of communication mechanism will offer a parallel explanation.

There is even evidence that plants have extrasensory awareness of people. If we accept this, we have to extend the sphere of consciousness from fauna to flora, and thereby to the entire race of life!

EXTRAPERCEPTUAL PERCEPTION

Another possibility that parapsychologists explore is whether extrasensory consciousness can enable us to know the perceptual qualities of something, independently of our senses. So that we might, for instance, know the color of a ball without seeing it. This is very different from that sentience that does not contain any perceptual qualities, and if it exists, it would be much harder to account for vis-à-vis aperceptual field theory.

There are two possible cases of this. One would be determining the color in the case that someone else knew it, and the other would be determining the color even though no one else knew it. The former case could be explained by telepathy, but the latter case is a ball of a different color. In order to explain that, should anyone be able to convincingly demonstrate it, we would have to go beyond the concept of the family of life to the family of existence. Even more, we would have to posit that a perceptual illusion could be known aperceptually and psychically, without first being perceived. That is a very great jump indeed!

Even if direct knowing is a true phenomenon, it would still be confined to aperceptual properties; perceptual qualities are dual and illusory and not-present in Oneness!

What could an aperceptual quality be? How would you know it? Even vibration and light, those two hoary standbys of mysticism, are perceptual qualities.

THE PROBLEM WITH PARAPSYCHOLOGY

This discussion points up the problem with research in parapsychology. By and large this research attempts to document the psychic knowing of perceptual or illusory qualities. The problem is there is no perceptual process in the knowingness of pure consciousness. To pure consciousness the queen of spades and the king of clubs are virtually identical. Even when reading the consciousness of another perceiver there is not much difference between these cards. This accounts for the hit-or-miss qualities of most parapsychological efforts. If the research was attempting to document aperceptual qualities, the effects would probably be much stronger. Of course, there are no aperceptual qualities per se, but there are states or forms of consciousness.

What has to take place in order for the perceiving individual to comprehend these forms of consciousness? The subconscious has to convert them into perceptual or quasi-perceptual terms. It does this though dreaming, the same dreaming process that translates the knowing of the Self when we sleep. Dreaming has a perceptual quality with an imaginary (rather than illusory) content. This subconscious function of translating the knowing of the Self is why most spiritual and religious knowing has such a mythic or fantastical content and why it is believed in so literally and passionately. It is dreamed (i.e., directly known and then comprehended by being converted into a quasi-perceptual form) rather than being perceived or come to by rigorous introspection and analysis. This is also the difference between most spiritual and religious knowledge and the investigations contained in this book.

IS EXTRASENSORY PERCEPTION AN EMERGING ABILITY OR A VESTIGIAL ONE?

If consciousness can enable us to know directly, bypassing our sensoriums, it might be considered an evolutionary potential. First consciousness, then the independent consciousness of the separate Self, and then the psychic dimension might be consecutive emerging phenomena. If this is the case, we humans could be at the evolutionary dawn of the psychic dimension (although even in this hypothetical case, the future of psychic abilities in the human gene pool would be uncertain, in that it would be dependent on establishing itself as an evolutionary advantage).

Because of the success of the scientific method in manipulating the world, Western men and women are entranced by their sensory perceptions and cognitive powers, and largely ignore *(mostly deny)* the psychic potentials of consciousness. In that sense tribal cultures and meditators may be ahead of the Western world in their recognition of the psychic dimension and the technologies they have devised for developing both consciousness and the psychic dimension, i.e., hallucinogens, shamanistic practices, meditation.

That we are at the dawn of a revolution in consciousness is a very popular idea; however, I doubt that it is completely true. Another, drearier prospect is more likely. Extrasensory awareness is found in various degrees in all societies. Although numerous persons are working with healing and various extrasensory capabilities, except for certain geographical pockets, they are overshadowed politically, economically, and informationally. In humankind as a whole, extrasensory awareness may be dying out. Like sight in a cave fish, it may fade through disuse. If so, this is tragic. While man was expanding and conquering his environment with technology, extrasensory means of knowing may have been relatively extraneous, but now that his survival is threatened by his own success and he needs to come into harmony with what is left of his environment, extrasensory perception may be just the tool he needs to resurrect!

Keep in mind that, like perception, extrasensory perception has its theoretical limits. Even in the most optimistic scenario, where the consciousness of one person is in direct psychic communication with the consciousness of another, or with a greater source of knowledge, if the communication is in perceptual form, it is illusory. If you intuit telepathically that Oneness is a field of green and gold with tiers of angels surrounding a glowing throne on which sits God in the form of an ear of corn, you can be certain you are dreaming, experiencing an illusion, a perceptual metaphor for what really is. Because whatever Oneness really is, you can be sure that it doesn't have perceptual qualities.

The other possibility, extraperceptual sentience, I believe is a real aspect of universal consciousness and as such within everybody's power. However, because it doesn't come in colors, it is widely overlooked, even by those who fancy themselves living at the frontiers of consciousness, i.e., coastal California.

CONSCIOUSNESS AS A HOMUNCULUS

Accounts of all manner of out-of-body experiences, including NDEs (near-death experiences have come to be so accepted that there is even an abbreviation for them) as well as the theory of reincarnation, all indicate that even out of body, mind, or self is a homunculus. That is, even without a body, without senses, without a brain, one's individual mind seems to retain a substantial part of its integrity, its embodied capacities and its identity. It does something like see, hear, and think. It has emotions. It recognizes and remembers. In NDEs it even recognizes previously departed loved ones who stand in greeting in the light at the end of the tunnel. Most remarkable among these assertions is the assertion that mind retains its original identity as an individual. To a substantial degree, a person, while out-of-body, even after death of the body and even through successive incarnations, remains uniquely and potentially consciously himself. These assertions, if true, present a conceptual challenge for perceptual field theory.

The idea of the homunculus is the ultimate nonexplanatory concept. It holds, in its simplest form, that the reason why we can sense, feel, think, and speak is that there is a little man within us who can do those things. If consciousness is a homunculus, that implies that the only reason we need a body is to carry out bodily functions. Either the senses and brain are not essential for the mind to perceive, remember, and think, or these functions are replicated in the mind in a portable version. Both these propositions are wildly improbable.

At this point in my understanding I can only go so far toward a solution for this problem, and my model falls far short of the mark. However, I think it is the right direction, so I am going to offer it for what it is. Also, I find that the process of getting something down on paper sometimes gets me to the next step in understanding.

Remember that we are positing that consciousness, pure or universal consciousness, is a fundamental, like electromagnetic energy. It is an aspect of Oneness. Insofar as consciousness inhabits a body, it takes on a form. That form is imposed by the brain. For a model, think of a movie projector. First, there is a light source. Then, the film modifies the light into potential images. Next, a lens focuses the light onto the screen, and finally the screen converts it into a viewable image. The light, of course, represents universal conscious energy. The film is the perceptual field that modifies consciousness into an image. If we view consciousness as a pure energy, capable of disembodied existence, the film should by all rights be a function of brain, dependent on body and experience.

Once the film has introjected information into the light, informed it into a potential image, the light holds that information as it radiates. Then, the lens can capture a portion of this light and focus it onto a screen, where it forms an image. The important point here is that the light holds information, holds an image. As a matter of fact, it seems to hold it indefinitely, no matter how much it diffuses or radiates. Telescopes can capture images of long-dead stars billions of light years distant. There is far less light to be had, but the information is potentially still there if we could capture enough light. If we had a telescope mirror a billion light years in diameter, we theoretically could recapture, in full detail, a life-size image of a star a billion light years distant.

If light can hold the information of an image indefinitely as it radiates, then it is conceivable that disembodied consciousness could hold the essence of an individual self once it is formed by embodiment. Now, of course, the self is not an image, but neither is the information held by the light an image, it only produces an image once focused onto a screen. The light is an amalgam of energy and information, informed energy, that has a center and a rapidly expanding periphery. It doesn't just carry the information to the screen; it *is* the information. The lens and screen just convert it into a viewable image. This is actually more than a metaphor in the case of the eye, where the lens and retina (screen) of the eye are indeed the way we know the information carried by light.

Correspondingly, the self is individuated, informed consciousness. Consciousness doesn't just carry the information of the self, it is the self. And just like the light, it can retain its integrity indefinitely as it radiates from the body whose experiences once informed it. Perception may be the lens that focuses the information of the self onto the screen of embodiment. We have a model then of how consciousness may be transformed into a self and sustain the integrity of the self indefinitely. So far so good.

However, there are vast and significant differences between a potential image and (the reports of what it is like to be) a disembodied self. These differences reveal the limitations in our movie metaphor. I'll address two of these differences.

The most compelling difference is that where the informed energy of the light holds the information of its material source, the informed consciousness of the disembodied self doesn't only hold the information of the embodied self, it functions like it. It is a homunculus. A self within, or in this case without, a self! Now, of course, since this is not light but consciousness in the full sense that we are speaking about, it is conceivable that one could have sentience without embodiment, even sentience modified by embodiment. However, it is still difficult to understand how that sentience could have ongoing perception, memory, thought, emotion, and awareness all without a body, senses, and a brain!

The other shortcoming of the projector metaphor that I want to touch upon is temporality. The light radiating from a source tracks the ongoing changes taking place in the source. If the source is changing, the image is not the same from one instant to the next. If you focus and sample the light simultaneously in different places in apparent space, you see different images from different times. However, people with out-of-body experiences seem to travel and experience themselves and the world as an intact self-homunculus, a self-sufficient consciousness independent of its source in the physical individual. Could it be that there are infinite, different, disembodied selves all experiencing themselves as the self, all radiating outward, like the samples of light taken at different distances from their source and that when they re-embody in the physical self, they reamalgamate into one experienced self again? It is possible but it is far-fetched.

DREAMING

There are a variety of accounts of out-of-body, near-death, and other psychic experiences which, if valid, would indicate that consciousness can function nonlocally, separate from the physical body of the individual. When trying to explain unproven phenomena, it is difficult to know how to proceed. Certainly it is folly to speculate how many angels fit on a pinhead in the absence of compelling evidence of the existence of angels. On the other hand, we have so many accounts of out-of-body and near-death experiences that I think it is necessary to account for them at least as real experiences, if not as real reports from the hereafter. If, for the purposes of this discussion, we accept nonlocal consciousness as a given, an interesting problem remains. If aperceptual field theory is correct, and perceptual qualities are generated by the function of a sensorium as a separate point of perception, how can disembodied consciousness know in terms of perceptual qualities (space, time, color, form, etc.) without a brain and sensorium at its disposal?

Again, there are two hypothetical cases of out-of-body and near-death experiences that I want to address. One is the case where there is a connection between the nonlocal consciousness and a viable bodymind of the host individual; the other is where there is no connection.

We know that in some cases quasi-perceptual qualities are generated by the mind independently of the sensorium. This is the case in dreaming and visualization, as well as some drug and mental illness-induced alternate states. Therefore we know that the mind can present aperceptual knowing in quasi-perceptual form. Let us refer to this capacity in all of its guises as dreaming. We don't know how the mind dreams, but just the unarguable fact that it does is adequate to account for the capacity of nonlocal consciousness to yield perceptual experiences. It does not, however, indicate that this quasi-perceptual knowing is real, that is, that it would be the same as the knowing of a live perceiver in the same place.

In the case of out-of-body and near-death experiences, there is still a live brain to interpret or translate the aperceptual knowing into quasi-perceptual experience, that is to dream. Therefore, we don't have to attribute this capacity to pure consciousness. Nonlocal consciousness can be sentient nonlocally, can travel or extend itself into other consciousness, or simply be aware of other apparent localities while the living brain is still there in the living body, the local mind is still there to dream the experiences.

Of course, if you accept that near-death experiences constitute complete disembodiment of consciousness and the physical host plays no further role, then you are attributing the capacity for dreaming to pure consciousness. Strictly speaking, there is no necessity for this. No accounts of NDEs for instance, have been reported by the permanently dead, nor have we any other indication that quasi-perceptual experiences are enjoyed by completely disembodied consciousness. Where there is experience, as far as we know or are likely to be able to know, there has to be an experiencer.

Another phenomenon should be taken into account but also with a grain of salt, namely apparent psychic communications of various sorts, channelings and messages from people who have died. It should be noted that, while it by no means solves the complete mystery, all of these communications involve a living person to host the disembodied consciousness. Whether or not dreaming can occur in pure disembodied consciousness is still unknown, but it is a distinct possibility that these communications occur because there is a living bodymind that is receptive to the disembodied consciousness and allows it to dream.

THE INTELLIGENCE OF THE UNIVERSE

16. PROTO-EVOLUTION AND THE INTELLIGENCE OF THE UNIVERSE

THE UNIVERSE CREATED ITSELF IN RELATION

Aperceptual field theory, exploring the role of perception in the universe, clarifies much about living gestalts. The problem of how the inorganic universe evolved to the degree of complexity that allowed the evolution of life is the subject of the speculations in this chapter.

On one level of discourse, perhaps the most basic that we can get to, all energy/matter has polarity and force, and/or is made up from components that have polar force. On another level, polar force is or results from electron spin. This polar force is magnetic in the sense that when electrons are polarized in a magnetizable material, they attract or repel similarly magnetizable materials. The same "magnetic" or polar force generated by electrons, or electron spin, seems to be universal. The earth and (probably) all heavenly bodies have magnetic fields, which implies that all space is suffused with weak magnetic fields coming from an infinity of directions.

Since the motion or spin of electrons generates magnetic force, it is probable that magnetic force is present in all existence and an attribute of all existence. Richard Gerbers in his book *Vibrational Medicine* summarizes extensive research showing that magnetic fields and the fields generated by psychic healers have parallel, positive effects on enzyme repair, crystal formation, molecular bonding, seed germination, and human healing, to cite a few instances. Considering that data, it seems probable that the energy of life, *prana* or *chi*, is a variant of magnetic force.

Units of energy/matter attract and repel each other and assemble in various ways according to their structure by virtue of their polar force. In this way organization is inherent in electrons and inherent in existence. Even life and individuated consciousness arise from the patterns that magnetic and electromagnetic forces make when they interrelate into complex organizations.

POLARIZED FORCE APPROACHES INTELLIGENCE

There is no dead, disorganized, entropic matter in the universe. Of course, there are aggregates of matter like dust, which on one level seem to be just there, totally disorganized and dead, but even these, on some level of organization, are aggregates of particles, every one of which in themselves has energy and organization. Every one in Oneness is on some level: molecular, atomic, stellar, living, etc., a holon or gestalt, an organization of energy.

Every gestalt in Oneness, regardless of its extent or complexity, whether an electron, a cell, a man, or a star is of itself a one in Oneness. As a one in Oneness it has its center. If you have a center, you have to have a periphery. So every one in Oneness has a center and a periphery (or boundary), (perhaps itself composed of many centers and peripheries). Each periphery is divided into two poles, positive and negative. This constellation of a center with a bipolar periphery is the irreducible duality of being. It is at once the organizing principle, the primal organization, and the fundamental building block of the universe. Whenever you have one organization apart, you have a center, and whenever you have a center, you have a periphery and potential poles. In it is the closest we can come to that doomed search for the "fundamental particles" that make up the universe.

Every (free) center also has spin (observable on the atomic level and then again on the astronomic level). The polarities are related to the direction of this spin. The positive pole spins clockwise; the negative pole spins counterclockwise. These polarities are not simply nominal; they either are or generate opposite magnetic fields.

Magnetic fields pervade the universe. All electrons and probably all heavenly bodies have spin, polarity, and a magnetic field. Amazingly enough, magnetic fields also constitute a second metabolism for all forms of life. Science has familiarized us with the biochemical metabolism whereby life forms metabolize nutrients and/or sunlight for heat, growth, repair, reproduction, and movement. Science has also documented that we have a bioelectric metabolism in the nervous system. What is just coming to light (in Western science anyway, the Indians and Chinese have been telling us this for hundred of years) is that we also have a magnetic metabolism.

Just as we have pathways for chemical circulation (blood vessels) and bioelectric information (nerves) we have pathways for the circulation of magnetic energy (meridians). These meridians branch off like capillaries into finer and finer channels bringing *pranic* or magnetic energy to every part of the body. (Meridians do not show up upon dissection. Perhaps they are lines of magnetic force, like you would see if you sprinkled iron filings on a sheet of paper and put a magnet under it.) Magnetic force penetrates and overlays matter and doesn't need physical channels. Magnetic force fields, radiating from the chakras, interact with one another to create complex circulation patterns. I suspect that the meridians are the lines of force radiating from the interacting patterns of these chrakral fields.

THE MAGNETIC BODY

Every cell is a magnet. Every organ and bone is a magnet composed of submagnets. The human body, as is the case with the body of every life form, generates its own magnetic field and has a polarity pattern. However, just as plants are dependent on light and all life forms are dependent on nutrients to sustain their metabolisms, our magnetic metabolisms, and the magnetic metabolisms of all life forms are dependent on nourishment from the magnetic energy coming from the outside. We are living in a sea of magnetic energy, generating from the magnetic fields of the earth, the sea, the air, trees, and all living things as well as heavenly bodies.

Just as life arose in the sea and the chemistry of our blood is the chemistry of the sea...life evolved in the magnetic field of the earth. Magnetic energy flows in our bodies, makes up our aura and radiates from our chakras.

In the same way that we have a mouth and digestive systems to take in nutrients, we have energy vortexes to take in fresh magnetic energy and discharge exhausted (disorganized or incoherent) magnetic energy. These vortexes in our magnetic field (sometimes called our aura) are called chakras. As is the case with electrons, the direction of spin of these vortexes determines the polarity of the field and whether the vortex is taking in or giving out magnetic energy. A number of problems can and do arise with our magnetic metabolisms, ranging from a deficiency of magnetic energy in the environment* to problems in taking in, circulating, balancing, and discharging magnetic energy.

POLARITY IS RELATIVE

Polarity and spin are relative; they are a function of position. When observed from above, a bar magnet in which the electrons are spinning clockwise has a positive or south field. When observed from below, the spin is counterclockwise relative to the observer and the field is negative or north. The absolute spin remains constant, but the relative spin reverses with the position of the observer. The

---

*NASA found that astronauts developed numerous metabolic problems in space. At first, they attributed these problems to weightlessness, but eventually discovered that they were caused by being outside of the earth's magnetic field. NASA started generating magnetic fields in manned spacecraft and the problems ceased.

difference between poles is solely dependent on which side of the magnet is being observed.

By this principle much of the behavior between two or more magnets can be explained. When you combine a stack of disc magnets NSNS (north-south-north-south), you are putting them together, them so they all spin the same way. Basically the bottom of one is spinning the same way as the top of one placed below it. They then stick together combining the strengths of their fields into one cylindrical magnet. If you separated them, it would be identical to cutting a cylindrical magnet into discs. If, however, you try combining magnets SS or NN the fields have very different effect; they repel one another strongly. Basically you are pitting the spin of the fields against one another, so that they are trying to reverse one another.

It is unclear why this would repel, but some intuitive help can be gotten by imagining the spins in other mediums than magnetic force. For example, imagine a body of water in which whirlpools of the same size with opposing spins are colliding. The collision would result in a big wave as they resisted one another, a situation analogous to the repulsion of the two magnets. Although we can't see anything in a magnetic field, it is clear that invisible forces are colliding. On the other hand, when we put a magnet together with an equal, unmagnetized quantity of the same material, then both poles are attracted to it equally. It is like a single whirlpool sucking in water.

The case of a broken bone is very interesting. It is known that bones are weak magnets and that in the case of breaks the edges repel one another, interfering with healing. Now according to the above explanation, we would expect the edges to attract one another, the break acting the same way as separating two disc magnets that were sticking together NS. However, this expectation is based on the expectation that the bone is polarized longitudinally, so that one end is north and the other south. However, bones are actually polarized laterally, from side to side, so that one side is north and the other south. A break divides them into two North or two South poles lying side by side (actually East East or West West), and repelling one another. Although they are still spinning the same way, at the point of contact they conflict. Imagine the front and rear wheels of one side of a moving car. The wheels are moving the same way but if you move them together until they touch they will collide and stop one another. (It is relational polarity* again: the front of one polarizes with the back of another. But where NS attract and NN and SS repel, EE and WW attract and WE repels {see diagrams}.

If North and South magnetic fields are intrinsically identical, it is difficult to understand how they could have different qualities. However, extensive research and clinical experience on animals and humans has established beyond question that the different magnetic fields have very different qualities and effects (the North has calming and healing effects while the South has stimulatory and energizing effects). If the fields don't differ absolutely, only relatively, then these different effects must be relative to the position of the subject within the field.

What is more, the two poles of magnets seem not to have different effects on magnetically neutral or nonpolarized materials, i.e., both poles equally attract a nonmagnet which is made out of magnetizable materials, whereas they neither attract nor repel nonmagnetizable materials. If we extrapolate from this, it follows that the effects of the different sides (polarities) of the magnet must be relative, not only to the positioning of the subject within the field, but also relative to the subject's magnetic field(s) itself.

Of course, magnets have other effects than attracting or repelling, but all materials have some magnetic field. It is well known that a strong magnetic field can influence or overcome a weak one, even to the extent of a strong magnet attracting a weak one when they are combined SS or NN. As a matter of fact, this is just my argument, that magnets have their effect on things by relating to their magnetic fields.

The difference between magnetized and nonmagnetized material is just the organization of its electrons. In magnetized materials some of the electrons are aligned so they are spinning the same way, whereas in nonmagnetized material the electrons are randomly aligned. The difference between a nonmagnetizable material and a

[*From these examples we see that polarity does not exist except as relationships between two force fields or directionalities.]

magnetizable one is that in the magnetizable material the electrons seem to be in a relatively fluid state in which they can be aligned by passing a magnetic field through them. In nonmagnetizable materials the electrons are more or less frozen into random patterns; therefore, they cannot be magnetized, nor can they be attracted by magnets, i.e., the spin of the fields is canceled out and cannot be co-opted by the field spin of the magnet. The sum "magnetic" energy or spin is the same in identical magnetized and nonmagnetized materials. However, in the nonmagnetized materials the electron alignment is entropic and the poles or spins cancel one another out.

Chakras

Chakras, the vortices of the human energy field or aura, are believed to usually spin clockwise taking in energy, and counterclockwise letting energy out.* If this is so, it follows that the field from a magnet, depending on the direction of its spin or polarity, as well as its strength, would either accelerate this chakral spin if it were going in the same direction, slow it, or even overwhelm and reverse it if were going in the opposite direction. So we can see that while a magnetic field is absolute and neutral in itself, it is polar in relation to another magnetic field, and has a specific effect on the chakral spin and energy metabolism of living beings.

Note: For vortex or spin to always attract, regardless of direction, we must be dealing with an external relational variable. A whirlpool always goes down, not up. It moves in relation to gravity. Tornadoes, on the other hand, are vortices that suck up. In their case there is an area of extreme low pressure in the middle that acts as a relative vacuum; thus, a tornado also operates in relation to gravity (indirectly). The external variable may be gravity or the magnetic field of the earth.

---

*The healing art called *pranic* healing rotates the chakras counterclockwise to cleanse the body of incoherent or spent energy.

RELATION

So we see that while both sides of a magnetic field are absolute and nonqualitative in themselves, introduce another magnetic field and suddenly polarity and relational qualities appear. The polarity and quality (e.g., NS) of one magnetic field is dependent for its very existence on the presence and position of another magnetic field. Thus, we can say that polarity is a relational or even protoperceptual quality.

This is a striking parallel to perception, which also polarizes (dualizes) and thus creates qualities, illusory qualities. As has been emphasized repeatedly throughout this book, the existence of a perceiver and the relative positions of perceiver and perceived not only determine whether the perceived is above or below, left or right, faster or slower, but they create these dualities, these relational qualities, these illusions, where none were before. In this sense the relationship of two (or more) magnetic fields to one another takes the principle of perceptual duality back to before the emergence of perceivers, which is, of course, before the emergence of life. It establishes relational polarity/duality as a quality of all being, of existence itself. Looked at from one perspective, relational duality is a protoperceptual phenomenon. Looked at from the opposite perspective, perceptual duality springs from relational polarity. The two phenomena are almost identical, follow an identical process. The only difference between them is that in perceptual duality the perceiver field is alive, and acts upon the relational qualities as if they were real. This is getting down to the Tao of being.

In summary, all being is composed of centers and their peripheries. These have spin and magnetic force and polarize in relationship to one another, attracting and repelling one another. This constitutes both a potential force for organization and an organizing principle: in short, an organizing potential. This organizing potential, in turn, gives us a way of approaching the twin cosmological problems of the spontaneous emergence of organization in Oneness and the evolution of life itself.

I am indebted to Duane Elgin, through his book *Awakening Earth*, for the idea that a *taurus* is the fundamental form and building block of the universe. A *taurus* is a fluid organization shaped like a dough-nut. Its center is open and its periphery is flowing force. One example would be a vortex, like a whirlpool or tornado. But an even more fundamental example would be a material body and its magnetic field. Every material body has a magnetic field around it, and this field forms the shape of a *taurus*. If you put a magnet under a film sprinkled with iron filings, the filings form a *taurus*. The *taurus* is empty (of magnetic force) in the center, whereas the lines of force themselves constitute the periphery or boundary. This idea of the magnetic *taurus* takes the ideas in this chapter a further step toward completion.

BEGINNINGS

From not thing, something comes

The most fundamental cosmological question of all, the one that has to eventually be answered for man to have a sense that he re-ally understands, is how did something come out of nothing. This book takes aim at different aspects of that question. I do not pre-tend to have the answer. Perhaps the whole answer, like Oneness itself will never be known in human terms, will in the final analysis prove to be unknowable. But I do know that the key to the riddle, as in most riddles, lies in how we ask the question. We are thinking about it and formulating it in an erroneous way and it is misleading us. How did something come out of nothing? Let us reexamine the question. Something and nothing, like beginning and end, are duali-ties, perceptual illusions, while thingness itself is only a perceptual category. It is obviously a trick question. How did one illusion, one perceptual category, come out of another. If we can figure out how to ask the question, indeed figure out what the question is in "real" terms, without perceptual illusions and perceptual categories, per-haps we can get around the paradox into which it has corraled us and begin to answer it. If we can't, perhaps there is no question! Perhaps the question, indeed the very problem, is an illusion.

Turtles

The problem of origins, of how something came from nothing, re-calls a story that I believe comes from William James. I paraphrase from memory. After a lecture on the history of science in which he mentioned that the earth was round and spinning in orbit, an elderly woman came up to him and disputed the point. "That's all very well for you to say, Mr. James," she said, "but everyone knows that the earth is flat and standing on the back of a giant turtle." "And what is that turtle standing on?" the lecturer asked. "Why another larger turtle," she replied, after a moment's hesitation. "And what is that turtle standing on?" the lecturer came back again. The women hesi-tated; then a sly grin came over her face. "You're very clever, Mr. James, and I see what you're getting at, but it's no use. It's turtles all the way down!"

A lot of the questions posed in this chapter and indeed in the book as a whole are related to that fundamental query of how did something come out of nothing. The principle of looking to the terms of the question for the answer applies throughout. As long as we re-main stuck in the universe of our perceptions, with its concomitant logical and linguistic syntaxes of duality, we are stuck with turtles all the way down. If we posit a creator, the question remains where that creator came from. If we posit a knower, the question remains who knows that knower. If we posit a basic building block or fun-damental energy, the question remains of what that was constructed from. If we posit the big bang, the question remains what banged and where it came from. If we get to the end of line with respect to causal attribution and say petulantly, well, it always was…though thwarted, the questions still remain, leaving us dissatisfied. What always was, how come, how did it get there, why is something here, why are we here, why isn't there nothing here? The dualistic logic of perception demands a nothing where there is a thing, as well as an antecedent, a cause.

What we need is a nonmaterial starting point, something that al-ways was there, not because it is a thing but because it is not a thing. But what could this "not a thing" be? Words and syntax are about to fail me, but try to see where I am going. What could a "not thing" be? What is and was always there? Idea, but with no one to hold the idea...principle...natural law...abstraction. Something like the Chinese concept of Tao...the way...the way things are...have to be...if and when they are. Something like a tautology...something that's true in itself. Tautologies are and were always there. Tautologies rest on nothing but themselves, they are intrinsically and self-evidently true. I am what I am. In the beginning was the truth? No, there was no beginning, just truth. Truth is the seed, that which is always, the eternal truth! But how could a tautology create a universe?

Let's try an example. Let's go back to my idea of centers. Any dimensional space imaginable is divisible into infinite points or centers.* That's a tautology; that's truth. (Any space of three or more dimensions, that is. A one-dimensional space is a point of itself. By the way, I don't mean the exact centers of a space, just centers of themselves.) Every center has a periphery. That's definitional, a tautology, a truth. If two or more centers share the universe they are in some relationship to one another. Tautology. If the centers spin, or indeed have any motion, the relationship of the motion depends on the relationship of the centers. Tautology! If the spin projects or generates a force, the relationship of the forces will be dependent on the relationship of the centers. Tautology.

Now for polarity. If the spin/force of centers adds or subtracts to one another, depending on relative direction of the spin, then the effects will depend on relative positions. Tautology. Therefore, polarity emerges as a function of the relationship between two or more spinning centers. (Refer to the discussion above.) If the (magnetic) force generated by a spinning center attracts or repels the force of another spinning center depending on relative spin directions, then the centers will attract or repel one another according to their relative positions. Tautology.

In this way centers will assemble themselves into various multi-

*Can you call Oneness a space, to say nothing of a dimensional space? Probably not, but I do not have any way of designating or conceptualizing a space that is not a space. Can the "not a space" of Oneness be divided up into centers? Your guess is as good as mine. We are out in space in more ways than one here!

centered organizations. Conjecture. In this way atoms could form out of charged particles and molecules could form out of atoms. Conjecture.

THE INTELLIGENCE OF LIFE

The equation between polarity and perception established earlier in this chapter creates a bridge between aperceptual and perceptual reality and provides an approach to the problem of the emergence of life from nonlife. The above topic, *Beginnings*, takes the problem of ultimate origins one step further. Now we address a question that has a significant bearing on magnetism, polarity, and the emergence of organization from chaos. It is how did the consciousness or intelligence of life come to be? Just as we question the dualities of something and nothing, and beginning and end, we need to question the dualities of conscious and unconscious, knowing and not knowing, sentient being and nonsentient being, realizing that they too, like something and nothing, are perceptual categories and illusions.

If we reject the dualities of consciousness and unconsciousness (in the sense of nonconsciousness), what we are left with? We are left with the alternative suppositions that consciousness never existed, always existed; or most puzzling of all, that both are true. Let us briefly examine these choices.

If consciousness doesn't exist, never existed, what are we to make of our experience of it? The only possibility left is that it too is an illusion, a perception. But a perception of what? In the final analysis there is only one thing to be perceived and that is Oneness itself. If Being is the common denominator of Oneness—i.e., there are many forms in Oneness, but they all exist, have being—then we may presume to conclude that consciousness is the perception, the illusory form, of Being. But even illusion has its reality, its substrate in the aperceptual realm. What is illusory about illusion is the quality of the experience, not that which is being experienced. So, following this line of reasoning, it is possible that in Being, there exists a substrate of the illusory experience of consciousness, leaving us with the question of what it could possibly be.

On the other hand, if consciousness, the same consciousness we experience and cherish, is real and always existed, even before the emergence of life, we are confronted with an excessively egalitarian challenge. Not only do we have to extend the very same consciousness we enjoy as humans to all animals and plants, including slugs, slime, and lichen, but we also must extend it to all manner of inorganic substances as well: rocks, crystals, atoms, stars. Not only could the person of strict Buddha conscience not eat animals, but respecting all sentient beings he could not eat plants, cut down a tree and use the wood, chisel something out of rock, or even use fire. He would be left with nothing to eat, nothing to wear, no place to live, without even ground to walk on. He could not even choose to die without violating the rights of those hoards of sentient beings, his organs, the cells they are made of, the chemicals they are made of, and the atoms that the chemicals are made of. There are only two ways out of such a procrustean enlightenment. The first is to declare that you don't care, that number one is all that is important to you and the other sentient beings can go hang. In which case you might just as well eat babies as tofu. The second is to demote consciousness, to posit that it is not all that it is cracked up to be, no big thing, not special, not sacred, not the most prized possession of the individual ego, in fact not individual at all. Rather it is universal, ubiquitous, ordinary, transferable, inexhaustible, indestructible; and not deserving of special treatment or even acknowledgment, let alone reverence. In this case, however, if we are not to hold consciousness sacred, is there any reason to hold life sacred?

Both suppositions, that consciousness never existed and always existed, are converging on the same territory, which brings us to the third supposition, i.e., that both are true! If consciousness is a perception of some aspect of our Being, as well as Being itself, an aspect at once eternal, universal, and ordinary, then both suppositions would be true. Consciousness never existed; we experience only the illusion of consciousness, the perception of Being. And illusion doesn't exist, not really! On the other hand, some not-thing, some substrate of the illusion of consciousness does really exist, has always existed. So what is this aspect of Being?

Let's go back to the summary statement of the previous section. All Being is composed of centers and their peripheries. These have spin and magnetic force, and polarize in relationship, attracting and repelling one another. Could this spin, this "magnetic" force, arising out of this one not-thing of a center and its periphery, be, among other not-things, the substrate of consciousness? Perhaps not, as it is, in its raw form as principle and process, force and potential, but as what it has become?

To continue with the summary statement...This constitutes both a potential force for organization and an organizing principle: in short, an organizing potential. So what has it become? It has become all the organizations in Being, all the ones in Oneness, electrons, atoms, molecules, planets, stars; cells, genes, plants, animals; humans. If this is the case, our consciousness would be the perception of what we are as a highly evolved interrelationship, a vast organization of organizations of polarized centers combining like a monumental, living tinker toy. And somehow in that organization of organizations has evolved our flesh and bone, our nervous system and brain, our physical body and our energy body...all composed of centers and their magnetic fields, magnetic *tauruses*, polarized and assembled in energetic relationship to one another, nourished in a sea of other external magnetic fields. Consciousness as we experience it would be the perception of this, while in reality it would also be the substrate, the no-thing that consciousness is.

In a very real sense, then, this force could be part of the intelligence of the universe. It is not the intelligence of the universe in the godlike way we think of intelligence, as something that knows... knows what to do...how to make things...what comes next...something that watches, balances, sees rights and wrongs. No, it is intelligence in a much more reactive sense, process, just what-comes-next way. It is intelligence as center-peripheries, spin, magnetic field, relational polarity, repulsion-attraction, tautology, the cosmos just doing its thing in the long march from chaos to systems to life. It is the organizing principle that combines and builds energy centers into their forms as atoms, molecules, minerals, cells, people, and planets. It is the force that makes up the life force that we perceive as consciousness.

Briefly summarized, magnetic force, spin, and relational polarity…are one part of the intelligence of the universe and the force that the entities we perceive as conscious are composed of.

PROTO-EVOLUTION

Another variable works hand in hand with relational polarity to make up the intelligence of the universe. Just as relational polarity is a protoperceptual variable, there is a proto-evolutionary variable and that is self-selection. Self-selection works largely by the laws of intrinsic stability. These are another set of tautologies.

Basically, energy centers attract and repel one other randomly through polarity, eventually trying out all the combinations that are mathematically and physically possible within the matrix of a given energy level. This is the way atoms and molecules are built. However, a number of variables determines which atoms and molecules endure and go on to build yet more elaborate structures. One of these is the intrinsic stability of the structure. Some atoms are structurally stable, while others have an tendency to jump into another form. Some molecules are relatively inert or combine only with themselves, while others have a tendency to combine with or be degraded by other molecules. These are stability factors. There are other stability factors like heat, pressure, the presence of catalysts and enzymes, whether they are in solution and what substance they are dissolved in, etc.

I call self-selection proto-evolution because like natural selection it determines what substances survive from a pool of variability (and some of these survivors go on to combine with others to create yet more elaborate substances). The difference between proto-evolution and evolution is that these substances are not alive and their survival does not depend on the success of their behavior (in the sense of self-interest).

Also, similarly to the way that perception determines evolution, protoperception determines proto-evolution. The difference here is that perception creates all sorts of illusory qualities relative to the perceiver, while in polarity there are no qualities, no illusions, and no perceivers. The only thing polarity determines is which *tauruses* stick together where. But this is sufficient. Although simpler and more mechanical than self-interest behavior, it is behavior nevertheless and it creates a stunning profusion of forms for proto-evolution to select from.

So we see that perception has strong antecedents in polarity, just as natural selection has strong antecedents in self-selection. I am forming a vision where perception comes from protoperception and evolution comes from proto-evolution in a continuum of process and form. The evolutionary process by which all organic forms develop is an amalgam of perception, self-interested behavior, and natural selection. Whereas the proto-evolutionary process, by which all inorganic forms developed, is a combination of polarity, random polar combinations, and self-selection. The two processes of proto-evolution and evolution are more a continuum than separate. Together they form a unified matrix that lights the way for a continuous accounting of the emergence of inorganic forms from energy centers, and organic forms from inorganic forms.

17. ONENESS, GOD, AND SPIRITUALITY

ONENESS AND RELIGION

Some people, after struggling through a few chapters of *Oneness Perceived*, ask me how does it tell us to better ourselves, assuming that any work of philosophy should do that at the very least. Others try to raise Oneness to a religious or mystical principle, or equate it with God. I, myself, following the inner logic of the book, have been increasingly veering off into the direction of physics, of which I know little, so it is with relief that I allow myself to be pulled up short in familiar territory, at least for the present, to address these questions.

Oneness is just reality. I would say physical reality except of course that physicality, with its overtones of fundamental matter, is just another illusion. Oneness has only a few characteristics that we can be reasonably sure of, most of then negative: it is one (i.e., non-dual), it is unknowable, the phenomena and laws of the Newtonian universe don't apply (that is, it is devoid of time, space, and other dimensions as well as their interrelationships), and finally it is.

Oneness is not a mystical principle of any sort, at least not if mystical principles are thought of as beyond the ordinary. If the spiritual dimension is real, I suppose Oneness encompasses it, since it encompasses everything that is real, but it is not the spiritual dimension as people ordinarily conceive of it. Indeed, I suspect nothing is. Neither is Oneness God in any of the usual senses of the word. It is a broader concept than God and a less personal one. It doesn't hold any secret for man, and it doesn't care a fig what he does or what happens to him. Oneness is simply what is, and it is a mistake to reify or deify it. One might as well worship DNA and strive to live according to the precepts of Planck's constant. However, if we ask the question what does Oneness have to do with God and spirituality, the answer is everything.

As Aldous Huxley illustrated in *The Perennial Philosophy*, a common vision originates and runs through almost all religious traditions. Such disparate traditions as Christianity, Judaism, Vedanta, Taoism, Buddhism, Zen, and Sufism as well as countless others spring from this vision. It is the vision of the founding visionaries, whether they be Jesus or Buddha, or any of the disciples, yogis, swamis, bodhisattvas, and sufis that recorded and added to the teachings of the world's major religions.

All these visionaries worked within the cultural contexts of their time and place as well as the belief systems and languages through which their perception was expressed, interpreted, and frequently distorted. Depending on these belief systems, as well as historical process and the quality of the priests, these spiritual traditions evolved into God-centered religions or enlightenment-centered ones, or then commonly split into factions, some of which were more God-centered and some which are more enlightenment-centered. So in Christianity, the epitome of a God-centered religion, where Jesus is thought of as the son of God, we find enlightenment-centered, mystical factions like Gnostic Christianity and Quakerism, where God is seen as in oneself. Whereas in Buddhism, the epitome of an enlightenment-centered religion, where Buddha is just a man who meditated under a tree until he discovered his Self nature, there are factions that enshrine gilded Buddhas and feed them saffron rice.

The God-centered religions preach an exterior deity who is variously the creator, organizer, guardian, moral authority, judge, punisher, and rewarder, whether here or in heaven. His "priests" admonish us to bow to his authority, supplicate his mercy, worship, have faith, and above all to believe.

The enlightenment-centered religions, on the other hand, do not revolve around a deity or his authority or the authority of his priests. Instead they revolve around a mystical vision, a perception of self and world, a realization of God within. Every person is potentially capable of realizing this vision by following certain prescribed disciplines and practices, thus in a sense becoming gods themselves, or at least realizing that about their nature which is holy and that about the universe which is sacred. The priests are teachers of these practices and guides to this perception, which presumably they all have first attained themselves. If God is anything in the enlightenment religions, it is a deified principle or a universal process. These principles are to be ascertained and perhaps aligned with, but not to be worshiped (although there is no accounting for the actions and beliefs of those whose zeal exceeds their understanding).

Whether a spiritual tradition has evolved into a God-centered, authoritarian form or an enlightenment-centered, empowering form, probably all spiritual traditions originate in realization. Whether this realization is called Satori, nirvana, epiphany, God-consciousness, self-realization, liberation, or enlightenment, it is more or less the same thing. For simplicity we will refer to all versions of this realization as enlightenment or enlightened perception. This realization includes understanding the unity of Oneness and consciousness, and the dualizing effect of perception. It is basically the same realization that *Oneness Perceived* has been written from.

ONENESS, GOD, AND EVERYTHING

Is God Oneness, Oneness God? It seems to be a proposition with which this book is continually flirting. Of course, Oneness is not God to people who conceive of God as a patriarchal figure taking a personal interest in their conduct and their fate. However, there are some more sophisticated notions of God that overlap with the concept of Oneness. Let's explore some of them.

One widely held notion of God is that it is everything! Some people have the idea that saying God is everything is the same as saying God is Oneness. However, this is a fallacy that ignores the distinction between aperceptual and perceptual reality which is at the heart of my vision. To say God is everything is to say that he is the sum of all possible or at least existing things (illusions). Since all possible things comprises an infinite set, it is saying that God is infinite, which is theologically praiseworthy, but it is also saying that God is illusory, which is anathema. Saying God is Oneness is preferable in that it asserts his universality and preserves his realness, but unfortunately it puts him outside of the category of that which is known or can be known.

If, despite this point, one stubbornly holds to the position that God is everything, one runs into more problems. First, the word "God" is superfluous as a synonym for everything; "everything" will do nicely. Second, everything is simply too broad a definition for God. A definition that indiscriminately takes in the entire apparent universe is useless. A definition implies a boundary. If God is everything, what's the big deal. If there is nothing that is not God, what possible use is God or even the idea of God to anybody? Why believe in it?

For the definition and therefore the concept to be meaningful and useful, a boundary has to be found between God and not-God. Is there a class of existence from which we can exclude the "God as everything"? Of course, if he is perceptual reality or appearance, we could exclude aperceptual reality or Oneness from our definition of God. Then if we posit a universe that contains both illusion and reality and exclude reality, we have a definition. God is illusion as opposed to (aperceptual) reality, a possible definition if not a satisfactory one.

Taking it the other way seems more promising. If God is Oneness, aperceptual reality, we can exclude illusion from our definition of God, and at least he exists in reality.

However, either way we run into some illogic. We know illusion exists (in our experience), and we infer that reality exists (even though we can't experience it). For any boundary between illusion and reality to be meaningful, they must coexist in one realm. There must be a potential juxtaposition. The question, then, is: in what realm do they coexist?

They don't coexist in our experience and they don't coexist outside of our experience. They don't coexist in reality and they don't coexist in illusion. As far as I can see they coexist nowhere. If they don't coexist, the concept of a boundary between them is nonsensical and we are left where we started out (unless, of course, you call nonexistence of coexistence a boundary).

For that matter, can we really say illusion exists? Certainly it doesn't exist in the same sense of the word that aperceptual reality exists. Of course it exists as illusion, but that is somewhat a contradiction in terms. Although illusion is signified by neural events and in that sense must exist in aperceptual reality or Oneness, that which the neural events signify does not exist in Oneness. On the other hand, we can only *infer* that aperceptual reality exists as a substrate to illusion, i.e., is that which perception is interpreting. (In fact, we know numerous examples, like color perception, in which the inference would be false.) Since reality or Oneness cannot be directly observed or otherwise known, we cannot say for sure it exists. On the other hand, since illusion is illusory, we can be sure it doesn't exist (at least if aperceptual reality is the criterion for existence). Interestingly there is a convention in physics that if there is no possible way of knowing something or getting information about it, it is held not to exist (as, for example, the universe before the big bang). Unfortunately, if physics were to strictly apply this rule to itself, it could not posit that physical reality exists, thus ending or at least redefining their mission as a science. Perhaps this is why they have not thought of it!

My position on this matter is that there is a base level aperceptual reality, but it is devoid of qualities and therefore we are devoid of ways of knowing it. (What a nonthing devoid of qualities might be like is beyond the scope of my imagination, qualitatively bound as I am.) Therefore, all qualities and dimensions we attribute to reality are artifacts of our senses or projections of our self-perceived dimensions; that is, they are qualities of ourselves.

Now, however, we are getting into hot water again. If we can't posit a whole in which reality and illusion coexist, what happens to our definition and what happens to God? If God is everything, all illusions, he is unreal, which is to say that he ceases to exist (save for the most undemanding of intellects). On the other hand, if God is Oneness, we have to, as always, take it on faith.

GOD IS IN EVERYTHING

A more plausible version of the "God is everything" position is "God is *in* everything." This can be generously interpreted as pointing to the Oneness underlying all appearance and in this sense it can be understood as a variation of the statement that God is Oneness. A problem with this, however, is that it rests on the aforementioned inference that Oneness exists as a substrate to illusion. If this were strictly true the statement would be acceptable, but what if it is not true? What happens to the statement that God is in everything if things are illusory, perceptual creations that have just a distant relationship to Oneness?

Why Define God at All?

I believe that there is no such thing as God outside of humankind, no absolute God. God is a human phenomenon. It seems to me silly, at this stage in man's understanding of the universe and his place in it, to posit that there is a God that has an objective existence outside of human experience and need. To the contrary, it seems self-evident that God is whatever men choose to call God. However, if God is not anything, if there is no one, specific, unique God to be discovered, why we are trying to define God in the first place? Why not just dismiss the whole question as a fantasy of primitive man and primitive minds?

There are several good reasons not to dismiss God out of hand. Not the least of which is that numerous good minds, even great minds, seem to believe in him or it. Also, he has been the subject of sense and nonsense, learned speculation and ignorant belief, reverence and awe throughout history. Another reason is that there are a number of feeling states that seem to compel people to belief and faith. The last reason is that there is still a lot we neither know nor understand.

So, although I firmly believe that even if there is no real, absolute God, there clearly is something to talk about and maybe even account for. Even if there is no absolute God out there, even if God is a just a human phenomenon, the human experience and conviction of God needs to be addressed.

GOD AND CONSCIOUSNESS

There are three categories of gods (God experiences): outer, inner, and meditative. The outer gods are primarily explanatory. They are the gods people have created to explain and account for what they don't understand. The inner gods are subconscious. People have experiences and identify them as coming from God. (Of course, this is in a sense explanatory as well.) The meditative experiences are not so much called God as identified with God or some indivisible principle of consciousness that seems to roughly correspond with what other people call God.

The outer gods represent natural laws and therefore tend to be masculine, paternal, implacable, and unsympathetic, God the creator, king, father, and judge. The sun and moon do not alter their course to suit man. These are also the gods of need, the gods men need to make sense of and regulate their world. The emotions these gods arouse are awe, fear, incomprehensibility, and a sense of personal insignificance. In the Judeo-Christian world, this is the God of the Old Testament.

The inner gods, those of the subconscious, tend to be feminine and maternal. They elicit not awe but adoration, and stand for tenderness, love, and compassion. They are Mary and strangely enough Jesus himself (who although a man was more maternal than paternal), as well as the gods of the natural world (assorted goddesses and nymphs), and of personal creativity (the muse).

A variation of the inner gods is provided by the emotional responses we have to the natural world. We witness the dawn and a feeling of awe comes over us. God is at work. This is not the attempt to explain why the sun rises and the birds start to sing by invoking God, this is invoking God to account for an emotional or aesthetic response.

Finally, meditators often equate with God the experience of luminous voidness or pure consciousness they get to in their meditations. However, it is important to be aware that this is by no means always the case. There is an equally strong tendency in the meditative traditions to consider meditation as experiential metaphysics, an attempt to realize the essence of both humanity and reality through meditation, the examination of meditative experience from postmeditative states, and the incorporation of ensuing insights into subsequent meditations. This is true of the teachings of Buddha and of Buddhism in general, although there are popular forms of Buddhism that have taken on devotional overtones.

Whether man makes God out of the need to explain why the sun rises, the need to explain his mystical experience, or just as another name for pure consciousness, whether he makes God consciously or subconsciously, it is clear he makes him to explain or at least to name. What does that imply? Are all the mysteries of the world, both outer and inner, destined for eventual classification and explanation? Is man's knowledge destined to someday be complete, and thus is God slated for obsolescence? Are God's days numbered? Or is there a mystery that will be always with us?…a mystery and therefore a need!

To take it another way: Does the fact that all gods, all forms of God, are at base names or explanations, mean that there really is no God? Or can there be another possibility? Can it be that at bottom man is positing God to explain God?

The explanatory God was always arbitrary, born of necessity. However, the old explanatory God of the prescientific age is no longer as necessary as it once was. He was born in a time when he was needed to explain and account for all we didn't understand. But he became an anachronism as we went into the age when science thought it would eventually know everything.

As it dawns on modern man that science may give him the power to "know about," but never to "know," the necessity for an explanatory God may reemerge. However, there no longer will be employment for God as a prescientific black box, the creator of life or the cause of the universe. All we will be left with will be the irreducible. What is the irreducible? It is the unperceivable, unknowable, the essence of being. Also, it is the process intrinsic to presence, that by which presence transforms, organizes, and perceives, that which Chinese philosophers call the Tao. Do we want to call the aperceptual God? Do we want to call universal process God? Put another way, do we want to call Oneness and its ways God? It is certainly a defensible, even attractive position.

However, it seems to me that when people invoke God they are in all honesty implying something more (and less) than Oneness and its Tao or process. The same people who, if pushed, defensively retreat to one or another of these nontheist positions (i.e., that God is everything, is in everything, is Oneness, is natural law, etc.), are only too quick when among coreligionists to resurrect the old God, to reattribute God with a personal interest in our individual conduct and fates, as well as with a moral standard, the powers of judgment, punishment and reward, and other attributes equally incompatible with these definitions. We should not try to have it both ways. If God is a personage, a deity, a thing, he certainly isn't Oneness. On the other hand, if God is just Oneness, does the word God convey a communicative advantage over the word Oneness? Certainly Oneness does not convey any of these qualities of concern and involvement that people are so fond of attributing to God.

Are the gods that religions believe in implicit indicators of their level of understanding of Oneness and illusion? If so, consider this: Judaism countered classical polytheism with monotheism, the one, paternal God, suggesting an equivalence between God and Oneness. Christianity, however, reinstated a limited polytheism, which was a throwback to the multiplicity of appearances and explanatory principles of perception. It pluralized the one God with Jesus, Mary, the Holy Ghost, and various saints (if you pray to it, it's a God), creating a religion where God the Father, the One, still got lip service but clearly took a backseat to his creations. An effete religion was created in Jesus's name, one where not living by the law but preserving the appearance of it kept you in God's grace. This became a religion not of the just man but rather the repentant child, the forgiven sinner, a religion not of implacable law but of indulgence, of saying you're sorry. This is not the religion of the Jewish God but of the Jewish mother.

One of the main contentions of *Oneness Perceived* is that there always will remain a mystery, an unknowable. This mystery is no less than the real nature of aperceptual reality, of Oneness. In a manner of speaking the mystery is no less than everything or even more accurately, of no thing. Off the edge of the perceptual map, beyond the flatland of knowledge, into the unknowable, will forever lie that space that the cartographers of science will be able to do no better than indicate with the legend "Here there be dragons." There will always be a mystery to explain, or at least to name, and therefore there will always be a position open for an explanatory God. In that sense, too, you could call Oneness God!

ORIGINAL PERCEPTION

There exists an almost universal preconception that enlightenment consists of seeing something, either God or ultimate reality. Following both this preconception and the thesis of this book, it is tempting to jump to the conclusion that enlightenment is the perception of Oneness. This mistake has misled many seekers back into the labyrinth of illusion just when they were at the threshhold of liberation.

If Oneness is indeed unknowable, made unknowable by the very act of perception, then enlightenment cannot be the perception of it. To hold that it is so is to misunderstand or ignore the relationship of perception and reality and invite magical thinking. Oneness cannot be known for two unarguable reasons. One, to perceive is to dualize and make illusory. Two, people know in terms of sensory analogs that themselves are illusory. Try to describe or conceptualize something you know without resorting to sensory analogs and you will experience the problem.

However, to hold to the position that enlightenment cannot be the perception of Oneness forces you into a choice. Either there is no such thing as enlightenment, which directly or by implication denies the basis of most of the spiritual traditions of the world, or enlightenment is something else altogether. In which case what could it be?

I have already introduced this subject in the chapter on "The Evolving Self" where I called enlightened perception original perception! I said there that while perception of Oneness (in the sense of real knowing) is an impossibility, perception from Oneness is not.

In the act of original perception, Oneness perceives itself as self and other, rendering itself dual and illusory. The self pole of this duality becomes the seed of self-concept. That is, it develops into self-concept through successive acts of perception. (The other pole becomes the world.)

Can a person really return from perceiving from self-concept to perceiving from Oneness? Let's consider it. Everyone is born into an individuated presence as a conscious point of perception. Then, additional perceptions fast overlay this given with self-concepts. This layer of self-concepts acts in lieu of its Oneness or core Self as a locus from which to perceive. Perceiving from self-concepts creates that level of illusion I call cognitive illusion.

It is possible to largely strip back these self-concepts (through certain psychotechnologies, i.e., psychotherapy, meditation, hypnosis, psychedelic drugs, etc.) and perceive from our core self. Perception without self-concepts, directly from the core or Oneness self, is Original Perception. I believe Original Perception is part of the unstated goal of most spiritual traditions and should be the goal of all psychotherapies as well. Original Perception imparts enormous clarity, serenity, and balance to human consciousness.

However, might there be something more to be attained? Can one go beyond, or should I say behind, his core self, his biogenetic given? Can one transcend the personal level and go to where he is just a point in Oneness perceiving? If so, this would be original perception in a cosmic sense. The person would be perceiving from a point that is devoid of qualities, impersonal, contentless, without self-concept or even self-reference. In that case we have to consider what the world would look like from such a point. We would expect a point in Oneness to be devoid of qualities, without even dimension or location. The universe it perceived would be devoid of qualities as well. What could that be like? Perhaps it is an awareness of nothingness without awareness of self.

Another, more extreme, possibility is that a person could reach the level where he does not perceive from a point in Oneness but instead knows as the whole of Oneness itself. In that case our identification would no longer be with self but with the entirety of Oneness. In keeping with this, we would expect perception and consciousness to undergo a cataclysmic figure ground reversal. Instead of peering out into a sea of Oneness from a point, we would sense points, likes grains of sand, imbedded in the limitless sea of Oneness that we are! From this perspective all things, however huge, would seem mere specks, all durations, however long, would seem mere moments, all energy events, however vast, would seem mere puffs of air.

But wait, doesn't this perspective seem familiar? Have we not read accounts of experiences that sound like this in the spiritual writings of the great traditions? Has this already been achieved by certain adepts through contemplation and meditation? Is this the reversal, the revolution of consciousness to which the great, historic visionaries, Lao-tzu, Buddha, Jesus, and countless others have come?

Perhaps this possibility of knowing from all Oneness is a human potential that has been reached and will be reached time and time again. Perhaps it is everyone's birth potential. Perhaps this possibility is the milestone in evolution that, more than anything else, more than the development of language and technology, marks the place of humanity in the cosmic scheme.

18. ONENESS, CONSCIOUSNESS, AND EXISTENCE

That which knows existence
Is identical to the existence it is knowing.
This is the underlying unity.

ONENESS AND CONSCIOUSNESS

How do we describe Oneness? Not by what it is, but by what it is not. Not a perceptual category, it is no thing. Devoid of physical characteristics, it is the void. Without qualities, it lacks dimension, materiality, space, location, velocity. Without past or future, it is eternally now. Neither here nor there, it is everywhere. It is only an inference, insubstantial, void and unknowable. Yet beyond argument it exists, because without it there would be no existence to perceive. To indicate that through void it exists, pervasive and omnipresent, we have to call it something. Another good name for it is presence.

Oneness cannot be known in its reality; it can only be perceived.

Perception, like a ray of sunlight piercing dusty air, makes the invisible motes glitter like fool's gold. But if you mistake it for the real thing, you are the fool. Perception gives Oneness its appearances, solidifies the ghost. In fact, all of Oneness's apparent dimensions and qualities, its materiality, space, location, movement, temporality, are given to it by the act of perception. Oneness takes on its substance by colliding with the substance of our senses and the cunning of our minds. Oneness cannot be known in its reality because there is no *thing* to be known.

Mysteriously, this insubstantial Oneness, this empty presence, this nonthing, can divide itself amoebalike into boundaried gestalts. Even more mysteriously, this *division* of nothing is not fully real; it is nominal. It is an acting division, an arbitrary boundary viewed from an arbitrary center. Oneness is all there is. Oneness can't come apart; it can just act as if it is apart. Through this nominal division of no thing into parts, one part of no thing can perceive and act on another. This is the way the universe interacts, sees itself, and evolves. It has to be this way, for the universe can only be tangible to itself as it acts in separation.

But now let's reflect…what have I just described? I have described a presence that is void, no thing, insubstantial, without qualities, dimensions, materiality, space, location, movement, temporality. Yet, through apparent division and self-perception, it is given the appearance of these things, given thingness itself. I have described a presence that can divide without really dividing, and by this nominal division engender parts that can perceive and act on one another, evolving more and more complex parts. I have described a presence that is unknowable in itself, yet can know.

Only one thing in our experience fits this description: Consciousness itself! Can it be that Oneness is Consciousness, Consciousness Oneness? Can it be that the deeper nature of this immaterial material, this insubstantial substance we have been calling Oneness, is Consciousness?

If true, the implication is truly amazing. It means that the essential nature of perception, though illusory as to form, is the same as the essential nature of that which is perceived. The subject is essentially the same as the object, context the same as content, perceiver the same as perceived. Oneness, Consciousness, is truly perceiving itself. *(At this point it seems fitting to capitalize the first letter of Consciousness, just as we do for Self, Oneness, and God.)*

Thus, the circle turns from illusion to reality again. Because if all is Consciousness, both perceiver and perceived, both duality and Oneness, then all forms of Consciousness are fully real (not equally material). In one sense the perceptual illusion is just as real as the underlying Oneness, and the second realm of reality is just that, a realm of reality. Perceptions, though illusory as to their referent in Oneness (i.e., they are not void and Oneness is), are essentially real. They are just what is created when Consciousness individuates into life and perceives itself from a particular vantage point. They are creations made out of the clay of Consciousness, just as are energy and matter, heavenly bodies and their gravity, you and I.

In a hologram, the interaction of two sources of informed energy (in this case light) create an interference pattern that yields an image, a virtual reality. Extending the metaphor of the holistic universe, if the two waves of informed energy consist of Consciousness instead of light, the image, the virtual reality that the interference pattern creates, is also Consciousness. It is as real as the sources it comes from. What's more, once formed it can be a source in itself. Virtual reality is as real as real reality, illusion as real as Oneness, perceptual experience as real as that being perceived. Everything is as real as everything else, and as real as every not-thing as well. Furthermore, everything is different, different in form and in formlessness, different in qualities and different in voidness. It's all different, yet it is all constructed of the same clay, and that clay is Consciousness. And the impulse that constructs the clay is also Consciousness. It is the same and it is different; it is illusion and it is reality.

At least two major enlightenment traditions, the Kashmir Shaivist, which flourished in Kashmir between the eighth and the thirteenth centuries, which in turn was a refinement of Vedanta, and the Chinese Chan (Zen) Buddhist, have come to this same insight in different cultural contexts. As a matter of fact, the reality of Consciousness and the equivalence of phenomena and the void are the principle differences between earlier forms of Vedanta and Kashmir Shaivism.

> God is Consciousness and bliss and ever one with His nature. Similarly God, in bondage as the embodied soul, always carries out the five processes on a small scale.
>
> The Svacchanda Tantra says that God's nature, even in the state of bondage, is Consciousness. The Lord takes on a body, prana, and sense organs of His own will and acts accordingly. He manifests the same objects outside that flash in His awareness (as) within Him(self). He performs the five processes in a limited way with limited power. When God, acting in the outer world through body, prana, and senses, perceives different objects in different instants of time and at different points of space, that is creation. Sustenance is the perceiving of an object for a length of time. Dissolution is the disappearance of an object into the mind, as when one object is replaced in awareness by another. Concealment of its true nature comes about when undifferentiated Consciousness differentiates itself into manifold forms. To vibrate once again as pure undifferentiated light, after manifesting as diverse objects, is grace or revelation.
>
> There is an important difference between the doctrine of Brahman, held by the followers of Vedanta, and this philosophy of Self-recognition. According to Vedanta, Brahman is the cause of the universe; He is ever pure, awake, and free. He is bliss. But the world is false, the result of ignorance. Only Brahman is real, and one becomes Brahman when false knowledge is replaced by true. On the other hand, the philosophy of Self-recognition teaches that the world is not false.
>
> From: *Nothing Exists that is Not Siva by Muktananda*, SYDA
> Foundation, South Fallsburg, NY, 1997

In the twelfth century, in a completely different cultural context, the Chinese Chan (Zen) master Kakuan created the Ten Bulls, a series of ten illustrated poems and commentaries detailing the journey to realizing One's true nature (symbolized as a bull). The journey begins with the realization that the bull is lost. It progresses through the tracking, finding, taming, and riding home of the bull. Then, in the seventh and eighth bull, appearances are transcended, and the seeker rests in the void of pure Consciousness. But in the ninth bull the circle turns and the reality of appearance is reaffirmed.

The commentary on the ninth bull goes like this: *"One who is not attached to form need not be reformed. The water is emerald, the mountain is indigo, and I see that which is creating and that which is destroying."* In other words, the apparent reality that has been seen through as just appearance has been penetrated further, and on another level reveals itself as real after all.

Thus, in seeing that Consciousness is the underlying nature of both Oneness and perceptual appearance, we have come, via an alternate route, to the ninth bull.

(The tenth bull is entitled *In the World,* wherein the seeker, having realized the unreality of appearance and the reality of the void, has gone beyond to see the reality of both. Having reached this, he gives up seeking and takes up ordinary life again, but his being has been transformed.)

CONSCIOUSNESS, THE UNIFIED FIELD

Is Consciousness the indivisible particle, the stuff of the universe, the unified field that physics is looking for? If so, this conclusion (which, as I said, was anticipated long ago by Indian philosophy) staggers the mind. Yet, it makes sense. It fits. What is more, as you explore its implications, you realize more and more that it is the conclusion of best fit.

In order for identifying Consciousness as the "stuff of Oneness" to be a theoretical advance and not just the substitution of one name of the unknown for another, it has to have additional explanatory value. It has to fit a larger number of observations. What more do we explain by equating the no thing that is Oneness with the no thing that is Consciousness? What additional observations fit? What questions are answered?

Perhaps most significant is that it accounts in some way for the phenomenon of knowing. That we know, that we are aware, that we are conscious is inexplicable. Our experience itself, just the fact that we experience, is unfathomable. Where did it come from, how did it come to be, how does it work? Furthermore, beneath the question of how we could know that anything is lurks the larger question of how anything could know that *it is*. If Oneness, the basic "stuff" of the Universe, is Consciousness, that may not fully answer these questions, but at least the answer is imaginable.

Yet another argument for Consciousness making up the unified field of reality is this. Consciousness fits the definition of Oneness *and vice versa*. It is monolithic. It cannot be reduced to a simpler form nor raised to a more complex one. Not a particle, it cannot be split into subparticles; yet it accounts for particles and subparticles. In itself it has no perceptual qualities; it is void. Yet, upon perception it takes on infinite qualities. No matter how you divide it, it is still Consciousness. No matter how you combine it, it is still Consciousness. It takes on different forms, but all forms of it are essentially Consciousness. It is as basic and as plastic as you can get.

Also, consider the role of meditation, real meditation where one sits in the void, in pure Consciousness without thought, feeling, or sensation. For thousands of years that has been regarded as the means of awakening to reality, the reality of the nature of the universe and the reality of the nature of oneself. Why is that so? How could immersion into the void, sitting without thought or feeling, lead to an understanding of the mysteries of Self and the universe? If that self-same void is Consciousness and as such is at once the nature of Self, the nature of the universe, and the nature of Oneness, it makes sense that immersing yourself in it would lead to realizing it.

If Oneness is Consciousness, that also suggests solutions for the apparent paradoxes of physics. First of all, it addresses the mystery of nonlocality because Consciousness is nonlocal. It illuminates the problem of the observer influence, because extending Bohm's holographic metaphor, phenomena are interference patterns between the Consciousness of the observer and the Consciousness of the observed. What is more, if all is Consciousness and distinctions between observer and observed are not real, merely a matter of perspective, then observer and observed form a unity that would be expected to change with changes in their interrelationship, *i.e., observation.*

Again, if everything is basically Consciousness, then light also is Consciousness. This addresses the particle-wave paradox of quantum physics. Light can alternatively appear as particle and wave because really it is neither. Both particle and wave are perceptual constructs, appearances or observations of light, which in turn are perceptual appearances of Consciousness.

If Oneness is Consciousness, that also obviates some of the problems of creation, namely origin and purpose. Teleological causation requires the illogical proposition of something existing in the nonexistent future, whereas creation implies an infinite regression (i.e., who created the creator, what caused the first cause). Both propositions get us into absurdity theory. However, the only remaining alternative to creation is to posit an *always was.*

Consciousness cannot be derived from any other state of being, material or energetic. It is almost inconceivable to get to Consciousness from anything or anything else. If Consciousness is, and it cannot be derived from something, there is a good case for positing that it *always was,* is the *always was.* We know Consciousness is, because we are conscious and that is the only way we know it. Therefore Consciousness probably *always was.* That this should be so is still a mystery to me. However, if Consciousness *always was,* questions like where did it come from, who created it, what existed before it, and what was it created for are nonsensical and do not have to be addressed.

A FINAL PROOF

Nothing can perceive itself. An eye cannot see itself. An organization in Oneness, a gestalt, a real Self, can know itself but it cannot perceive itself. By the same token it can perceive the rest of Oneness, but it cannot know it. That is to say, it cannot know all of Oneness while being a separate organization in it. It can only know all of Oneness while being one with it. It has to give up its (self-perceived) separation to know. The boundaries between Self and other are themselves a matter of self-perception.

These self-evident principles, which I first expounded in chapters 13 and 14, if accepted, further suggest that Oneness, in all its manifestations, is consciousness. Furthermore, they suggest that perception, though another order of reality, is in the larger context real. In order for self-perception to constitute a necessary and sufficient condition for the separation of Oneness into real Selves apart, perception has to be real; it has to be a function of the selfsame reality that defines Oneness, whatever that is. Furthermore, since perception is a function of consciousness, consciousness has to be an aspect of essential stuff of the universe, the immaterial material of Oneness, as well as the material of materiality in all its forms. How else could perception, a function in and of consciousness, manifest the matter and energy of a real Self? Only if consciousness partakes of the same nature of matter and energy, can it manifest matter and energy.

CONSCIOUSNESS AND EXISTENCE

Again consider the mystery of why anything exists at all, why in fact existence exists. Even if we accept a creator for all else (despite the attendant issue of who or what created the creator), we must reject the explanation of a creator for existence. A creator for existence would definitionally precede existence and therefore could not exist. This points us in the direction of the eternal now. If we accept time as the eternal now, we are forced to conclude that existence, the essence of what exists now, always existed. Now what could have always existed? Energy, matter, gravity, light; it doesn't make sense. Where did existence come from, and where did what it came from come from? Why is something here in the first place? If you remember, I discussed this question in chapter 16, "Proto-Evolution and the Intelligence of the Universe." My answer, for better or worse, was that something that was here all the time was something that was true in itself, true in its own terms no matter what.

If something always was, neither created nor caused, then what fits this description? What is infinite and indestructibly true in itself? One possibility would be tautological propositions. Propositions that are definitionally true, propositions that are statements or equations of unity, of *Oneness!* Notice here that we are implicitly creating one of those equations. One with three parts.

Oneness = Consciousness = the always was

To make this point clear, let's look at something more familiar. An infinitude of points can fit on a line. Such propositions, because they are definitional, independent of matter or energy, are eternal. Stated or unstated, they are always true and thus always exist, at least potentially. But if propositions are independent of matter and energy, what are they dependent on? For instance, the above proposition certainly doesn't depend on the existence of a line or points on it, for these are also propositions. If anything, it depends on Consciousness, both to posit and to know these propositions. Propositions are not material or energetic. Their substance resides in their terms and their terms, in turn, rest if anywhere in Consciousness. Without Consciousness, no propositions exist. So we have encountered another turning of the circle. That which always exists is that which is true in itself (like the tautological propositions inherent in the unity of that Oneness that is Consciousness).

Tautological statements are definitionally or propositionally true in that they posit the conditions for their own validity. In other words, if there are points and a line, then it is true that an infinite number of points can fit on a line because a line is a two-dimensional extension and a point does not have any two-dimensional extension. If Oneness is, in fact, a unity bifurcated by perception in infinite ways, then each dualization, each cross section of Oneness has its own conditional or propositional reality. And this is itself a statement of the unity underlying the duality. For instance, Einstein's relativity theories, equations about the convertibility of energy and matter, are statements of the underlying unity of energy and matter in Oneness.

THE ULTIMATE TAUTOLOGY

In some way "why existence exists" is a nonquestion, traceable to an implicit assumption of duality between existence and nonexistence. This nonquestion is the ground of all illusion, all religion, and all natural philosophy. Simply and unequivocally, existence exists because nonexistence cannot exist. A thing can nonexist but existence cannot. Nonexistence is a contradiction in terms and the statement "nonexistence cannot exist" is the ultimate tautology.

When you get to the ultimate tautology, you have come to the end of the line. If you take it seriously, it ends duality, ends thought. It is the master koan. Hold it in meditation and you will be plunged into the void of nonduality. There simply isn't anyplace else to go!

Why does existence exist?
Because nonexistence cannot exist!

Why does existence exist?
Because nonexistence cannot exist!

There's nowhere else to go
Except
Beyond words, Behind thought
Dropping out of time
Hurling out of space
The instantaneous journey without end
To where you always were.

CONSCIOUSNESS AND EXISTENCE ARE EQUIVALENT

Existence offers another argument, albeit roundabout, for the identity of Oneness with Consciousness. Without Consciousness, is there existence? Certainly there is no way to know. Existence seems to be dependent on Consciousness, for without someone or something to be conscious of being, without Consciousness to reflect the universe, you cannot even say the universe is there. But is existence itself dependent on Consciousness, or is only the Consciousness of existence dependent on Consciousness? It seems incredible that existence itself is dependent on Consciousness, but there is that guideline in modern physics again, which states that if there is no way of conceivably knowing something, it cannot be posited to exist. Since without Consciousness existence cannot be known to exist, if you buy this guideline, without Consciousness existence cannot be held to exist. Even if you reject the rigorous position and hold that existence can exist without Consciousness, what could it possibly matter? Mattering, like existence itself, seems to be irretrievably hooked up with Consciousness.

In a very real sense then, the existence of anything, even Oneness itself, is dependent on Consciousness. Which brings us to the converse position that existence not only depends on Consciousness, but that Consciousness depends on existence. Without existence it is obvious that Consciousness cannot exist. So existence and Consciousness are codependent.

Which brings us to ask whether Consciousness and existence are equivalent. Remembering that other guideline of physics, which states that if it is theoretically impossible to tell the difference between things, they can be assumed equivalent, is it possible to differentiate existence and Consciousness? This is an improbable question to ask because existence with its material implications, and Consciousness with its intangible and vitalistic implications, seem so far apart in quality. However, once asked, it is an easy question to answer.

Can a situation be imagined where there is one without the other; where there is existence without Consciousness or Consciousness without existence? Nonexistent anything, even Consciousness, is certainly a contradiction in terms. Whereas there are simply no grounds for deeming existence to exist without Consciousness. Can anything exist in the absence of Consciousness? Again, there would be no way of knowing, so there is no basis for presuming it can. So existence and Consciousness co-occur and codepend. Are there any other means of differentiating them? I can't think of any! If there are no means to differentiate existence and Consciousness, they probably should be considered equivalent and basically names, aspects, or viewpoints of the same presence.

Consciousness and existence are equivalent. Cs = Ex

If Consciousness and existence are equivalent, how does this imply that Oneness is Consciousness? If Consciousness and existence are equivalent, which we have already discussed, and Oneness and existence are equivalent, then Oneness and Consciousness are equivalent.

If Cs = Ex and Ex = O, then Cs = O. O = Oneness.

But are Oneness and existence equivalent? Can you imagine a situation where there is one without the other? Certainly, where Oneness exists there is existence. If Oneness exists, if anything exists, existence exists. So the presence of Oneness does entail existence!

Reversing this, does existence entail Oneness? At the risk of being simplistic if not sophistic, existence is a common denominator, it transcends all boundaries. Everything that exists has existence in common. In this sense if no other, existence inescapably entails a level of Oneness. So let's say that existence entails Oneness as well as the other way around. This being true, then Ex= O, and the whole three-part equation is true!

However, where you have Oneness, you have the potential for duality. Where does duality come into the picture? *If duality could exist independently of Oneness, then existence and Oneness would not be equivalent.* Duality exists (in some sense); yet its existence is dependent on (the perception of) Oneness. Since duality does not exist without Oneness (although Oneness might exist without duality), it must be seen as an alternate form or appearance of Oneness. The clear implication, then, is that both Oneness (always) and duality (when it emerges) are equivalent to Consciousness. (This is in agreement with our intuitive sense of things which feels Consciousness to be the stuff of everyday, dualistic experience). Thus, Consciousness, if it is different from Oneness in any way, differs in that it is an even more basic level of existence than Oneness, because it is equally the stuff of Oneness and duality. Oneness is the primary level of existence, but it shares the playing field with duality. So we establish, albeit torturously, the position that Oneness and duality are both equivalent to Consciousness. Furthermore, in the course of doing this we have glimpsed an even more basic truth. We have seen that Consciousness is indistinguishable from existence itself.

This is a conclusion of extraordinary portent. If true, it reverses the way most of us think about Consciousness. I think it's safe to say that most of us are used to seeing Consciousness as an emergent phenomenon, a mysterious achievement of higher life forms or even the exclusive domain of man. It is even, according to some, the highest achievement of the universe! We see it as something to be studied, explained, accounted for, held in awe. We also see it as our most prized possession, an essential part of our individual selves. Now we are positing that nothing could be further from the truth. Consciousness is not the end point, but the starting point. It is as basic as existence itself because it is existence itself. Everything that exists is Consciousness because existence is Consciousness.

> *That which knows existence*
> *Is identical to the existence it is knowing.*
> *This is the underlying unity.*

CONSCIOUSNESS AND BEING CONSCIOUS

In chapter 8 I posited an equivalence between Consciousness and life, stating that since there is no way to tell them apart, they must be deemed aspects of the same presence. What is more, both Consciousness and life are also equivalent with active self-interest and perception. Now we are looking at deeper equivalences, those between Oneness and Consciousness and existence. On the surface the equivalence between Consciousness and existence seems contradictory. Nonliving existence does not display perception and active self-interest, whereas life does. This difference constitutes a way of telling them apart, therefore suggesting that Consciousness cannot be equivalent to both life and existence. What is the truth?

The resolution lies in the difference between Consciousness and being conscious. Because we are conscious, we anthropomorphize Consciousness. We confound Consciousness with the quality of our human awareness. Of course, there is Consciousness in our human awareness, but this is being conscious of. It is complicated with many hierarchies of Consciousness knowing Consciousness and many levels of content. Consciousness in and of itself is a far simpler thing. At base it is just a function or aspect of the identity, the isness of existence. Consciousness is the sentience of being. Sentient beings, beings apart, life, is a late development, an emergent phenomenon. The phenomenon of beings being conscious is not the same as Consciousness. Consciousness is the clay of existence, whereas being conscious is the state of being alive. Sentient beings are able to be conscious because they are made up out of Consciousness. Being conscious, however, is a form in Consciousness, constructed out of Consciousness but apart from it.

The Consciousness we experience is not only an experience of, it is also dual and illusory, i.e., conscious, unconscious. Therefore, it is clearly a perceptual artifact. Conscious experience is an experience of other consciousnesses. However, it is not real as to its object, but illusory. The Consciousness that we are and all existence is, is nonreflective. It is not experienced, just experience. It is not experienced and not an experience of because it is fundamentally undivided. It knows but it does not know it knows because there is no part apart to know. It is only when there arises division, individuation, life, and perception that there arises awareness, something knowing something else and (oftentimes) something else knowing back. Advanced meditators all tell us that the true Self is that which persists unchanged though awakeness, dreaming, and deep sleep. They are referring to this level of Consciousness unperceived.

WHEN A TREE FALLS

Oneness, Consciousness, Existence, God, whatever you choose to call it, however you choose to think of it, is present everywhere, at all times. It is omnipresent in all dimensions: time, space, materiality, energy, etc. Let's call this omnipresence just presence. Every thing, every perceptual quality is a slice of that presence, a perceptual abstraction. For example, when physicists see the interconnectedness of matter and energy, they are just penetrating their own illusions, those perceptual abstractions that created the illusions of matter and energy in the first place. In this they are approaching the nature of reality from the wrong direction. They are reasoning as if perception is reality, as if their perceptions of separate energies and things are real, and they are just discovering new attributes of them. They are reasoning from the illusion to the reality, and this is why the pictures they get of reality are so complicated. In order to remedy this situation one must reason from (aperceptual) reality, not to it, because it is the center. The sun doesn't revolve around the earth.

The principle that duality is Oneness perceived is a major shift of perspective, one that recognizes Oneness rather than phenomena as the center. It is a shift that compels a reorganization of thought in all arenas of human endeavor, from science to religion, from thinking about the world to thinking about oneself.

Compared to perceptual illusion, aperceptual reality is comparatively simple. It is completely void, completely without thing, form, or distinction, nonlocal and atemporal. Which is only to say it is devoid of perceptual qualities. It is pure existence, pure Consciousness. Unfortunately, to the same degree that it is simple and void, it is also, in itself, unknowable and unfathomable. The perceived world originates there in potential, yet it is unobservable, it can only be inferred. However, the fact that reality is unknowable is no excuse for accepting illusion as reality. This would be compounding ignorance with self-deception. We need to become open to the non-dual, nonlinear, nonqualitative nature of reality. We should not only know ourselves and the universe in perceptual terms, we should also try to envision reality directly, both the inner and outer realities, and then figure out how they are translated into appearance by perception.

This entails breaking our addiction to the scientific method, overcoming our epistemological materialism and going back to investigating reality through *knowing* itself. It requires rigorous introspection, impeccable inference, intuition, concentration, and meditation. We need, in fact, to develop a new wisdom tradition. Previous wisdom traditions were prescientific and not only devoid of means for establishing the validity of hypotheses, they were not even aware of the concept of validating hypotheses. The next wisdom tradition will be postscientific. While throwing off the mesmerization of modern science with illusion, it will retain its emphasis on validation. In fact, it will reinforce the validation process by rigorously incorporating the philosophy of science into the doing of science and the validation process into metaphysics.

This all has bearing on that famous question, "If a tree falls in the forest and there is no one to hear it, does it make a sound?" This is a trick question, a Western koan. On the surface it is a straightforward query, but embedded in it are some of the most ubiquitous illusions of perceptual reality. So much so that analyzing the question will be an exercise in enlightened thinking.

The question "Does it make a sound?" is not only the question of whether Consciousness is necessary to perceive existence, it is also the question of whether Consciousness creates existence (existence being both phenomena and noumena). Is a conscious observer necessary for the occurrence of the tree falling to exist?

Let us begin by dividing the discussion into two questions. The first is: "Did anything at all happen?" The second is: "Did that which was perceived happen?" The naive, intuitive view is that, of course, something happened; the tree fell noisily. Conscious observation is merely the means by which someone hears it.

In complete contradistinction to the view that something happened is the rigorous but counterintuitive view that *if it is impossible to know about something, it doesn't exist.* Taking this view, the only possible answer is no, it didn't happen, no sound was made. Without Consciousness, without an observer, nothing exists. Consciousness creates existence in the sense that without Consciousness, nothing can be known. In this line of thinking we are actually redefining existence as Consciousness of.

We have already seen, however, that existence and Consciousness cannot be rigorously distinguished from one another. If all that exists is Consciousness itself, then certainly *Consciousness of* is also Consciousness?

Which brings us to the second question, namely: something happened, but was it the tree falling and did it make a sound? Of course something happened, but is the event itself identical to its appearance by an observer? Was that which happened a tree falling, making a sound? This returns us to the perceptual viewpoint that we have been espousing all along. Existence exists, but it is devoid of qualities. Conscious perception is the means by which an observer becomes aware of happening and imbues happening with qualities, in that sense, recreating it as a happening thing. The tree falling and the sound it creates are perceptual artifacts, illusory creations. However, there does exist a presence, one that is transformed by perception into a tree falling and making a sound. Something happens, but without a perceiver that thing is not a tree falling or the sound it makes. It is not a thing happening; it is just happening.

However, there is still a third reading of the question. This finally gets us to consider the possibility that the Consciousness of the observer actually plays a role in creating the occurrence in reality (as distinguished from perceptually encoding the occurrence into appearance). Getting into the twilight zone of the holographic model we ask, is the Consciousness of the observer actually playing a part in the creation of the forest, not only the appearance of the forest but the aperceptual forest itself?

The holographic model developed by David Bohm states that the universe is like a hologram in that it is an interference pattern of energy waves. In so much as the forest is made up of conscious entities, it may be also made up of entities radiating the (magnetic) force of consciousness. Axiomatically, every observing or radiating Consciousness effects every other Consciousness. Following this model, we could hypothesize that the *energy wave* of the observer is creating an interference pattern with the *energy wave* of whatever is already out there, actually cocreating the observed universe at the very moment it is being observed.

By this formulation we are hypothesizing that both observer and observed are radiating Consciousness, they are both sources of conscious energy waves and their interaction is creation. Looked at this way, the question of whether the observer cocreates the reality of the forest seems as self-evident as the question of whether the doughnut affects the hole. Looked at this way, the observer is another part of the forest. Thus, we might restate the old adage, "It is difficult to see the forest for the trees" into, "It is difficult to see the trees (observers) for the forest."

Which gets us beyond the original question and into a fourth possibility. If Oneness equals Consciousness, even nonlife is Consciousness and may interact with and affect other consciousnesses, alive or not. Since everything is fundamentally Consciousness, alive and not alive Consciousnesses might both play an *active* role in creating observed reality. We are now inquiring whether reality itself, the void substrate of the perceived happening, is being simultaneously cocreated not *only* by observing Consciousnesses but also by every center of consciousness. Which paints a picture of infinite gestalts of Consciousness, living and not living, crisscrossing their energy paths to make infinitely varied and observable interference patterns.

If we accept that not only the observer and the trees are real, but the rocks and the earth are real as well, that all are conscious energy interacting with other conscious energies, we get to a further implication. All of them play a part in cocreating their own reality and the realities that follow.

So if a tree falls in the forest and there is no one to hear it, does it make a sound?

* * * *

We have come to our limits, the limits of humanity, the limits of perception, the limits of separation. All perception is illusion, creates illusion. Human knowing is an anthropomorphism and that is that. We humans are like creatures of light in a universe composed totally of light. But we are blind from birth and light is a quality hopelessly beyond our imagining. Because of this handicap we have all had to become applied physicists. We comport ourselves according to principles and theory. We observe the effects of one illusion on another and rely on our observations. In our sky of light we all fly blind, relying totally on the instruments of our senses.

With this book we acknowledge the limits of our knowing, and then, I hope, go back to seeking. There is sadness, great sadness in accepting our limitations, but there is liberation as well, liberation from a certain kind of striving, striving to know as Gods. There is another benefit as well and that is a kind of sophistication, call it wisdom. If we accept that everything is a cloak of illusion that perception wraps around us, perhaps our emphasis will shift from knowing facts to understanding process, from seeing separate things to understanding relationships, from conquering our world to husbanding it, from ignoring the role of perception to taking it into account. Perhaps we all, scientists and generals, clerics and physicians, presidents and businessmen, you and I can stop trying to use the universe and be satisfied just being of it.

AFTERWORD: TOWARD ORIGINAL PERCEPTION

Can you know Oneness?…only as the void
Can you perceive from Oneness?…that's the whole point
Is Perception from Oneness being God?…if you choose to call it that

DE-VOID

Why is the void de-void, what is it, and why go into it? These questions have been addressed throughout the text, but perhaps not all together and perhaps not simply enough. The void is void because it is *devoid* of perceptual and cognitive qualities. Nothing more and nothing less. That does not mean there is no existence there, just that there is no thing there (thing as a perceptual category).

So what is the void? The void is Oneness, or more accurately the experience of Oneness. Why? Because in one sense Oneness is all there really is! Perception and cognition, the tools of the mind, dualize. They create a spectacle of qualities, things to enchant and entrance, color and form, time and space. But these things are illusions. All that is real, prior to perceptual dualization, is Oneness.

Why go to the void? Because you are already there! It is the lost kingdom of reality, the reality of who you are, who everyone is, what everything is. The void is the ground of all existence. How did you lose this kingdom of reality? Simply through becoming entranced by perception, through becoming identified with the perceiving mind, and ultimately through confusing your real Self with your perception of self, your self-concept.

Why go to the void? Because there, beyond past and future, beyond cause and effect, beyond your life history, beyond your situation, beyond thoughts and emotions, lies freedom; freedom from and freedom to. Freedom from negative thoughts and emotions, freedom to continually recreate yourself in the ongoing present without fear, and without being weighed down by the baggage of a false identity.

Why go to the void? For knowledge. The perceiving mind is outside and apart from, but the void is inside. Therefore, it knows. It knows reality, although there is no One apart to know (which, of course, is part of reality's voidness).

The outside is always apart from, looking in, perceiving, dualizing, confined to its viewpoint. The inside, however, is one with... Perception is knowledge of...Knowing is knowledge as! There are boundaries to the outside, but there are only connecting layers to the inside. The consciousness of your individuated Self is the first layer, but connected to that is the consciousnesses of other people, other sentient beings, other life forms, the cosmos, and finally universal, undifferentiated consciousness itself. The void is the mystic gate through which you can realize your greater identity, your identity with the all. The deeper you go into the void, the further you go out into universal consciousness, toward the vastness of being. Truly you go in to go out.

How do you get there? Ordinary consciousness is full of hiatuses, gaps in the thought stream through which the stillness, the now, the void shines, like glimpses of blue sky through the clouds. Go through any one of them and you are there. Then use your understanding to resist being pulled back. Or alternatively, punch your own hole in the clouds. Stop thinking, absolutely. An instant will suffice. Then escape through the opening you have made, enter, and stay. Don't be upset if you get pulled back down. After doing it once you will know how. The second time will be easier.

ORIGINAL PERCEPTION AS GOD

If we reject or go beyond the definitions of the last chapter, if we're not satisfied to say that God is everything or in everything, that God is Oneness, that God is the way things work, then what more could God be? There is another definition of God that I want to advance, which is God as a perceptual process. The idea stems from the concept of original perception. The basic premise of original perception is that although Oneness cannot be perceived or known (without rendering it illusory), it can be the locus of perception. It, rather than a self-concept, can be perceived from, can be the knower. (Perceiving from Oneness is the same as perceiving from the void.) This process of perceiving from Oneness, from your Oneness, I call original perception.

If God is a human experience, I want to nominate individual perception, the process of perceiving from Oneness, for the position. Original perception is not the experience of God, it is experience as God. When a person is perceiving from his core self, from his existence in Oneness rather than his self-concept, that process, that amalgam, that person, in a manner of speaking, is God. The person, for the time he is in original perception, has ceased to be an individual and is a direct channel to the universal. It isn't really that the individual has become God so much as he has stopped stopping being God. The individual has returned to being God. His consciousness has detached from the individual level and returned to Oneness. This reverses the ordinary process of personal development, by which consciousness progressively alienates from Oneness and focuses on the individual. If God is Oneness; being God is Oneness Perceiving.

(Individuality is just an overlay on Oneness, the illusion of separateness parlayed into an identity. To perceive from Oneness is, to some degree, to function from Oneness. This functioning from Oneness confers extraordinary attributes and powers on the God/individual: calm, serenity, heightened intuition, psychic perception, healing, and other powers emerge! These attributes and powers emerge because when one is perceiving and functioning from original perception, one is perceiving and functioning from a universal reality that works in different and expanded ways from our isolated "individual" reality. In this way individual mind has the ability to directly access universal mind.

ORIGINAL PERCEPTION, PSYCHOTHERAPY, AND ENLIGHTENMENT

Human perception typically originates from a self-concept instead of the core Self or Self in Oneness. The essence of Original Perception is the letting go, the dissolving of all of these self-concepts, whether temporarily or permanently, so that perception can be directly from Oneness. In that regard the pursuit of Original Perception has much in common with various meditative and spiritual disciplines as well as with some forms of psychotherapy.

(The same phenomenon of perception originating from a self-concept exists to a lesser extent in higher animals. It is easy to see how perception in humans originates from a self-concept, but more difficult to imagine among animals. However, one example makes apparent how pervasive self-concept is among the animal kingdom. That example is the pecking order or dominance hierarchy. Almost all social species exhibit some sort of pecking order phenomenon, whereby some animals have dominance over others. The interesting thing about this order of dominance is that it does not necessarily reflect reality. Weak animals frequently dominate stronger ones. Although the pecking order is subject to challenge and revision, these revisions do not always keep pace with changes, and pecking orders tend to endure long after they cease to reflect real relationships in the prowess of individuals. In other words, various social species, from dogs to chickens, have a social order that is at least partially maintained by self-concept rather than real interrelationships.)

Numerous strategies for getting away from self-concepts and getting to original perception have been developed over the ages. Vedanta, Buddhism, Sufism, even sects of Christianity and Judaism practice them. All are based on fundamental meditative or devotional practices. These vary on how effective they are at accessing the core or Oneness Self, but most of them achieve of some degree of success. Unfortunately, however, most of them share the same shortcoming. Although they access the core Self, they accomplish it by inducing alternative states of consciousness rather than permanently releasing memories and their associated self-concepts and response patterns. There is a hidden assumption that as the Oneness Self is realized, the inappropriateness of the self-concepts will become apparent and fall away. This is an attractive theory that, for want of a better option, has guided the meditative practices of the religious traditions of east and west for thousands of years. It would be nice if it were true, but unfortunately it isn't. It ignores the Tao of the Subconscious. It is more difficult to will away unwanted memories, attachments, and self-concepts than it is to will away unwanted weight. In fact, if you don't know how, it is almost impossible. Even after the point where the meditator sees these subconscious self-concepts as counterproductive and fallacious, dissolving them is far from automatic and requires specific, direct techniques, techniques that have just begun to be developed.

Because the meditative techniques of the various religious and meditative traditions don't permanently clear self-concepts but rather go beneath them, they make little headway on the subconscious level. (Subconscious traumas, perceptual mistakes, learnings, and conditionings are an inescapable part of every person who has been born into a body and therefore starts life with the illusion of separateness and its resultant self-concepts.) At the subconscious level reside the pitfalls to grace. Because their paths don't address the psychological dimension, adherents of the wisdom traditions strive to remain in a meditative state and avoid anything in life that might tempt them into falling from grace into self-concept and ordinary humanity. At best this is a monastic path, while at worst it becomes fanatical.

The attainment of Original Perception

In the West our psychological and technical bias has combined with our growing spiritual awareness, developing new syntheses of East and West, science and spirit. Psychosynthesis, the transcendental psychotherapy founded by Alberto Assagioli, is arguably the most effective established school of psychospiritual therapy. Transpersonal hypnotherapy, in the hands of an enlightened practitioner, can also be a very effective means of approaching original perception, whereas schools of therapy such as psychoanalysis that only address the personal or ego level fall as short as disciplines which only address the spiritual level. *(It's interesting that both Psychosynthesis and hypnotherapy share an emphasis on working with subconscious visualizations with many meditative practices, with Tibetan Buddhism in particular.)*

The West has generated other approaches to perception from Oneness as well: other psychospiritual therapies, psychedelic drugs, biofeedback, sensory deprivation, etc. All of these have a modicum of efficacy and validity. However, as psychospiritual and ethical systems capable of guiding the spiritual evolution of the whole person, they vary tremendously.

I have been working with another, more direct approach to Original Perception through the release of traumatic memories (and other perceptual distorters). Traumatic memories entrain people in the past. People perceive ongoing occurrences through traumatic past occurrences and combine them into a metacategory that includes what has happened in the originating traumatic occurrence, what has happened in all "like" occurrences, what is happening in the present occurrence. When they identify a present occurrence as fitting into this metacategory, all the feelings and responses from the originating occurrence on up are triggered. People become locked into a trance of past consciousness and emotion in which objective and appropriate judgment, emotion, and response become difficult if not impossible. (Memories that are not associated with traumatic or at least intense or challenging events, and the person's responses to them, do not entrain the past nearly so strongly.)

Original perception is a more or less permanent state of perception from Oneness. It is attained when most of the traumatic memories, their entrained self-concepts, and their associated response patterns are released. This clarifies perception, first so that it is "in the present" and eventually so that it is without self-concept, the self-concept one would ordinarily perceive from. As I have said, there are two broad strategies for accomplishing this. One is the way of meditation or spiritual discipline. In this strategy, concentration on a point, whether it is breathing, a mantra, or anything else, gets you out of your mind, or more precisely, the part of your mind in which your self-concepts reside. The shortcoming of this strategy is impermanence. In order to remain in that place you have to keep on meditating, and the challenges of ordinary life tend to bring you back to your ordinary, historically formed perception.

The other strategy is unlearning, deliberately releasing all of your self-concepts. The advantage of this strategy is economy of effort and permanence, at least relative permanence. Instead of going out of your mind, you stay there and instead banish your self-concepts.

How do you unlearn self-concepts?

Since the origins of psychoanalysis and psychotherapy, it has been widely assumed that catharsis and/or insight have been sufficient conditions for psychological change. (This has led to perpetual psychotherapy leading to breakthrough after breakthrough, without really reaching to the clear space of functioning wholly in the boundaryless present.) However, new understandings of the subconscious, coming from clinical hypnosis and other sources largely outside of the academic and clinical disciplines of psychology and psychiatry, have revised that assumption. It has come to be understood that the subconscious, like overwrite-protected computer memory, learns or associates situation, action, and outcome in one exposure, but under ordinary conditions never unlearns or forgets it. Because of the aforementioned catharsis/insight assumption, little or no attention has been paid to the process of unlearning or intentional forgetting, at least in ordinary life. *(Of course, there is a body of literature studying extinction in lab animals, but that is only partially relevant because the conditions for controlled extinction do not exist in everyday life.)*

However, there is a strategy of release or unlearning that does work, which I have been working with for a few years. The process of subconscious unlearning takes place as a dialogue with the subconscious (usually in an altered state of consciousness). It has two broad phases, identification and release. The identification phase also has two parts. First, through dialoguing with the subconscious, it is ascertained whether there is a memory, response pattern, or identity taking control of responses in the present. Second, the specific memory that is taking control of the present has to be identified. This done, the therapy advances to the release phase.

In the release phase the subconscious is instructed by the therapist to let go of the identified memory. The therapist or client then checks to see whether it has done so. When confirmation is gotten, that release cycle is over. The attainment of Original Perception requires many release cycles over time, and usually some maintenance, as memories and self-concepts are never fully cleared and new ones tend to arise. Sometimes the treatment cycle goes further and a new memory (learning) is put in the place of the released one, either through visualization, hypnotic suggestion, affirmation, or simply incorporating insight. However, this is not necessary. A life lived in the present, in a state of original perception, will furnish affirmations in short order.

Original Perception, its theory, and how it is to be attained and used will be the subject of a forthcoming book.

APPENDIX

THE ILLUSION OF PROBABILITY AND THE IMPLICATIONS FOR SCIENCE

In the real world, any event that has not happened is so improbable as to be impossible, i.e., the meeting of my wife and I depends not only in our being at the same concert at the same time, waiting on line for an ice cream cone with all the circumstances attendant on that, but also on the evolution of human life on earth and the evolution of the universe with all the circumstances attendant on those unlikely occurrences. One way of looking at it then is summed up in the question: What is the possibility of arriving at a predetermined event in a field of infinite possibilities. Not only are the possibilities infinite in any given instant, but they are infinite multiplied by a span of time that is itself either infinite or measured in hundreds of billions of years, depending on how you look at it. A predetermined outcome dependent upon an instant of infinite possibilities multiplied by infinite time is extremely unlikely. Even more unlikely than that famous speculation that if a chimp bangs on a typewriter long enough he is going to flawlessly type the Encyclopaedia Brittanica. It is just not going to happen.

The probability of any predetermined event occurring, not selected from preexistent choices circumscibed in time and number,
but "materializing" at all, from an undefined beginning of time and
existence is 1/infinity (although the probability of any particular
thing happening that has already happened is 1/1).

Which leads to two conclusions. One, it is impossible for any
particular thing to happen and therefore it won't. Clearly an insup-
portable position, although I suppose like all things absurd, it will
find its champions. Two, everything that has ever happened was
fully determined and inevitable, an idea that flies in the face of our
sense of the chaos and opportunism of existence, although millions
of people believe it!

The other way to go is to question the applicability of probability
theory to reality or to open systems. Probability theory is a branch
of mathematics that assumes and studies random occurrences in a
finite and known field of separate possibilities. The model at its simplest is exemplified by a bag with five different colored marbles in
it. Picking blindly and at random, one has a 1 in 5 chance of picking
the blue marble. If he then puts all the marbles back in the bag, he
has a 1 in 5 chance of picking the blue again.

When you apply probability theory to reality, you are assuming
that the field of reality is the equivalent to that arbitrary, mathematical field represented by the bag of marbles, a finite and known or
knowable universe of predetermined, separate, and equal possibilities to randomly choose from.

But perhaps this is just not the case. Perhaps reality is *not* just an
enormous bag of marbles randomly choosing themselves. Perhaps
this is not just an oversimplification but a misrepresentation and a
grievously misleading one at that. Instead, picture reality as one
unified, all-encompassing, infinitely big system where nothing is
separate and everything is an aspect of everything else. Next, consider that the entire system is constantly, simultaneously changing
in every respect. Then, consider that every aspect of every new form
has almost every dimension and quality you have ever experienced,
conceived, measured, or even heard about: form, color, brightness,
temperature, speed, location, temperature, rate, radioactive decay,

hardness, smoothness, malleability, elasticity, beauty, time, space, size, you name it, the list goes on and on. Now, consider that every quality and dimension of each aspect of every new form is a perceptual illusion. There is something real there but you in fact don't know, can't know, and for the most part can't even begin to ascertain what it is. Next, consider that not only don't you know what the reality behind these aspects or things is, but for the most part your very impressions of what an aspect or thing consists of are themselves perceptual illusions and that actually all perceived aspects are simultaneously one, fewer, many more, and completely different than you perceive them to be from your individual viewpoint. To complicate the picture, consider that for the most part the states of this infinitely faceted whole consist of "aspects" that have never existed before and are never to exist again. Then, to top it off, remember that the qualities of these aspects are projections of the qualities of the perceiver rather than the thing perceived. Consider this and you've got the problem.

Can we reduce this complex, unknowable, and rapidly evolving reality to our model of a bag of marbles, however many marbles it contains, thus making it fit into the probability theory model? Scientists and statisticians have been doing it for years, but the closer we examine it, the worse it seems to fit. Probability theory, based as it is on the model of a finite universe of randomly determined, separate, and known or at least knowable possibilities, implicitly imposes numerous and untenable assumptions on reality. We can question at least seven assumptions that are in some way essential for conventional probability theory.

a.   That reality consists of probabilities.
b.   That they are random.
c.   That they are separate or independent.
d.   That they are finite in number, and constitute a finite field.
e.   That they are known or knowable.
f.   That they are preexistent.
g.   That the circumstances of this field can be reconstituted and the results replicated.

1. Probability

First we come to the question of probabilities. Let us return to the paradox that although it is impossibly improbable that any given event happen before it happens, everything that has happened has happened. If this paradox holds and nonexistent occurrences are impossibly improbable, they can't be dealt with by a theory of probability. On the other hand, if everything that has happened was a necessary and fully determined occurrence from the precedent conditions, just next, all things that have occurred were inevitable and probability theory still does not apply.

Fire a reality arrow into the heart of this paradox.

The problem is practical as well as theoretical. If everything is fully determined, all we have to do is know all the precedent conditions and fully understand the implications of them and we could conceivably predict what comes next. However, it is inconceivable to do this in a reality or open system. There are too many variables, most of them are unknown, and virtually none of them are understood to the requisite degree. To appreciate the magnitude of the problem, consider predicting just what effect an unprecedented change in the sequence of a gene would have on the organism. Then consider the enormous complexity of millions of years of evolution. For a simpler example think of the problem of forecasting tomorrow's weather in NYC, then contemplate the difficulty of forecasting the weather a year from tomorrow. The chain of events is impossible to predict. All we can do is make a rough statistical selection from past weather conditions at that time of year.

An open system is one where the variables are not preselected and limited either by definition or experimental control. In this sense, all reality systems are open. In another sense, though, all reality systems are closed. If, as is our premise, all perceived variables are really just qualities or aspects of Oneness, then everything is just an aspect or perception of one thing. A universe consisting of one thing can hardly be termed an open system. Therefore, the explanation that there are just too many unaccountable variables at work is superficial. The deeper explanation is that there is only Oneness evolving. When we see reality as Oneness evolving, all problems change and we have not one but two sources of variation and unpredictability.

The first source of variation is the evolution of Oneness itself. That, we have seen, is a source of infinite variability and almost infinite unpredictability, since almost all of its evolved forms are, on one level or another, novel. Furthermore, although the evolving forms themselves may be absolutely determined, the infinite variablity of the open system precludes prediction.

The other source of variation, as we have already seen, is perception itself. Perception creates illusions, and illusions are also infinite. Qualities, time, space, events, even thingness are perceptual illusions and therefore as numberless and evanescent as a play of light and shadow.

2. Randomness

Two, we come to the question of randomness. The discussion rests on the preceding one. If there is no probability there is no randomness. If an occurrence is impossible randomness could hardly apply. In the same vein, if an outcome is fully determined by precedent conditions which in turn are determined by precedent conditions, where is the randomness? Only in the limits of our knowledge.

3. Independence Of Variables

Three, we come to the question of the independence of variables. This too rests on the original discussion and the model of Oneness, but it bears repeating. If, instead of consisting of numerous things, existence consists of one thing ever changing in the eternal present, all seemingly independent variables are really aspects one thing. Every isolated thing or event is just an isolated perception of a transient phase of Oneness. The misconception that reality consists of independent variables corresponds to the perceptual dualization of Oneness into separate things and separate events occurring in separate moments of time.

Now of course one could argue that whether the variables are independent things or aspects of one thing makes no difference statistically. One could treat aspects as if they were independent and come out with the same result. However, this is an argument that itself can be evaluated statistically. That is, sometimes it would sort of hold true, and sometimes not. If all variables are aspects of Oneness, you would expect changes in any one variable to be accompanied by changes, however subtle, in all variables. You would expect all real variables to co-vary. The problem is that in a real system not only would you have no way of assessing the magnitude or direction of most of the aspects, but there are no real boundaries between aspects. You could never assume true or even acceptable independence of the particular aspects that you chose to look at from the infinite field you were blissfully unaware of.

4. Finiteness

Again, following the original discussion, reality presents neither a finite or an infinite field, or alternatively it presents both. It depends on whether you are looking at it aperceptually or perceptually. It is finite in the sense that Oneness is one thing, but in that case there are no separate probabilities. On the other hand it is infinite because both the fields of Oneness and of illusion are infinite *(i.e., there are both infinite aspects of Oneness and infinite illusions)*. Both these assertions run contrary to probability theory's assumption of a finite field of separate probabilities.

It is a corollary to this that in an open system the number of variables cannot be determined. As we have already seen, the number of qualities and even the quality of thingness itself is an artifact of perception and subject to infinite multiplication, division, and redefinition.

5. Knowability

Now for the question of the knowability of variables. In the aperceptual perspective, the aspects of the field cannot be known. In the perceptual perspective, that which we know is illusory and evanescent. We cannot know anything but illusion, which means we cannot, in reality, know anything at all. Either way we do not have a knowable field.

6.   Preexistence

Now we come to the assumption that outcomes are selected among predetermined or preexistent events. This is the most significant problem of all in the applicability of probability theory to reality systems. In the marble analogy, we know the marbles are in there and what colors they are. They are preexistent, and only their choice is chance. But in the evolution of Oneness, all events are perceptions of the original and transient forms that Oneness is passing though. Some were never before seen, and some are never to come again. They are not preexistent. We are not talking about a random choice out of a preexistent, finite field: a known quality present in known quantities. It is not the choice of them but the very materializing of them that is at issue. The choice of a particular ear of corn being picked randomly out of a bushel is a very different matter than the coming into existence of an ear of corn. The coming into existence of a specific ear of corn, indeed the evolution of corn, is not a probable or replicable event, no matter what the odds. It is definitely a unique occurrence in an infinite field.

7.   Replicability

Finally we come to the assumption that the circumstances can be reconstituted and the events replicated. In the analogy of the bag of marbles, we can put the marbles back in the bag, thereby reconstituting the relevant circumstances, and the probable sequence of events will be replicated. With reality systems, however, we are dealing with unique events in a unique field. We cannot destroy the species that is corn and expect it to evolve again no matter how long we wait. It is not a replicable event. We cannot restore the state that Oneness was in immediately prior and leading up to the evolution of corn. They are not reconstitutable circumstances. Oneness is not a bag of marbles, and the evolution of a form in Oneness is not comparable to a blue marble waiting to be randomly chosen.

IMPLICATIONS

Rigorously speaking then, probability theory is ultimately inapplicable to the task of describing the nature of reality. The usefulness of probability theory, though considerable, is limited. It is a technique. Just because one can describe and predict occurrences probalistically in a branch of science does not imply that it is fundamentally probabilistic. If this is correct, it has radical implications for those aspects of science and scientific methodology that are now seen as fundamentally probabilistic. Evolution and quantum physics as well as the scientific method itself spring immediately to mind, but I am sure that other natural scientists will have other candidates in their specializations.

This discussion comprises an interesting illustration of the main premise of perceptual field theory, i.e., all things are just separate and illusory perceptions of Oneness. We perceive seven characteristics of apparent reality and take them as assumptions. They are probability, randomness, independence, finiteness, knowability, preexistence, and replicability. Based on these assumptions, we create a strategy, methodology, and mathematics for doing science. Then I come along and one by one argue against these assumptions. But my argument is the same in every case. It is that reality is not like that, that we are unconsciously describing perceptions in every case. Seven assumptions, one argument. Why? Because there are in truth infinite perceptions but only one underlying reality. Both the scientific method and probability theory are procedures based upon complex perceptions of groups of only slightly less complex perceptions. The argument against all these assumptions is a return to the model of aperceptual reality.

REASONING BACKWARD FROM THE NATURE OF METHODOLOGY TO THE NATURE OF REALITY

A principal difficulty with the sciences that tend to be studied using statistical methodology is that they come to be described in probabilistic terms and eventually their reality is conceived in those terms.

Thus quantum mechanics assumes that physics, and by extension ultimate reality, follows probabilistic laws. Evolution assumes that all life was evolved probabilistically. However, if this discussion holds true, probability will turn out to have less validity as a description of reality systems and be seen only as one useful technique for studying them.

EVOLUTION AND PROBABILITY

What does this say for evolution? Evolution is a probalistic model. In a nutshell, it holds that certain genetically determined traits of organisms convey a competitive advantage in survival and/or reproduction and thus the genes come to predominate in the gene pool of a "species" while less advantageous traits and their underlying genes tend to disappear. Thus species tend to evolve toward these advantageous traits and away from the disadvantageous ones. It further says that all genetically determined traits tend to distribute according to a bell-shaped or probabilistic curve and that species tend to evolve toward the most advantageous combined expression of all traits.

This beautiful and elegant theory has vast explanatory power (although not much predictive power). Since Darwin, it has defined the way science thinks about life and creation, and has undermined, religious creationism. However, a lot of people, even scientists, have an intuitive problem with it. They can't imagine, following this one principle and given the infinite possibilities and permutations of life, how evolution could have ended up creating the specific forms it did. It just doesn't seem possible. Life forms yes, but these specific forms no. It seems utterly impossible, considering all the random and probabilistic factors at work that evolution should specifically produce a pin oak or a human being. Teleological notions keep rearing their improbable heads. Thus we return to the *paradox* that began this discussion, before something occurs it is impossibly improbable, the chance of its occurrence is 1/infinity. After it occurs, it is inevitable and the chance of its occurrence is 1/1.

It is the problem of the chimps and the encyclopedia again. The chimps would produce a lot of text, and each production could be considered a product of chance, but they just wouldn't re-produce a given encyclopedia. It is not theoretically impossible, just inconceivable.

What is the solution to this paradox? Not surprisingly, it is our old friend, perception. Reality seems different from different points of view. Before and after are as neat a pair of perceptual dualities as you would ever hope to find. Viewed from before, things are unpredictable and any given outcome impossible; viewed from after, things are inevitable. What is the truth, neither or both?

Where does probability theory fit into this? Is it looking at things from before or after? Actually it is a confounding of both points of view. The concept of probability is a subtle möbius. The seven assumptions of probability theory are clearly looking at things from afterward in their assumption of a known and finite universe. However, this hindsight is used to construct a predictive method, a way of looking at things from before they happened. Even ex post facto research relies on the predictive method, i.e. do the occurrences match or differ from those that one would predict if there were no significant differences. Is this valid?

BEYOND THE SCIENTIFIC METHOD:
TWO APPROACHES TO APERCEPTUAL REALITY

Triangulation

Before and after are multiple viewpoints. Is combining multiple viewpoints a good strategy for getting at the truth? I think it is, but only to a limited extent. The observation of where viewpoints intersect is the means by which we locate things in space. Two viewpoints suffice to locate things in two dimensions and three suffice to locate things in three dimensions. In navigation it is called triangulation. If one knows the time of an occurrence in space, that locates it in four dimensions.

There is a lot of nonsense written about dimensions...how many dimensions exist, what they are, the existence of geniuses who can visualize and think in multiple dimensions we ordinary mortals don't even suspect, and for the topper, dimensions that are outside of the laws of nature as we know it and that confer extraordinary powers to those able to perceive and negotiate them.

According to perceptual field theory there is only one dimension in reality and that is Oneness. Even location and time are illusory. Of course, one dimension hardly merits being called a dimension, since what is a dimension but a division in reality, and if you haven't any divisions what is the sense of having a word for them.

On the other hand, illusion, perceived reality, is full of dimensions. In fact, it is nothing but dimensions, they just keep materializing infinitely. But what is a dimension; even in perception their nature is uncertain. A dimension is nothing more or less than a qualified viewpoint (a qualified viewpoint is a perception from the point of view of a quality, or onto which the quality is projected). Thus the dimensions of space are established from the point of view of the perception or the perceiver. The time dimension is established from the point of view of the present plus an arbitrary beginning point in the cognitively perceived past. The temperature dimension is established from the point of view of the perceiver or measuring instrument plus some starting point, like the freezing point of water and so on. Each qualified viewpoint is in fact another dimension.

Looked at this way, we realize that all of us perceive in simultaneous multiple dimensions after all, and it is no big deal. When we remember a smelly, white horse galloping in from the north and being reined in at the stable yesterday in the evening light, we are perceiving simultaneously, in a minimum of ten dimensions, location in three-dimensional space, time, chemical (smell), color, direction, speed, acceleration, and light. Then, if we think about it (cognitive perception) and look at it from the viewpoints of our thoughts, we realize that we are generating all sorts of cognitive dimensions as well: beauty, control, mastery, grace, harmony, power etc.

All that is vaguely although commonly thought of as a dimension is, according to aperceptual field theory, nothing more or less than a viewpoint or perspective. Furthermore, viewpoints and qualities are the same thing. They all constitute dimensions and they all are illusory. Therefore, if we knew the temperature at which something occurred, that would constitute a dimension, and if we knew its density, chemistry, refractiveness, radioactivity, direction, and velocity, those would all constitute additional dimensions. The four dimensions of location and time that we deem principal are really arbitrary selections based on the arbitrary equation of the space-time illusion with reality. Every viewpoint or perceptual quality is equally a dimension and equally illusory.

Looked at like this, it is apparent that the human mind is superbly equipped for perceiving in multiple dimensions simultaneously as well as overlaying them as traits on a selected perception and forming a combined impression of the whole. In fact, it cannot do otherwise. On the other hand, it is equally apparent that it also creates all of the dimensions it perceives through the very act of its own perception. There is, however, a limit to even the human mind's ability to assimilitate and integrate dimensions, particularly if these dimensions are fed to us as facts and rather than our own perceptions. Which brings us to a dilemma, because the present direction of modern culture is to amass and communicate as many facts about as many things as possible, far outstripping the mind's ability to create intelligible gestalts.

How Many Blind Men Will It Take to See an Elephant (Mapping)?

Triangulating the unknowable, reality, may be our best strategy for locating and describing it.

All perceptions are illusory, but extensively delineating the shared source of multiple perceptions is useful. Even though it comes no closer to revealing the underlying reality.

Probability theory, conventional logic, causal reasoning, the scentific method, and perceptual thinking as a whole have gotten us far, very far indeed. However, increasingly, as the problems considered by science and philosophy become deeper, they have begun to mislead us, creating wild goose chases, presenting us with insoluble paradoxes, and fragmenting all rigorous investigation into increasingly inpenetrable subspecialties. The question is, How can we go deeper, to approach aperceptual reality, to know of it in a rigorous, synthetic, conceptual way despite never being able to know it in any direct or perceptual way?

The program I am going to propose is nothing new. Investigators of reality have been doing it for centuries, even millennia, just like the scientific method was used intuitively long before its formulation. What I am going to propose is a formulation of this method so that people can use it consciously and methodically as well as intuitively and so it can take its place as a respectable way of doing science.

My proposal is beautifully illustrated in the ancient fable of the blind men and the elephant. Five blind men touch an elephant, one his leg, one his tusk, one his tail, one his trunk, and one his side. The first says an elephant is like a hairy tree, the second like a polished branch, the third like a little snake, the fourth like a big snake, and the fifth like a rough wall.

Which blind man is right? None of them and all of them. The orginal point was that each person was limited to his own viewpoint, and therefore limited as to what he could know. But in this age of computers, digitalization gives us another perspective. Immediately we go to the question: How many blind men will it take to see an elephant? The fable stays the same but the moral changes. Certainly a few million blind men, each touching a spot on the elephant, the locations of their hands and what they felt tracked by a computer and converted into pixels, should enable the computer to form a pretty good 3-D image of the elephant, accurate down to the eyelashes, that it could then project on a screen, measure, rotate, analyze, and even animate.

In science we tend to assume that only one viewpoint is right, vying among ourselves to be the first to discover it and be awarded the Nobel Prize. In reality, however, every viewpoint is equally invalid and valid. (Not every theory.) It is invalid in the sense that it is partial, dual, and illusory. But it is valid in the sense that there is a lawful, understandable, and sometimes even reversible process by which a specific perceiver converts an aspect of aperceptual reality into an individual perception. There is a reality underlying every viewpoint. There is something universal in every perception, in that all perceptions are dualizations from a sole viewpoint. Also, there is something specific to the individual perceiving organism in every perception, since that perception is processed through the perceivers sensorium or cognitorium and since the perceived quality is a projection of a quality of the perceiver.

What the computer is doing is taking every available viewpoint, however partial and illusory, keeping track of each one and imaging an elephant that satisfies them all. This suggests a program for doing science. It consists of three parts: The first is taking every available viewpoint and assuming they all are valid (subject to checks. Some of the greatest theoretical advances followed the discarding of false viewpoints that were distorting all prior attempts at understanding). The second consists of building a model that sums them all. The third consists of understanding that this model is perceptual and as much as possible reconciling it with aperceptual reality. This last step is called *Enlightenment.*

When we create a three-dimensional map of something, we call it a picture or image and we call the process visualizing, picturing, seeing, or something of that sort. What should we call that unknowable, unimaginable map of something that we get when we take all possible viewpoints as a sample of the infinite viewpoints available. I propose to call it a virtual entirety, the process of of reaching this virtual entirety…virtualization.

The first, taking all viewpoints, I call *Triangulation,* since the way you locate something in space is by triangulating in between three or more points. However, in triangulating reality we take all possible viewpoints. The second, creating a model that satisfies all viewpoints, I call *Mapping* (it is well to remember that the computer could not have imaged the elephant if it did not know where all of the hands were).

How is this different from what science does now? Probably not very. However, it is very different from what science thinks it is doing! It is a return to taxonomy, to the description and classification of reality, but on a much more complex level and without the illusion that we are knowing anything.